Marguerite Patten

The Family Cookbook

Edited by
Hyla O'Connor

CHARTWELL BOOKS INC.

Acknowledgements

The publishers would like to acknowledge the help of the following in providing photographs:
American Dairy Association: White lemon cake 95, Pumpkin orange chiffon pie 114, Lemon chiffon pie 115; **American National Live Stock and Meat Board:** Standing rib roast with popovers 21, New England boiled dinner 26, Herbed pork chops 27, Chicken salad Veronique with tongue 63; **American Poultry and Egg National Board:** Chinese vegetable soup 50, Seafood pizza 83; **Argentine Beef Bureau:** Argentine beef soup 64; **Argo Corn Starch:** Sour cream lemon pie 111; **Birds Eye Ltd:** Berries on a cloud 101; **British Egg Information Service:** Pastel de Tortillas 73; **Cadbury Schweppes Ltd:** Chocolate soufflé 119, Gooseberry sparkle 125; **California Apricot Advisory Board:** Fresh apricot pie 108; **California Strawberry Advisory Board:** Strawberry bonanza shortcake 89, Strawberry custard pie 114; **Chiltonian Ltd:** Composite photograph 9; **Danish Agricultural Producers:** Glazed forehock of bacon 29, Danish open sandwiches 56–57; **Dutch Dairy Bureau:** Cheese soufflé 78; **Eden Vale Ltd:** Cottage cheese salads 61; **Fruit Producers' Council:** Chicken peach salad 60, Fruit snow 125; **John West Foods Ltd:** Corn chowder 67, Emergency shelf omelette 73; **Herring Industry Board:** Preparing herrings 34, Normandy Herrings 41; **National Dairy Council:** Haddock and mushroom scallops 40; **New Zealand Lamb Information Bureau:** Composite photograph 19, Roast lamb with apricot nut stuffing 22; **Pasta Foods Ltd:** Composite photograph 11; **Pillsbury Company:** Coconut fudge cake 97; **RHM Foods Ltd:** Ham en croûte 29, Green salad 58, Shrove Tuesday crepes 77, Old English chicken pie 80, Pizza 83, Pancake 105, Cherry flan 112, Peach gâteau 124; **Spanish Green Olive Commission:** Paella salad 62; **Tabasco Sauce:** Roast pork with prune and apple stuffing 22, Creamed turkey duchesse 46, Corned beef plate tart 81; **Walls Ice Cream:** Composite photograph 121; **T. Wall & Son (Meat and Handy Foods) Ltd:** Sausage twists and sausage cheese savories 14; **White Fish Authority:** Sole Sevilla 36, Goujons of fish 39.

This edition first published in the USA 1977 by
Chartwell Books Inc.
a division of Book Sales Inc.
110 Enterprise Avenue
Secaucus, New Jersey 07094

© 1977 Octopus Books Limited

ISBN 0 7064 0653 2

Produced by Mandarin Publishers Limited
22A Westlands Road,
Quarry Bay, Hong Kong

Printed in Hong Kong

Contents

one

HORS D'OEUVRE & SAUCES

In this chapter you will find the first course of a meal, the hors d'oeuvre, or meal starters, as they are often called today. This course is a very important one, for it can turn an everyday meal into something special. It is a leisurely course, where everyone should relax, ready to enjoy his meal.

Although an hors d'oeuvre generally consists of a light cold or hot dish, and could be fruit juice only, the choice is important. If the hors d'oeuvre is too solid and highly flavored, then it spoils one's appetite for the main course to follow. The hors d'oeuvre, like the dessert, should complement the main course. It should have a refreshing flavor, so that if your family and guests are not particularly hungry the piquant taste of this beginning to the meal whets their appetites. In order to enjoy the first course, time the

cooking carefully for your main dish so you can linger over the start of a pleasant meal. Almost any kind of food could be served as an hors d'oeuvre and pages 8–15 give a very varied selection together with ideas of *just when* that particular kind of meal starter would be ideal.

Can you make perfect sauces? All too often when I pose this question I am told that it is "so difficult to make a smooth sauce." That is not true. It takes both time and patience to achieve perfection in saucemaking but it is *not* difficult. It is important to appreciate *why* sauces curdle or *why* they become lumpy and these points are dealt with in the last part of this section. It is also important to know *how* to put right an error when making a sauce, whether it is to correct seasoning, texture or consistency.

Interesting and well seasoned sauces can turn a simple dish into a superb one and mastering the art of saucemaking is an important part of cooking.

I hope you will enjoy all the recipes in this section and that they will help you to cook better, with fewer problems of meal planning and preparation.

Fruit Plus

When you plan a really substantial main course and a rather creamy dessert, choose a fruity hors d'oeuvre. The refreshing flavor will give everyone an appetite to appreciate the meat or fish course that follows.

Certain fruits and fruit juices are served so frequently that they could be dull. Melon, grapefruit, orange juice—all of these are very pleasant, but there are many occasions when they would be improved with a new look.

Blue Print

Serving Fruit for an Hors d'Oeuvre

Never oversweeten the fruit or fruit juice. If you do it makes it rather like a dessert.

Present it in an interesting way, i.e. melon should be cut as the sketches opposite, fruit juices should be served in frosted glasses and topped with mint leaves, which both smell and look attractive.

Try to have an unusual mixture of flavors when serving fruit, as the recipes on these pages.

● **AVOID** *Making you fruit hors d'oeuvre too sweet.*
● **TO RECTIFY** *Sprinkle a little lemon juice or dry sherry over the fruit if you have added too much sugar.*
● **SHORT CUT** *Use canned grapefruit segments and mix the liquid from the can with a little sherry or lemon juice.*
● **TO REDUCERS** *An ideal hors d'oeuvre on most diets.*

Melon balls with lemon sauce

Melon

Throughout most of the year one is likely to be able to purchase some kind of melon. The most usual are honeydew, crenshaw, casaba, cantaloupe and Persian. The pink-fleshed watermelon is less suitable for a first course, except in the melon cocktail (page 13).

To buy melon, feel it and it should appear heavy for its size. Press gently but firmly and the melon should give at either end, so indicating it is ripe.

Prepare by slicing or halving and removing the seeds The usual accompaniments are sugar or salt and lemon wedges.

Although melons may not be kept in the refrigerator, they are improved by being chilled before serving or serving on a bed of crushed ice.

Melon Balls with Lemon Sauce

1 melon (see below); 2 lemons; little water; 1–2 tablespoons sugar. *To garnish:* sprigs of mint; lemon twists.

Buy a ripe honeydew, Persian or cantaloupe melon. Halve the melon, remove the seeds. Take a vegetable scoop and make balls of the flesh, see Sketch 4. Chill these. The rather untidy pieces of melon at the bottom of the fruit can be used for the sauce. Grate enough rind from the lemons to give about 2 teaspoons. Squeeze the juice, measure and add enough water to give $\frac{2}{3}$ cup. Simmer the rind with the liquid and sugar for about 5 minutes. Pour over the odd pieces of melon, then put through a food mill or puree in a blender. Taste and add more sugar if wished. This is not really necessary, for the sauce should be both thick and fairly sharp. Spoon into the bottom of 4–6 glasses and top with the melon balls. Garnish with mint and lemon. *Serves 4–6.*

Melon and Crème de Menthe

Sprinkle balls of melon or a slice of melon with a little crème de menthe.

Melon and Pineapple

Freeze canned pineapple juice until lightly frozen; do not allow it to become too hard. Put at the bottom of glasses and top with diced melon or melon balls.

Melon and Prosciutto

Put slices of melon, this time with the skin removed, on plates with curls of Prosciutto. Garnish with a slice of lemon and serve with freshly ground black pepper.

Grapefruit

This is one of the most refreshing hors d'oeuvre and particularly good if you are dieting. Grapefruit, like melon, should feel heavy for its size. Do not buy very light colored fruit unless you can store them for a while, for they are inclined to be underripe and lacking in sweetness and flavor. Halve the grapefruit and separate the segments, discard the pith and seeds. Serve with sugar and decorated with cherries.

Jamaican Grapefruit

Halve the fruit, remove the segments, put into a bowl. Blend with a little brown sugar and rum. Pile back into the grapefruit shells, chill and serve very cold, or put back into the shells, top with a little brown sugar and butter and heat under the broiler.

Grapefruit and Avocado

2 grapefruit; 2 avocados; 2 tablespoons oil; good pinch dry mustard; pinch salt; shake pepper; pinch sugar; 1 tablespoon white vinegar or lemon juice; lettuce.
Cut the peel away from the grapefruit, then cut into segments. Make the dressing before halving the avocados. Blend the oil with the seasonings and sugar, then the vinegar or lemon juice. Halve the avocados, remove the pits and skin. Cut into slices. Put in the dressing so they do not discolor. Arrange small lettuce leaves on 4 or 6 individual plates. Top with the sliced grapefruit and avocados. *Serves 4–6.*

Avocado Vinaigrette

2 ripe avocados (see method); lemon juice; dressing as above, but you need to make a little more. *To garnish:* lettuce.
To choose avocados feel gently all over the fruit; it should yield to the gentlest pressure; or better, allow to ripen at home.
Halve the avocados, remove the pits, sprinkle lightly with lemon juice if there is even a slight delay in serving as the fruit discolors badly. Fill the holes where the pits were with the dressing. Garnish with lettuce leaves. *Serves 4.*

The recipes pictured and described on this page use fruits in unusual ways. The dishes are equally as suitable for an informal party as for an hors d'oeuvre. If serving as an hors d'oeuvre, pass each dish round the table with crisp crackers, as shown in the picture, to counteract the rather rich flavor of the fillings.

Avocado Cream Dip

2 avocados; 2 tablespoons lemon juice; 3 tablespoons mayonnaise; 1 very small onion or 2–3 spring onions; 2 tablespoons sour cream; 2 tablespoons heavy cream; seasoning. *To garnish:* shelled shrimp or salted peanuts.
Halve the avocados, remove the pits. Spoon the pulp into a bowl; be careful not to break the skins, as these will be used for holding the filling. Add the lemon juice at once so the pulp does not have an opportunity to discolor. Mash thoroughly, then blend in all the other ingredients; the onion or onions should be chopped very finely. Return the mixture to the 4 halved shells and top with shrimp or nuts. *Serves 4, or 8–12 if part of a mixed hors d'oeuvre.*
To vary Add 2–3 oz. chopped shrimp to the mixture.
Use cream cheese instead of heavy cream and add finely chopped nuts to the mixture.

Smoked Herring and Grapefruit Dip

2 slices lean bacon; 1 small onion; 2 fairly large grapefruit; 1½ cups cottage cheese; 6 tablespoons heavy cream; 2 tablespoons chopped parsley; 1 can smoked herring fillets; seasoning.

Fry or broil the bacon until crisp; leave two larger pieces for garnish, then chop finely. Chop or grate the onion. Remove the tops from the grapefruit and scoop out all the pulp. Press this through a strainer to extract the juice. Mix the juice with the cottage cheese, the chopped bacon and onion and the cream. Blend thoroughly, then add the parsley and the well drained flaked herring fillets. Keep two pieces of herring for garnish. Season the mixture very well, then pile back into the grapefruit shells. Garnish with pieces of bacon and herring. *Serves 4, or 8–12 if part of a mixed hors d'oeuvre.*

Melon and Pineapple Dip

1 cantaloupe; 1 lb. (2 cups tightly packed) cream cheese; ⅔ cup plain yoghurt; 1 tablespoon tomato paste, 1 can pineapple chunks; 2 tablespoons chopped parsley; seasoning.
Cut the top off the melon, scoop the flesh from this slice. Remove the seeds then scoop out all the pulp; use a dessertspoon or a melon scoop, as shown in Sketch 4 opposite. If using a scoop, save a few melon balls for garnish. Blend the cream cheese, yoghurt and tomato paste until smooth. Stir in the melon pulp, well drained pineapple chunks and parsley. Mix thoroughly, add a little pineapple syrup from the can if the mixture is too stiff. Season well. Spoon back into the melon shell and top with melon balls. *Serves 8, or 12–16 if part of a mixed hors d'oeuvre.*

Storing and freezing *Grapefruit and melon store well for some time, although melons ripen quickly in hot weather. Put into a refrigerator for a short time before serving. Whole melons and whole grapefruit do not freeze well, but segments of grapefruit or melon balls, packed in sugar and water syrup, freeze very well for a limited time. Avocados also ripen quickly, so use soon after purchase. They can be kept for a few days in a refrigerator and can be frozen whole. Use as soon as they have defrosted. The avocado must be ripe when frozen.*
To use leftovers *Leftover fruit can be added to salads.*

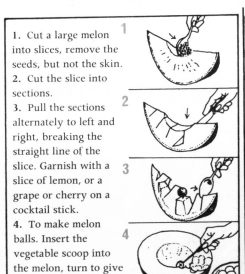

1. Cut a large melon into slices, remove the seeds, but not the skin.
2. Cut the slice into sections.
3. Pull the sections alternately to left and right, breaking the straight line of the slice. Garnish with a slice of lemon, or a grape or cherry on a cocktail stick.
4. To make melon balls. Insert the vegetable scoop into the melon, turn to give a ball.

Avocado dip, Smoked herring and grapefruit dip and Melon and pineapple dip

Salad as Hors d'Oeuvre

Practically every type of salad can be served as an hors d'oeuvre. The simplest salad can be delicious if the food is fresh and presented well.

Firm fresh tomatoes, sliced and topped with a little oil and vinegar and chopped onion, chives and parsley, are an excellent beginning to the meal. Hard boiled eggs and tomatoes make a very satisfying as well as attractive salad. Slice firm tomatoes, as shown in the picture, season, and insert slices of hard boiled egg in between each cut. Serve on a bed of lettuce with mayonnaise to taste.

Stuffed hard boiled eggs (see also page 70) are another type of salad that can be prepared and served very easily.

Blue Print
Serving Salad for an Hors d'Oeuvre

Salads can be surprisingly filling and substantial, so let the salad you serve at the beginning of a meal be fairly light textured or allow small portions only. It should be well seasoned and flavored to stimulate the palate.

A salad can be as varied or as simple as you like, but should not repeat the ingredients that follow in the main course. For example, if you are serving meat, fish or poultry with a tomato sauce, you should avoid adding tomatoes to the salad you present as the first course. You will find many salads suitable for a meal starter on pages 58–62. Some of the salads on these pages are based on pasta and these would be unusual and ideal if the main course was rather light, for they are very sustaining.

● **AVOID** *Too substantial salads; they should be light and interesting in both color and texture.*

● **TO REDUCERS** *Choose the low calorie ingredients — tomatoes, cucumber (fresh or pickled), green salad — where possible.*

Storing and freezing *These salads are better eaten fresh. They can be covered and stored for a short time in the refrigerator.*
To use leftovers *Serve in smaller dishes and with a fresh garnish.*

Smoked Salmon and Egg Salad

4 eggs; little mayonnaise; about $\frac{1}{4}$ lb. very thinly cut smoked salmon; 1 lemon; cayenne pepper; seasoning; lettuce. *To garnish:* watercress; tomatoes.

Hard boil the eggs, remove from the boiling water, plunge into cold water and crack the shells. Remove the shells while the eggs are still warm as it is easier to mash the yolks. Halve the eggs lengthwise. Remove the yolks from the whites very carefully, put the yolks into a bowl and mix thoroughly with enough mayonnaise to make a soft creamy consistency. Chop the smoked salmon finely and blend with a squeeze lemon juice and a shake cayenne pepper. Put into the whites. Season the egg yolk mixture and put into a piping bag with a $\frac{1}{4}$-inch rose tip. Pipe the mixture on top of the smoked salmon and arrange on a bed of lettuce. Garnish with watercress and small wedges of tomato. *Serves 4, or 8 if part of a mixed hors d'oeuvre.*

Italian Salad

5 oz. pasta, preferably spiral shaped; seasoning; 4 oz. can pimiento; $\frac{2}{3}$ cup crushed pineapple; $\frac{1}{3}$ cup currants; 2 tablespoons olive oil; 1 tablespoon white wine vinegar.

Cook the pasta in well seasoned boiling water for about 8 minutes or until tender. Drain, rinse in cold water and drain again. Add the pimiento, pineapple plus the juice from the can and the currants. Stir in the oil, vinegar and a generous amount of seasoning. Pile into a dish. *Serves 6, or 12 if part of a mixed hors d'oeuvre.*

Pasta Slaw

3 oz. spaghetti rings; seasoning; $\frac{1}{2}$ small white cabbage; 1 small green pepper; 1 medium-sized carrot. *For the dressing:* 4 tablespoons mayonnaise; 1 tablespoon sour cream; 1 tablespoon cider vinegar; 2 teaspoons sugar.

Cook the pasta in well seasoned boiling water for 10–12 minutes until tender. Drain, rinse in cold water and drain again. Shred the cabbage very finely, dice the green pepper (discard the core and seeds), grate the carrot coarsely. Mix the ingredients for the dressing together, add the pasta, then the remainder of the prepared ingredients. Chill well before serving. *Serves 6, or 12 if part of a mixed hors d'oeuvre.*

Summer Salad

$\frac{1}{4}$ lb. elbow macaroni; seasoning; 1 medium-sized can tuna; $\frac{1}{3}$ cup raisins; $\frac{1}{4}$ cup walnuts; 1 eating apple; 2 stalks celery; 3 tablespoons mayonnaise; lettuce; chopped chives; lemon juice. *To garnish:* celery leaves.

Cook the macaroni in well seasoned boiling water for 8 minutes. Drain, rinse in cold water and drain again. Add the flaked fish, raisins, chopped nuts, cored and sliced, but not peeled, apple (reserve a few slices for garnish), chopped celery and mayonnaise. Mix thoroughly and season well. Line a dish with lettuce and pile the salad on top. Sprinkle with chopped chives and garnish with the reserved apple slices, dipped in lemon juice, and celery leaves. *Serves 4, or 8 if part of a mixed hors d'oeuvre.*

Garden Salad

$\frac{1}{4}$ lb. elbow macaroni; seasoning; 2 table-spoons olive oil; 1 tablespoon white or brown cider vinegar; pinch sugar; pinch dry mustard; 3–4 green onions; 2 stalks celery; 1 small green pepper; $\frac{1}{4}$ lb. Swiss or processed cheese; 4 tablespoons mayonnaise. *To garnish:* 2–3 tomatoes.

Cook the macaroni in well seasoned boiling water for 8 minutes. Drain, rinse in cold water and drain again. Blend the oil, vinegar, sugar and mustard. Toss the macaroni in this. Add the chopped onions and celery, diced pepper (discard the core and seeds) and diced cheese. Mix with mayonnaise, season well and pile into a dish. Garnish with wedges of tomato. *Serves 4, or 8 if part of a mixed hors d'oeuvre.*

Maryland Salad

2 oz. shell pasta; seasoning; $\frac{3}{4}$ cup cooked corn; 1 small red pepper; 2–4 tablespoons mayonnaise; a little onion salt.

Cook the pasta in well seasoned boiling water for about 10 minutes. Drain, rinse in cold water, then drain again. Blend with the cooked corn, diced red pepper (discard the core and seeds), mayonnaise and seasoning. Allow to cool thoroughly then serve in a flat dish. *Serves 4, or 8 if part of a mixed hors d'oeuvre.*

To vary Add peas or mixed vegetables in place of the corn. Add chopped ham.

Egg and tomato salad

Smoked salmon and egg salad

Italian salad, Summer salad, Pasta slaw and Garden salad

11

Mixed Hors d'Oeuvre

A selection of the dishes in this section would make a splendid hors d'oeuvre, but on this page are a wide variety of simple ingredients to give an ambitious looking tray from which to choose.

Select a mixed hors d'oeuvre if you have plenty of time to prepare the dishes and if your main course is fairly light. In the hors d'oeuvre tray opposite there is a good balance between vegetables and fish with a little meat. I doubt whether many people would have quite as large a selection as this so you will also find a choice of six ingredients with ideas to make them more exciting for special occasions and a very simple hors d'oeuvre consisting of just four dishes.

Blue Print

Perfect Mixed Hors d'Oeuvre

Plan a good mixture of different colors and textures.

Be adventurous about your mixture of ingredients, never mind adding fruit to the vegetables; for example, balls of melon, slices of grapefruit and fresh orange.

Keep a good balance between the amount of vegetables, fish and meat.

If you have separate hors d'oeuvre trays, then serve each ingredient or prepared dish in an individual container; but if you do not possess these, then I would arrange the basic mixed hors d'oeuvre on plates. Serve the ingredients really chilled, but if you add one hot dish, such as hot filled pancakes, fish cakes, hot shrimp in sauce or browned butter, this adds to the interest of the meal starter.

● **AVOID** *Having all food in mayonnaise. It makes the first course too substantial and rich. Leave some vegetables, meat or fish quite plain if you have others in a dressing. It is, however, usual to serve hors d'oeuvre ingredients in their dressings and not add these at the table.*

● **TO RECTIFY** *If your hors d'oeuvre selection seems rather rich, then have bowls of lettuce, endive and watercress to counteract this.*

● **SHORT CUTS** *Use some of the ready prepared ingredients in addition to those given, i.e. pickled gherkins, walnuts, onions, canned anchovy fillets, flaked canned tuna or salmon. Use diced cooked vegetables, by themselves, or put into a dressing; this can be mayonnaise or oil and vinegar.*

● **TO REDUCERS** *Concentrate on the plain vegetables, meat like salami and avoid the ingredients in sauces.*

Storing and freezing *It is essential that a good hors d'oeuvre looks fresh, so prepare at the last minute. Keep the dishes covered and store in the refrigerator. The frosted cocktails are excellent for storing in the freezing compartment of a refrigerator or home freezer. Bring out some time before required so the mixture is not too hard.*

To use leftovers *Add any leftover hors d'oeuvre to mixed salads. Return the cocktails to the freezer.*

Frosted tomato cocktail

An Hors d'Oeuvre Tray

Sliced celery—this could be blended with mayonnaise and chopped hard boiled eggs.
Pickled red cabbage.
Pickled herrings with onion rings.
Asparagus—cooked, tossed in seasoned oil and vinegar and topped with strips of pimiento.
Cottage cheese—mixed with chives.
This could be blended also with diced ham and cooked vegetables for a most colorful dish.
Liverwurst—sliced.
Corn—cooked or canned, with stuffed olives. This could be blended with chopped chicory, red and green peppers and a little well seasoned oil and vinegar.
Salami—sliced.
Coleslaw—this particular version was made with shredded cabbage and grated carrot blended with well seasoned mayonnaise and a little lemon juice (or vinegar) to give a softer, more piquant sauce.
Sliced well seasoned tomato—topped with parsley (oil, vinegar and chopped chives could be added).
Flowerets of *partially* cooked cauliflower—topped with sieved egg yolk. The vegetable could be tossed in mayonnaise (the chopped egg white could be mixed with the peeled shrimp—see below).
Halved dill pickles.
Canned sardines on lettuce.
Rolls of boiled ham—these can be rolled round mixed vegetables in mayonnaise.
Peeled shrimp in tomato mayonnaise (page 18).

Take Six Hors d'Oeuvre

1. Serve a variety of sliced salami and garlic sausage. Garnish with celery leaves.
Special occasion suggestion: Dice and serve in walnut mustard sauce, i.e. mix mayonnaise with Dijon mustard and chopped walnuts.
2. Canned artichoke hearts tossed in well seasoned oil and vinegar.
Special occasion suggestion: Top the artichokes with cones of smoked salmon wrapped round shelled shrimp.
3. **Cheese and carrot salad** Mix equal quantities of coarsely grated cheese and carrot.
Special occasion suggestion: Blend with shredded white cabbage, raisins, mayonnaise and chopped almonds.
4. **Potato and pepper salad** Toss diced cooked new potatoes, diced celery and red pepper (discard core and seeds) in well seasoned oil and vinegar or mayonnaise.
Special occasion suggestion: Add diced gherkins, capers and chopped green onions.
5. **Beet salad** Cut cooked or canned beets into neat strips, blend with finely chopped onion, oil, vinegar and seasoning. Top with onion rings.
Special occasion suggestion: Add chopped apple and a very little diced cooked duck or chicken.
6. **Herring and onion salad** Cut Bismarck, cooked or rollmop herrings into neat pieces. Mix with diced apples, chopped onion and blend with plain yoghurt or sour cream. Garnish with sliced apple (dipped in lemon juice) and watercress.
Special occasion suggestion: Add a small quantity of white wine to the yoghurt or sour cream, or use mayonnaise and wine blended together. Add diced dill pickles.

Four Simple Hors d'Oeuvre

Bean and salami salad Rub the salad bowl with a cut clove of garlic. Mix diced salami and cooked broad beans together. Toss in oil and vinegar. Season well.
To vary Diced frankfurters, ham or garlic sausage may be used instead.
Orange herring salad Blend segments of fresh orange and soused or rollmop herrings together. Season well. Put on to a bed of lettuce.
To vary Use portions of smoked trout or smoked mackerel with orange or other fairly sharp fruit. Serve with prepared horseradish.
Vegetable salad Niçoise Mix sliced or quartered tomatoes, tiny cooked whole or sliced new potatoes, diced cooked green beans and black olives. Toss in oil and vinegar and season well.
Mushroom rice salad Cook long grain rice in boiling salted water until just tender. Drain and toss in well seasoned oil and vinegar. Allow to cool then blend with strips of green pepper (discard the core and seeds), sliced raw button mushrooms and white or black raisins.

To vary Add chopped anchovy fillets. Add pine nuts or blanched almonds.
Mix with cooked peas, flaked salmon and diced cucumber.

Frosted Tomato Cocktail

Although this cocktail can be served to everyone at the beginning of a meal, without the choice of an alternative, I occasionally have made it part of a mixed hors d'oeuvre, for it balances the rather rich flavor of foods in mayonnaise. In this case scoop out balls of the frosted mixture and serve on a bed of lettuce.
2 lb. ripe tomatoes; 5 tablespoons water; seasoning; good pinch sugar; little lemon juice; Worcestershire sauce to taste. *To garnish:* lettuce or mint.
Chop the tomatoes. Put into a saucepan with the water, seasoning and sugar. Heat for a few minutes only so you can extract the juice. Put through a food mill, add lemon juice, Worcestershire sauce and any extra seasoning or flavoring required (celery salt, cayenne pepper and a few drops Tabasco sauce can be added). Put into the freezing tray and freeze lightly. Either spoon or scoop on to lettuce leaves and make part of a mixed hors d'oeuvre, or chop lightly (as the picture) and spoon into chilled glasses and top with mint leaves. *Serves 4–6, or 8–12 if part of a mixed hors d'oeuvre.*
To vary
Frosted melon cocktail The red-fleshed watermelon is ideal for this. Halve the melon, remove the seeds and scoop out the flesh. Mix with lemon juice, a little sugar, then taste. You may like to add seasoning to make it more piquant in flavor and/or a few drops Tabasco or Worcestershire sauce. Freeze and serve as the tomato cocktail.

Four simple hors d'oeuvre

13

Meat Hors d'Oeuvre

You will find that meat hors d'oeuvre are extremely popular, even when the main course consists of meat or poultry.

Blue Print

Choosing Meat Hors d'Oeuvre

With the very wide selection of garlic sausages, salami, etc. available, this can be a very simple course to prepare. Arrange the various kinds of salami (or choose all one kind) on a dish and garnish with lettuce and tomato. Serve with mustard.

touch of originality, serve with Cumberland sauce (see page 27).

Prosciutto or other smoked ham makes a luxurious meal starter. It can be served by itself or it blends well with melon, fresh figs or pears.

Undoubtedly pâté is popular with most people and the recipe on this page is particularly quick and easy.

Small portions of some of the meat or chicken salads given on page 63 would also be very suitable. Modern food is often very informal and the slightly unusual version of sausage rolls would be a practical and inexpensive beginning to a meal.

Sausage twists and Sausage cheese savories (above)

For Family Occasions

Sausage Twists

1 lb. small chipolata sausages. *Puff pastry made with:* 1 cup flour; pinch salt; $\frac{1}{4}$ lb. butter and water to mix (or buy $\frac{1}{2}$ lb. frozen puff pastry). *To glaze:* little beaten egg.

Broil, fry or bake the sausages for about 6 minutes until partially cooked. Allow to cool. Make the pastry and roll out until wafer thin. Cut into strips and roll round the sausages, as shown in the picture. Put on a baking sheet. Brush with beaten egg. Bake for 15 minutes towards the top of a very hot oven, 450–475°F. Reduce the heat after 7–8 minutes if necessary. Serve with mustard or one of the sauces below. *Serves 8 as an hors d'oeuvre.* These sauces are all cold, but could be heated in the top of a double boiler or bowl over hot water.

Onion mustard sauce Blend $\frac{2}{3}$ cup mayonnaise with 2–4 tablespoons chopped green onions (use the white part only) and 3–4 teaspoons Dijon mustard or use half this quantity of prepared English mustard. Top with the chopped green stems of the onions.
Deviled tomato sauce Blend $\frac{2}{3}$ cup mayonnaise with 2 tablespoons tomato paste or ketchup and 2 tablespoons half and half or light cream. Flavor with a few drops Tabasco and/or Worcestershire sauce. Top with parsley.

Pineapple sweet sour sauce Blend $\frac{2}{3}$ cup mayonnaise with 2–4 tablespoons syrup from a small can pineapple. Add 2–3 teaspoons vinegar, 1 teaspoon prepared mustard and the diced pineapple.

Chopped Liver

Generous $\frac{1}{2}$ lb. calf's or chicken livers; 4 tablespoons rendered chicken fat or butter; 2 eggs; 1 small onion; seasoning. *To garnish:* lemon; parsley.

Sauté the liver in the hot fat or butter until just tender. Hard boil the eggs. Mince or chop the liver with the onion. Add to the chopped hard boiled eggs and season well. Allow to cool, pile on to a dish and garnish with lemon and parsley. Serve with hot toast and butter. *Serves 4–5.*

Fried Garlic Sausage

Many garlic sausages can be served hot, particularly the Spanish chorizo, and sliced blood sausage makes an excellent hors d'oeuvre. It is important that the sausage is not dry, so sauté quickly.

Dip the slices of sausage into a very little flour and sauté in hot fat for a few minutes. Serve garnished with tomatoes and lettuce.

For Special Occasions

Five Minute Pâté

Generous $\frac{1}{2}$ lb. calf's liver; 4 tablespoons butter; seasoning; 2–3 tablespoons cream; 2–3 tablespoons sherry or brandy.

Cut the liver into small pieces. Heat the butter in a pan and sauté the liver in this for several minutes only. Either mince or chop very finely while warm and blend with the other ingredients, or puree in the blender with the seasoning, cream and sherry or brandy. Allow to cool and serve with hot toast and butter. *Serves 4–5.*
Note If the mixture seems too stiff for the blender blades, then add a very little extra hot liquid (cream, stock or brandy). If you add the liver gradually to the liquid, though, it should blend easily.
To vary Add 1 crushed clove garlic to the liver when sautéing in the pan.
Add 1–2 gherkins to the mixture in the blender.
Use chicken livers instead. Pig or lamb liver could be used, but this needs slightly longer cooking.
Cover with a layer of melted butter to prevent it from drying.

Ham Mousse

Envelope plus 1 teaspoon unflavored gelatin; $1\frac{1}{3}$ cups chicken or ham stock; 2 eggs; $\frac{3}{4}$ lb. lean ham; $\frac{2}{3}$ cup mayonnaise. *To garnish:* lemon; tomatoes; lettuce.

Soften and then dissolve the gelatin in the stock. Separate the eggs and beat the egg yolks for a few minutes. Add the warm aspic liquid, whisking hard as you do so. Cool, then add the ground or finely chopped ham and mayonnaise. Leave until the mixture stiffens slightly then fold in the beaten egg whites. Spoon into an oiled mold and allow to set. Turn out and garnish with wedges of lemon, tomato and lettuce. *Serves 4–6.*
To vary Add lightly whipped cream flavored with sherry or lemon juice in place of mayonnaise.
Use tomato juice instead of stock in which to dissolve the gelatin.

Cucumber cheese mold

Mainly Vegetable Hors d'Oeuvre

Many vegetables are served as an hors d'oeuvre, the most usual and appropriate being artichokes and asparagus. These vegetables can be served hot with melted butter or cold with a vinaigrette dressing. Many other vegetables are served as part of salads and these are described on pages 10–13.

Cheese is not often part of an hors d'oeuvre, but it is included in both the recipes pictured on this page. The cheese is used delicately so it does not make too substantial or too strongly flavored a dish.

Vegetable cheese pie

For Family Occasions

Vegetable Cheese Pie

4 tablespoons butter or margarine; 4 large tomatoes; 2 onions; $\frac{1}{2}$ cup mushrooms; small can asparagus tips; seasoning; $\frac{3}{4}$ lb. (1$\frac{1}{2}$ cups) mashed potatoes. *For the cheese sauce:* 2 tablespoons butter or margarine; 4 tablespoons flour; 1$\frac{1}{3}$ cups milk; $\frac{1}{4}$ lb. (1 cup) grated Cheddar cheese. *To garnish:* 1–2 tomatoes.

Heat 2 tablespoons butter or margarine and sauté the 4 peeled chopped tomatoes, onions and mushrooms until softened. Mix with the drained asparagus tips and seasoning. Put into 4 individual dishes. Add the rest of the butter or margarine to the potatoes and season. Put into a piping bag with a $\frac{1}{4}$-inch rose tip and pipe a border round the edge of the dishes. Make the cheese sauce as page 17. Spoon over the vegetables. Brown under the broiler or in the oven and serve at once garnished with sliced tomato. *Serves 4.*
To vary Use flaked cooked fish instead of the selection of vegetables.
Use one vegetable only instead of the selection in the recipe.
Use a béchamel sauce (see page 17) for the base rather than the white sauce given above.

For Special Occasions

Cucumber Cheese Mold

1 lemon; 1 envelope plus 1 teaspoon unflavored gelatin; 1$\frac{1}{3}$ cups water; 1 large cucumber; $\frac{2}{3}$ cup mayonnaise; $\frac{1}{2}$ lb. cream cheese; seasoning. *To garnish:* cucumber; watercress; lettuce; tomatoes.
Grate the rind from the lemon; use only the top "zest". Soften the gelatin in the lemon

juice. Add the lemon rind to the water, heat and pour over the gelatin. Stir until the gelatin has dissolved. Strain, if wished, to remove the pieces of lemon rind. Allow to cool, but not set. Dice the cucumber finely, remove the seeds and the peel if the latter is tough. Blend the cucumber with the mayonnaise and cream cheese. Gradually beat in the cool liquid gelatin mixture. Season well. Spoon into an oiled mold and allow to set. Turn out and garnish with cucumber, watercress, lettuce and sliced tomatoes. Serve with mayonnaise or tartar sauce (page 18). *Serves 6–8, or 12–16 if part of a mixed hors d'oeuvre.*
To vary Use a lemon flavored gelatin instead of unflavored gelatin. This gives a slightly sweet flavor which is very pleasant. Add 2–4 tablespoons very finely chopped or grated onion to the gelatin liquid.

Mushroom Cocktail

Generous $\frac{1}{4}$ lb. (1–1$\frac{1}{2}$ cups) button mushrooms; $\frac{2}{3}$ cup yoghurt; $\frac{1}{2}$ tablespoon olive oil; 1 tablespoon lemon juice or white wine vinegar; 1 tablespoon chopped chives; 1 tablespoon chopped parsley; seasoning (optional); lettuce. *To garnish:* paprika.
Wash, dry and slice the mushrooms very thinly. Blend the yoghurt, oil, lemon juice or vinegar and herbs. Add seasoning if wished. Shred the lettuce very finely. Put into 4–6 glasses. Blend the mushrooms with the sauce. Spoon on top of the lettuce, garnish with paprika. *Serves 4–6.*
To vary Light cream or mayonnaise may be used in place of yoghurt. The latter is rather thick, so blend with a little cream.
Mix mushrooms and shrimp in the recipe above.

Danish Cucumber Boats

1 medium-sized, but fairly thick, cucumber; 2 tablespoons oil; seasoning; 2 tablespoons lemon juice; $\frac{1}{4}$ lb. smoked salmon; little grated horseradish; 3 eggs; 2 tablespoons heavy cream; 2 tablespoons butter. *To garnish:* $\frac{1}{2}$ red pepper; lettuce.
Remove the peel from the cucumber and slice lengthways. Cut into about 12 segments and remove the seeds, creating small boat shapes. Chop the seeds and pieces removed very finely. Blend the oil, seasoning and lemon juice. Sprinkle the cucumber with this dressing and leave for about 20 minutes. Drain the cucumber. Fill each boat with chopped smoked salmon, spread with a little grated horseradish. Season the beaten eggs, add the chopped cucumber and cream. Heat the butter in a saucepan. Scramble the eggs and spoon over the smoked salmon. Garnish with thin strips of red pepper and serve on a bed of lettuce. While the scrambled egg may be served cold, this is a very pleasant hors d'oeuvre with *cold* cucumber and salmon and *hot* egg topping. *Serves 4–6.*

Storing and freezing *All these recipes should be served freshly cooked or freshly prepared.*

Through the various chapters of this book are recipes for sauces that are needed for a particular dish. In this and the next pages, basic entrée sauces are described with easy and interesting variations that can be served with various foods. An indication of the dishes with which they blend is given with each sauce.

Blue Print

Making Sauces

The following points are the most important when making any sauce.

1. Use the correct proportions for the consistency required, but if you have misjudged the amount of flour or liquid, this can be adjusted:
a) If too thick add more liquid.
b) If too thin thicken by cooking down in an open pan.
2. Cook the flour adequately. If a sauce is cooked for too short a time, there is a floury taste which spoils the flavor. The times given in the Blue Print Recipe are minimum and a little longer cooking will be an advantage.
3. Stir the sauce as you add the liquid.
4. Stir as the sauce thickens to keep it smooth and prevent it sticking to the pan.
5. Taste to make sure the sauce is adequately seasoned.
6. Never let a sauce boil if adding egg or egg yolk; the sauce will curdle (become lumpy). Cook very gently. Other ingredients can cause curdling to a white or similar sauce, i.e. lemon juice, vinegar, wine, sour cream.
7. Do not let a skin form on a sauce. There are two ways of preventing this:
a) Cover with very damp polyethylene wrap. Remove the wrap when ready to heat the sauce.
b) Use less liquid in making the sauce than stated in the recipe. Make the sauce, allow to thicken, then pour the cold liquid on top. This acts as a barrier between the sauce and the air. You will need a good layer of liquid so hold back about 25%. Stir the liquid slowly into the sauce before heating.

● **AVOID** *A lumpy sauce. An undercooked sauce. A greasy sauce.*
● **TO RECTIFY** *Whisk a lumpy sauce hard and the lumps should come out. If not, strain the sauce or whirl in a blender and reheat. Taste a sauce and if it has the roughness of uncooked flour or cornstarch, return to the heat for a little longer. A greasy sauce indicates too much butter (or other fat) to the amount of flour, so blend a little extra flour with cold liquid, stir into the sauce and continue stirring until thickened.*
● **SHORT CUTS** *Use the quick method of saucemaking or sauce mixes.*
● **TO REDUCERS** *Sauces should be avoided.*
Storing and freezing *A sauce can be kept for 1–2 days then reheated. Cover with damp paper to keep it as moist as possible. Heat gently to serve. You will probably need to add a little extra liquid to give the desired consistency. It is a good idea to whirl the sauce in the blender after or before heating. Sauces can be frozen but they may separate as they are reheated. The possibilities of this happening are less if you make the sauce with cornstarch (allow 2 tablespoons cornstarch in place of each 4 tablespoons flour) or potato flour (allow the same measurement as when using flour). Whisk or blend the defrosted sauce if it does separate or add a little extra flour or cornstarch mixed with cold liquid and cook slowly, stirring all the time, until the sauce thickens again.*

Caper sauce

Terms Used in Saucemaking

Roux This means the butter and flour mixture, which can be called a liaison. Stages 1–3 in the Blue Print Recipe for white sauce show how this is used.
Consistency The thickness of a sauce.
Coating consistency The sauce coats the back of a wooden spoon (shown in the picture).
Thin consistency The sauce pours easily. This is often used when adding a sauce to vegetables to make a soup. Follow the Blue Print Recipe but use 1 tablespoon butter or margarine and 2 tablespoons flour to 2 cups milk.
Panada or binding consistency The sauce is very thick. This is used to bind ingredients together, e.g. in rissoles and fish cakes (instead of an egg). Follow the Blue Print Recipe but use 4 tablespoons butter or margarine and 8 tablespoons flour to 2 cups milk.

Blue Print Recipe

White Sauce

For a coating consistency
2 tablespoons butter or margarine · 4 tablespoons flour · 2 cups milk · seasoning ·
1. Heat the butter or margarine in a fairly small saucepan. Do not overheat, otherwise the butter or margarine darkens in color.
2. Remove from the heat, stir in the flour.
3. Return to a low heat and stir for several minutes until the roux forms a dry looking ball.
4. Once again take the pan off the heat and gradually blend in the liquid.
5. Stir briskly with a wooden spoon as you do so.
6. Return once again to the heat and bring steadily to the boil, stirring or whisking all the time as the sauce thickens.
7. Add *a little* seasoning and continue stirring for 4–5 minutes. Taste and add more seasoning if required.
To serve A white sauce blends with most foods—eggs, fish, poultry, vegetables. *All recipes based on this make about 2 cups sauce.*

Adaptations

Blending method Use the same proportions as in the Blue Print Recipe for white sauce. Blend the flour carefully with the liquid. Put into a saucepan. Add the butter or margarine. Bring gradually to the boil, stirring all the time. Cook as Stage 7 of the Blue Print Recipe. This is found to be an easier method of making the sauce for some people.
Quick method Use the same proportions as in the Blue Print Recipe for white sauce.

Making white sauce

Proceed as Stages 1–3. Take the pan off the heat, add *all* the liquid. (It is better if the liquid is boiling.) Return to the heat. Allow the liquid to come to the boil and whisk sharply. Continue as Stage 7.

Using cornstarch If you wish to use cornstarch instead of flour, remember cornstarch thickens more than flour, so use 2 tablespoons cornstarch in place of 4 tablespoons flour. Although a sauce made with cornstarch thickens more quickly than one made with flour, it is important to cook it for some minutes.

When all milk should not be used in a white sauce

I prefer using half milk and half vegetable stock, or at least some vegetable stock, when making a sauce to coat vegetables. In this way you retain more of the flavor of the particular vegetables.

Use *some* fish, meat or poultry stock in the sauce when making a white sauce to serve with these foods, see velouté sauce below.

Recipes Based on White Sauce

In each case the proportions for the basic sauce are as the Blue Print Recipe. The flavorings are added at Stage 7, unless stated to the contrary.

Admiral sauce—for fish dishes.
Add 1 tablespoon capers, 1 tablespoon chopped parsley, a squeeze of anchovy paste, ½ teaspoon grated lemon rind and 1 tablespoon lemon juice.

Anchovy sauce—for fish dishes.
Add enough anchovy paste to give a definite flavor and color to the sauce. Be sparing with the salt.

Aurore sauce—for fish dishes.
Make white or béchamel sauce. Flavor with a little paprika and ½ teaspoon chopped tarragon. For luxury occasions, add 3 table-spoons pounded red lobster coral (roe).

Béchamel sauce—A more sophisticated version of white sauce and used as a basis for other sauces in place of white sauce. Warm the milk with a piece of celery, carrot, onion and bay leaf for 2–3 minutes. Leave in the pan for about 30 minutes, strain, then add enough milk to give 2 cups again. Proceed as white sauce. If desired you can flavor with a little grated nutmeg at Stage 7 of the Blue Print Recipe.

Bohemian sauce—for meat dishes (particularly beef).
Use half milk and half white stock. Add 1–2 teaspoons grated horseradish. This sauce can be made by omitting the flour, heating the butter or margarine and milk and thickening with ⅔ cup soft white bread crumbs, then adding seasoning, grated horseradish and a little cream.

Caper sauce—generally served with boiled lamb, but can be used with fish, ham or chicken.
Add 1 tablespoon capers (chopped or left whole) and a little vinegar from the bottle.

Cardinal sauce—for fish dishes.
Blend pounded lobster coral into a very creamy béchamel sauce.

Celery sauce—excellent with chicken or turkey.
Make white sauce with half milk and half celery stock (from boiling finely chopped celery). Add ½ cup chopped cooked celery and a little heavy cream.

Cheese sauce—to serve with fish, vegetables, meat, eggs.
Add a little prepared mustard to the thickened sauce or good pinch dry mustard to the flour. Stir in 1 cup grated cheese (Cheddar, Dutch Gouda or Gruyère—or use rather less Parmesan). Heat, do not boil.

Duchesse sauce—for boiled ham.

Blend 4–5 tablespoons chopped tongue and ⅔ cup sliced mushrooms sautéed in 2 tablespoons butter into the sauce.

German sauce—for chicken or veal.
Make the sauce with half milk and half white stock. When thickened, blend 2 egg yolks with 3–4 tablespoons heavy cream. Stir into the sauce. Cook gently, *without* boiling, for several minutes.

Mornay sauce—as cheese sauce above or for a richer sauce use a béchamel sauce foundation.
Add 1–2 tablespoons cream blended with 1 egg yolk with the cheese.

Mustard sauce—to serve with herrings, very good with fried or broiled chicken.
Blend from 1 teaspoon to 1 tablespoon prepared mustard with the sauce or add ½–2 teaspoons dry mustard to the flour.

Onion (soubise) sauce—excellent with many meat dishes, particularly roast lamb.
Boil 3 finely chopped onions until tender. Strain the liquid. Use 1 cup of this and 1 cup milk to make the sauce. Add the chopped onions to the thickened sauce. Add a little cream, cayenne pepper and/or grated nutmeg if desired.

Shrimp sauce—for fish or egg dishes.
Add 4–6 tablespoons whole or chopped shrimp to the sauce.

Velouté sauce—for steamed or boiled chicken or other meat dishes.
Make béchamel sauce with half chicken stock and half milk or all chicken stock if preferred. When thickened, blend in 4–5 tablespoons heavy cream mixed with 1–2 tablespoons dry sherry. Heat gently *without* boiling.

White wine sauce—for fish, chicken or veal dishes.
Flavor a white or béchamel sauce with a little white wine.

Cold Sauces

The most famous of all cold sauces is mayonnaise, and while excellent commercial mayonnaise is available the homemade variety has a flavor that it is difficult to surpass.

Blue Print Recipe

Mayonnaise

2 egg yolks · $\frac{1}{2}$–1 teaspoon prepared mustard or Dijon mustard · $\frac{1}{4}$–$\frac{1}{2}$ teaspoon salt · good shake pepper · pinch sugar (optional) · 1 cup olive oil · 2–3 tablespoons vinegar (white or brown cider or wine vinegar) or lemon juice · 1 tablespoon boiling water (optional).

To make   Put the egg yolks, seasonings and sugar into a mixing bowl. Beat well with a wooden spoon or with a whisk. Add the oil drop by drop, beating all the time. When the oil has been incorporated, whisk in the vinegar or lemon juice. Taste once or twice to make sure you are not adding too much for *your* taste. Add the boiling water gradually at the end to give a very light creamy taste.
To serve   Cold with salads.
To make a piping mayonnaise   Add up to 1$\frac{1}{4}$ cups oil; the more oil added the thicker the mayonnaise.

● **AVOID**   *Adding the oil too quickly; if you do, the mayonnaise curdles.*
● **TO RECTIFY**   *Put another egg yolk into a bowl and whisk the curdled mayonnaise very gradually into this. Be sure the egg yolks and oil are at room temperature; if the eggs come from the refrigerator, the mayonnaise is more likely to curdle.*
● **SHORT CUTS**   *Use an electric beater. A blender is even quicker.*
● **TO REDUCERS**   *Avoid the oily mayonnaise and use the yoghurt dressing on this page.*

Mayonnaise in a Blender

Ingredients as the Blue Print but the order of adding these is different. Put the egg yolks, seasonings and sugar into the blender; switch on for a few seconds. Add the vinegar or lemon juice. Use the smaller amount the first time you make this. Switch on until blended. Switch to a low speed and pour the oil in *very steadily*. Taste and add any more vinegar or lemon juice required on low speed; then add the water.

Sauces Based on Mayonnaise

Andalouse sauce—especially good with shellfish.
Add 1–2 tablespoons fresh or canned tomato paste and 1 finely chopped red pepper (discard the core and seeds) to the thickened mayonnaise.
Aioli (garlic) mayonnaise—for all salads.
Add 1–2 cloves finely chopped or crushed garlic to the thickened mayonnaise. Taste and add a little extra lemon juice if desired.

Green mayonnaise—especially good with fish salads.
Add freshly chopped herbs plus a little green coloring, or put a spinach leaf and the herbs into the blender when the mayonnaise has thickened. Switch on until the herbs are chopped and the spinach blended.
Lemon mayonnaise—to serve in place of mayonnaise.
Add extra lemon juice and a little finely grated lemon rind to the thickened mayonnaise.
Tartar sauce—for all fish dishes.
Add up to 1 tablespoon chopped parsley, $\frac{1}{2}$–1 tablespoon chopped gherkins and 1–2 teaspoons whole or chopped capers to the thickened mayonnaise. If making the mayonnaise in the blender, add the sprigs of parsley and whole gherkins to the thickened mayonnaise. Switch on until chopped, then add the capers.
Tomato mayonnaise—especially good with cheese or meat salads.
If making in a blender, add 1–2 peeled, seeded tomatoes to the mayonnaise when thickened. Switch on until the tomatoes are blended. If mixing by hand sieve tomatoes or use tomato paste.

Yoghurt Dressing

Blend seasoning, a little prepared mustard and 1 crushed sugar substitute tablet into 1 cup unflavored yoghurt. Add $\frac{1}{2}$–1 teaspoon finely grated lemon rind and 1 tablespoon lemon juice. 1 tablespoon olive oil may also be blended into the yoghurt to give a richer flavor. *Serves 4.*

French Dressing

Gradually blend 2 tablespoons olive or other good salad oil (corn oil if wished) into a little dry or prepared mustard ($\frac{1}{2}$–1 teaspoon). Add a good pinch of salt, shake of pepper, a pinch of sugar and 1 tablespoon vinegar or lemon juice.

Vinaigrette Dressing

This is often given as another name for French dressing, but this is not quite correct—it is French dressing plus 1–2 teaspoons freshly chopped herbs. A teaspoon finely chopped shallot or onion and 2 teaspoons chopped gherkin may also be added.

Storing and freezing   *Mayonnaise keeps well in the refrigerator for several weeks. Keep well covered so the mixture does not dry. French dressing keeps almost indefinitely which is why you can make a large quantity and store it in a screw topped bottle. Shake before using. I prefer to make vinaigrette dressing freshly. Mayonnaise will not freeze; it separates badly.*

Mayonnaise

two

MEAT COOKERY

Meat is one of the most popular and important protein foods in most countries of the world. It is also one of the most expensive and, in order to make the best use of meat, it is worthwhile learning about the various cuts and grades, and to recognize them in the butcher's shop or supermarket so you may choose the best kind of meat for each and every purpose.

When one is busy, the quick cooking cuts of meat for sautéing and broiling are an obvious choice. Because these are tender cuts they are appreciably more expensive than meat for stewing. The Blue Prints on pages 23 and 24 give information on the best way to broil and sauté meats to make them as tender and appetizing as possible. One of the secrets of success when sautéing and broiling meat is to seal the outside of the meat quickly, so the meat remains moist, which is why the Blue Prints stress the importance of this. I hope they will also give some new suggestions of the meats that may be sautéed and broiled. For example, the obvious choice when one wants a Wiener Schnitzel is veal, but fillets of pork are

cheaper and really have more flavor than veal.

Nothing is more imposing than a really good roast; again this demands high quality, but if you make use of the slow roasting method on page 20, you can use the slightly cheaper cuts of meat. Stuffing and interesting accompaniments not only add flavor and help to keep the meat moist but enable one to serve more portions from a roast, and many fruits, vegetables and herbs can be used in stuffings and sauces.

Every country has its own traditional way of cooking meat and in countries where the quality of meat is not perhaps as good as one would wish, the cooks have become experts in slow cooking to tenderize meat by braising or boiling. There is a variety of such recipes from pages 26–28. Be adventurous in the vegetables and fruit you add; acid fruit is like wine, it gives flavor and helps to tenderize meat.

Never feel that specialty cuts are less interesting or nutritious than other cuts. The very wide variety of textures and flavors provided by these meats (liver, sweetbreads, tripe, kidneys, brains) make them appetizing and adaptable.

When one is making a fairly complicated meat dish, or buying a large quantity of meat, it is a good idea to freeze part of the dish or some of the meat to use on future occasions. On most pages in this part you will find information on home freezing of the meat or the completed dish.

I hope you enjoy the various meat dishes in this section and it will help you to provide greater variety to family meals.

There is nothing to beat the flavor of a succulent roast; when you buy expensive cuts, there is no point in dressing-up the meat, except to serve it with appropriate sauces and stuffings.

In most homes today the accepted method of roasting is in a roasting pan in the oven; purists argue that this is not roasting, it is baking and that the only correct method is to cook the meat on a turning spit over open heat. If you have a rotisserie attachment in your oven use this, for you do obtain more even browning over the whole roast than in a pan. If the rotisserie is under the broiler, then the cooking times are the same as given for fast roasting. If in the oven, you can select which method you prefer—high-or low-temperature cooking.

For top quality meat you may choose the heat at which you cook this. Although most sources recommend roasting at constant temperature, I personally prefer high-temperature roasting, for I believe the meat retains more flavor although it may shrink a little more in cooking. If the meat has been chilled, frozen or is of slightly cheaper quality, then the slower cooking is better for you achieve a more tender roast.

The table that follows the Blue Print assumes the meat is at room temperature.

● **AVOID** *Trying to roast cuts of meat recommended for stewing; these need long, slow cooking to break down the fibres and make them tender.*
Overcooking—this destroys flavor and texture and dries the roast. Roasting with no fat at all; this also dries out the meat and destroys flavor.
● **TO RECTIFY** *Look at the roast during cooking; if there is too much fat, pour away any excess. Dried meat is spoiled meat, so you must camouflage it with sauce or gravy.*
● **TO REDUCERS** *A sensible way to cook meat; avoid the fatty outside, stuffings and thickened sauces or gravy.*

Roasting Meat

Blue Print Recipe

Roasting Meat

To prepare Buy meat to give a minimum of $\frac{1}{2}$ to $\frac{3}{4}$ lb. per serving (including bone). Allow $\frac{1}{3}$ to $\frac{1}{2}$ lb. for boneless roasts and $\frac{3}{4}$ to 1 lb. for such cuts as spareribs. Defrost frozen meat. Dry the meat and season. Make any stuffing required. Put the meat in the roasting pan, foil or on the spit (boneless cuts should be placed on a rack). Lean cuts of meat with no fat covering should come with a layer of fat tied around them.

To Cook

1. IN AN OPEN ROASTING PAN Allow the times given under each meat. You can baste with a little fat during cooking if wished. This means spooning some of the hot drippings over the meat. The advantage of this is that it keeps the meat moist and encourages it to crisp, but it is not essential.

2. IN FOIL You need to wrap the meat in the foil and to time as under each meat, but you must allow about 20 minutes extra cooking time or set the oven 25°F higher. If you wish the meat to crisp and brown, open the foil for the last 20–30 minutes. There is no need to baste during cooking.

3. IN A COVERED ROASTING PAN Try and use one large enough to give some space above and around the meat. This means the fat splashes the lid, drops back on to the meat and so is self-basting; it will brown well. If required to be crisp, the lid should be removed for the last 20–30 minutes. Allow higher temperature or extra time as for foil.

4. SPIT ROASTING Time as for slow or fast roasting, but melt the fat and brush over the whole. Baste if wished during cooking.

5. FAST ROASTING The chart gives roasting times for low temperature slow roasting. If you prefer to fast roast, set the oven at 425–450°F. After 15–20 minutes, lower to 375–400°F. *For beef* (use fillet, sirloin, rib), 15 minutes per lb. and 15 minutes over for rare, 20 minutes per lb. and 20 minutes over for medium to well done. *For lamb* (all cuts) 20 minutes per lb., 20 minutes over. *For pork* (all cuts), 25 minutes per lb., 25 minutes over. *For veal,* 25 minutes per lb. plus 25 minutes over. The weight should include any stuffing.

To serve Hot with seasonal vegetables and sauces or stuffings as on page 22, or cold with salad; many of the stuffings are also good cold.

Good Gravy

Gravy can make or break a roast. It should incorporate the delicious flavors from the roasting pan.

To make If you have stock from meat bones, then use this as the basis of the gravy, but if no meat stock is available then use vegetable stock, obtained after straining the vegetables. This contains valuable mineral salts, so it is nutritious as well as being a

Roasting Constant Low

CUTS	APPROX. WEIGHT (LBS)
Beef	
Sirloin tips (high quality)	$3\frac{1}{2}$ to 4
	4 to 6
Standing rib	6 to 8
(Ribs which measure 6	
to 7 inches	4 to 6
from chine	
to rib tip)	
Rolled rib	5 to 7
Delmonico	4 to 6
(Rib eye)	
Rolled rump	4 to 6
Tenderloin (half)	2 to 3
Tenderloin (whole)	4 to 6
Lamb	
Leg	5 to 8
Shoulder	4 to 6
Rolled	3 to 5
Cushioned	3 to 5
Rib	$1\frac{1}{2}$ to 3
*Pork, fresh	
Large roasts	over 3
Small roasts	under 3
Rolled roasts	
Spare Ribs	
Picnic shoulder	5 to 8
Boston shoulder	4 to 6
Leg (fresh ham)	
Whole, bone in	12 to 16
Whole, rolled	10 to 14
Half, bone in	5 to 8
Veal	
Leg	5 to 8
Loin	4 to 6
Rolled shoulder	4 to 6

*See page 29 for cured ham.

Roast lamb
with rosemary

source of flavor. Allow about $1\frac{1}{3}$–2 cups gravy for 4 people; the amount depends upon personal taste.

When the meat is cooked, pour away all the fat from the roasting pan except for about 1 tablespoon. If convenient, make the gravy in the meat pan; if not, pour the fat and any residue of tiny pieces of meat, and scrapings into a saucepan.

For a thin gravy   Blend 1 level tablespoon flour into the fat.

To cook   Heat for a few minutes or until the roux turns golden brown. This is quite a

risky business as it can burn, so you may like to add a little gravy browning (and flavoring) instead and just use the flour as a thickener. Gradually work in about 1 cup stock, bring to the boil and cook until slightly thickened. Strain and use.

For a thick gravy   Proceed as above but use nearly 2 level tablespoons flour to 2 tablespoons fat.

Beef and lamb are usually served with a thin gravy; pork and veal are usually served with a thick gravy.

If serving rare beef, the natural juices that flow from the meat may be served instead of gravy.

Standing rib roast with popovers

Meat at Temperatures

OVEN TEMP. CONSTANT (°F)	INTERIOR TEMP. (°F)	APPROX. COOKING TIME (MIN./LBS.)
300–325	140 (rare)	35
	160 (med)	38
	170 (well)	40
300–325	140 (rare)	30
	160 (med)	33
	170 (well)	35
300–325	140 (rare)	23 to 25
	160 (med)	27 to 30
	170 (well)	32 to 35
300–325	140 (rare)	26 to 32
	160 (med)	34 to 38
	170 (well)	40 to 42
300–325	140 (rare)	32
	160 (med)	38
	170 (well)	48
350	140 (rare)	18 to 20
	160 (med)	20 to 22
	170 (well)	22 to 24
300–325	150–170	25 to 30
425	140 (rare)	45 to 50 (Total)
425	140 (rare)	45 to 60 (Total)
300–325	175–180	30 to 35
300–325	175–180	30 to 35
300–325	175–180	40 to 45
300–325	175–180	30 to 35
375	170–180	35 to 45
325–350	170	30 to 35
325–350	170	35 to 45
325–350	well done	$1\frac{1}{2}$–$2\frac{1}{2}$ Hrs. total
325–350	170	30 to 35
325–350	170	40 to 45
325–350	170	22 to 26
325–350	170	24 to 28
325–350	170	35 to 40
300–325	170	25 to 35
300–325	170	30 to 35
300–325	170	40 to 45

Well chosen accompaniments provide extra flavor, counteract undue richness, as with pork, give a moist texture to drier meat, such as veal, and turn a merely good roast into a memorable dish. Make a pocket in the meat and put in the stuffing, or spread on boned meat, roll and tie firmly, then roast. *Always calculate the total weight of meat plus stuffing for cooking time.* If preferred, put the stuffing into a separate dish and bake in the oven for 40–50 minutes, basting it with the drippings.

● **AVOID** *Too dry stuffings.*
● **SHORT CUTS** *Use the blender to make crumbs, or buy packaged stuffing or bottled or canned sauces.*

TO SERVE WITH BEEF

Horseradish sauce: Whip $\frac{2}{3}$ cup heavy cream, gradually beat in $\frac{2}{3}$ cup light cream and 2–3 teaspoons lemon juice or vinegar. Add 4–5 tablespoons grated fresh horseradish, seasoning and 3–4 teaspoons sugar. *Serves 5–6.*
New look: Blend 3–4 tablespoons shelled chopped walnuts with the sauce.

TO SERVE WITH LAMB

Apricot nut stuffing: Drain a 1-pound can of apricots, reserving juice; chop the fruit and blend with $1\frac{1}{2}$ cups soft bread crumbs, 3–4 tablespoons chopped peanuts or walnuts, 4 tablespoons softened margarine and the grated rind and juice of 1 orange and 1 lemon. Season well and bind with some of the reserved juice and 1 egg. *Serves 4–5.*
Pineapple nut stuffing: Use canned pineapple instead of apricots.
Mint sauce: Chop enough mint leaves to make about 1 cup, add 3–4 tablespoons sugar and 4–5 tablespoons vinegar. *Serves 4–5.*
Onion sauce: Peel, chop and cook 2 large onions in $1\frac{1}{3}$ cups well seasoned water. Strain and reserve the liquid. Make a sauce

Accompaniments to Roast Meat

with 3 tablespoons butter, 6 tablespoons flour, $1\frac{1}{3}$ cups milk and $\frac{2}{3}$ cup onion stock. When thickened, add the onions and season well. *Serves 5–6.*

TO SERVE WITH PORK

Apple sauce: Simmer peeled, sliced apples in a very little water until soft. Put through a food mill or puree in the blender. Sweeten to taste.
New look: Add ground cinnamon, a little dried fruit or orange segments to the sauce, or serve an orange sauce (page 30).
Sage and onion stuffing: Peel, chop and cook 2–3 large onions for 10 minutes in $\frac{2}{3}$ cup water. Season well, strain, then blend with $1\frac{1}{2}$ cups soft bread crumbs, 1–2 teaspoons chopped fresh sage or $\frac{1}{2}$ teaspoon dried sage and $\frac{1}{4}$ cup melted butter. Bind with onion stock and/or an egg. *Serves 5–6.*
Prune and apple stuffing: Soak 1 generous cup prunes overnight, drain, pit and chop. Mix with 1 cup soft bread crumbs, 2 peeled, diced raw apples, grated rind and juice of 1 orange, seasoning, 1 teaspoon ground cinnamon, 2–3 tablespoons chopped parsley and 1 egg blended with $\frac{1}{2}$ teaspoon Tabasco sauce. Tabasco is very hot, so reduce to $\frac{1}{4}$ teaspoon if wished. *Serves 7–8.*

TO SERVE WITH VEAL

Parsley and thyme stuffing: Blend 2 cups soft bread crumbs, $1\frac{1}{2}$–$2\frac{1}{2}$ tablespoons chopped parsley, $\frac{1}{2}$ cup melted butter, 1–2 teaspoons chopped fresh thyme or good pinch dried thyme, grated rind and juice of 1 lemon and 1 egg. *Serves 5–6.*

Franconia or Pan-roasted potatoes

These are the favorite accompaniment with most roasts. Select medium-sized potatoes and peel. Parboil in salted water for about 10 minutes and strain. Roll the potatoes in the hot fat in the roasting pan (around the meat) or roast in 4–6 tablespoons heated butter, lard or clarified drippings in a separate pan. Cook for approximately 1 hour, turning frequently. If the roasting temperature is too low for browning, turn oven to 400°F while the roast rests and finish browning.

A Perfect Yorkshire Pudding

Although this is the classic accompaniment to roast beef, many people enjoy it with other roasts. Beat 2 eggs with 1 cup milk. Then beat in 1 cup flour and $\frac{1}{2}$ teaspoon salt.

There are two ways of producing the perfect Yorkshire pudding. The traditional way is to lift the meat from the roasting pan and pour away all the fat, *except* about 1 tablespoon. Pour the batter into the pan and cook with the meat on a trivet, or on the shelf above. Alternatively to give a very well-risen pudding, put about $\frac{1}{4}$ cup drippings in a 9-inch square pan. Heat, then pour in the batter. Cook in the top part of the oven until well risen and brown.

You cannot cook a Yorkshire pudding slowly, so it is only possible if you raise the oven temperature during the last 10 minutes of the roasting time. The oven must be hot, 450°F. Pour in the batter, cook for 10 minutes at this temperature, then remove roast and lower heat to 350°F. Cook for about 20 minutes longer, lift out, cut in squares and serve immediately. It may also be baked in individual glass custard cups.

Roast pork with prune and apple stuffing (left)

Roast lamb with apricot nut stuffing (below)

Mixed grill

Broiling is undoubtedly one of the best methods of cooking small cuts of high-quality meat, for they retain the maximum flavor and are more easily digested than sautéed meats.

Blue Print Recipe

Broiling Meat

Broiling Meat

Turn on the broiler, so it is very hot before cooking commences, except for ham steaks.

To prepare To broil tomatoes and mushrooms put into the broiling pan, top with a little melted butter or margarine or fat, season. Broil for a few minutes, then put the meat on the rack of the pan and cook with the meat; or see Mixed Grill.

Choose The same cuts of meat and time the cooking as for pan-broiling on the next page. Season the meat if wished. Brush lightly with a little melted butter or olive oil.

To cook Broil quickly for 2–3 minutes, or until the outside is sealed. Turn the meat with tongs; do not pierce with the prongs of a fork as this allows the meat juices to escape. Cook quickly for 2–3 minutes on the second side. Lower the heat slightly and/or move the broiling pan further away from the heat and continue cooking until meat is tender. A very thick steak can be broiled easily as you can move the broiling pan away from the heat after sealing the outside.

To serve With broiled tomatoes, mushrooms or maître d'hôtel butter and watercress.

● **AVOID** *Broiling too slowly or putting the food under a cold broiler (with the exception of ham steak, where the broiler rack is only heated when the ham is put under to prevent the fat curling); Allowing the food to dry-baste well with melted fat. Serve broiled food as soon as it is ready.*

● **TO RECTIFY** *If the broiler is too cool, remove the pan, heat the broiler until red and glowing, then replace the pan; If the broiled meat is dry, top with a sauce or maître d'hôtel butter.*

● **TO REDUCERS** *An ideal cooking method.*

Mexicali Lamb

1 tablespoon oil; $\frac{1}{2}$–1 tablespoon vinegar; 1 tablespoon tomato paste; 1 tablespoon prepared mustard; seasoning; good pinch garlic salt; 4 large or 8 small lamb chops; 4 tomatoes.

Blend the oil, vinegar, paste, mustard and seasonings. Halve the tomatoes, brush meat and tomatoes with oil mixture and broil as Blue Print. Serve with French fried potatoes and mushrooms. *Serves 4.*

Mixed Grill

4 lamb chops (in the picture are leg chops); 4–8 sausages; 4 tomatoes; about 12 mushrooms; seasoning; little oil, margarine or butter; 4 slices Canadian bacon. *To garnish:* watercress.

Put the chops and sausages on the rack of the broiling pan. Halve the tomatoes, wash and dry the mushrooms (there is no need to skin good quality mushrooms, simply cut the base of the stalks). Season lightly. Put the vegetables on to the rack, as in the picture, or into the broiling pan, see Blue Print. Brush the food with melted margarine or butter or with oil, cook as the Blue Print until meat is nearly tender (by this time the vegetables can be removed and kept hot if there is not much space on the rack of the broiling pan). Add the Canadian bacon, cook for a further 2–3 minutes. Arrange on a hot dish with watercress. *Serves 4.*

For Special Occasions: Add halved lamb kidneys, fingers of lamb or calf's liver, steak and fried eggs. Serve with maître d'hôtel butter.

Maitre d'Hôtel Butter

4 tablespoons butter; little grated lemon rind (optional); 1 tablespoon chopped parsley; 1–2 teaspoons lemon juice; seasoning.

Cream all the ingredients together, chill. Form or cut into pats. Put on the meat just before serving. *Serves 4.*

Storing and freezing *Keep uncooked chops and steaks for 2–3 days only in the refrigerator, but store good stocks in the home freezer. Separate with squares of waxed or greaseproof paper; peel-off as required and broil or pan-broil as pages 24 and 25 from the frozen state.*

To use leftovers *Broiled or pan-fried meats are not good reheated but can be used for tasty sandwiches.*

23

Sautéing & Pan Broiling Meats

Sautéing and pan broiling are methods of cooking that can be used for tender pieces of meat 1 inch or less in thickness as well as for hamburgers. Thicker cuts should be broiled. Cuts are outlined in the table below. Both methods use high heat, the essential difference between the two being that pan broiling uses no fat other than that rubbed on the surface of the pan, while sautéing uses a small quantity of fat. The former method is particularly good with non-stick pans. Extremely thin slices and coated meats should be sautéed.

Wiener Schnitzel

Blue Print Recipe

Sautéing and Pan Broiling Meat

Choose a good-sized heavy skillet; too light a pan is inclined to overcook the outside of the meat before it is cooked through to the center. The amount of butter or fat suggested for sautéing is enough for 3–4 portions, but this must vary according to the amount of natural fat on the meat. If sautéing in butter, add a few drops of olive oil; this lessens the possibility of the butter burning and discoloring.

To prepare Season the meat if wished. Coat as individual recipes. Tie fillet steaks into a round to make into tournedos if following a recipe that requires these (the butcher will do this for you). If sautéing mushrooms and tomatoes as an accompaniment, prepare these and either sauté in a separate pan or sauté before the meat if the meat is to be very rare. Keep the vegetables hot while cooking the meat. If the meat is to be well done, it may be sautéed first, lifted on to a hot dish and kept hot while the mushrooms and tomatoes are sautéed.

To cook Heat the butter, or butter and oil, or other fat in the pan. Add the meat and cook quickly on one side, turn with tongs (do not pierce with the prongs of a fork as this allows the meat juices to escape). Cook quickly on the second side, lower the heat and continue cooking as the timing in the table.

To serve Garnish with sautéed mushrooms and tomatoes or with watercress, parsley, lettuce or as the individual recipes.

● **AVOID** *Cooking too slowly—this leaves the outside of the meat greasy and pale; Too much fat—you will end up frying the meat;*

Overcrowding the pan—the meat will steam instead of sauté; Not wiping the meat dry—it will not brown.

● **TO RECTIFY** *If the meat does not begin to cook the moment it is put in the pan, raise the temperature immediately; pour off excess fat.*

● **SHORT CUTS** *Have the meat cut thinly or in very small slices.*

● **TO REDUCERS** *If you cannot pan broil or use a non-stick pan, broil the meat, particularly if following a fat-free diet.*

Wiener Schnitzel (Scallops of Veal or Pork)

Choose four $\frac{1}{4}$-pound veal cutlets or filleted pork chops or steak. As Blue Print PLUS seasoning, $\frac{1}{2}$ cup flour, 1 egg, 1 cup fine soft bread crumbs, 1 lemon and a little chopped parsley. The meat must be about $\frac{1}{4}$-inch thick, so flatten with a heavy, flat object if necessary. Coat the meat slices in seasoned flour, then beaten egg and bread crumbs. Refrigerate so crumbs will adhere. Cook as the Blue Print, allowing a total cooking time of about 10 minutes. Garnish with slices of lemon and chopped parsley. If the lemon and parsley are put on the meat in the pan and warmed for 1–2 minutes, the maximum flavor can be extracted. For a more elaborate garnish, top the lemon slices with chopped hard-boiled egg, capers and anchovy fillets. *Serves 4.*

Veal Parisienne

As above, but add $\frac{1}{2}$ teaspoon powdered sage to the bread crumbs for the pork, and $\frac{1}{2}$ teaspoon thyme and $\frac{1}{2}$ cup chopped parsley to the bread crumbs for the veal. Cook as for Wiener Schnitzel.

TABLE FOR BROILING

CUTS		APPROX. COOKING TIME RARE	TOTAL TIME MED.
Beef			
Rib or rib	1 in.	15	20
eye steak	1½ in.	25	30
	2 in.	35	45
Club steak	1 in.	15	20
	1½ in.	25	30
	2 in.	35	45
Porterhouse	1 in.	20	25
steak	2 in.	40	45
T-bone steak	1 in.	20	25
	2 in.	40	45
Tenderloin,	1 in.	15	20
Filet mignon	1½ in.	18	22
Sirloin steak	1 in.	20	25
	2 in.	40	45
Ground beef			
patties	1 in.	15	25
Lamb, chops			
Rib, loin and	1 in.	not	12
leg and steaks	1½ in.	usually	18
	2 in.	served rare	22
Pork, fresh			
Chops-rib, loin	¾–1	always	
sirloin, blade	in.	cooked	20–25
Pork, smoked			
Ham slice,	½ in.	well	10–12
tenderized	1 in.	done	16–20
Loin chops	¾ in.		15–20
Canadian style	¼ in.		6–8
bacon	½ in.		8–10
Veal Not generally broiled			

The term "frying" has become synonymous with shallow- and deep-fat frying, the only difference between the two being the amount of oil used, and that in turn is determined by the size of the utensil. In either case, the meat is covered with oil. A deep skillet, electric frypan, kettle or electric deep-fry pot may be employed. With deeper fat, a basket is used to contain the food being cooked. Frying is used largely for coated meat mixtures such as croquettes and rissoles.

Blue Print Recipe

Frying Meat

Prepare the meat as the individual recipes. Preferably, use a vegetable oil and never have the utensil more than half filled. Heat steadily to 375°F or until a cube of day-old bread turns golden brown in just over $\frac{1}{2}$ minute (no quicker). If shallow frying, add food; if deep frying, lower the basket into the fat. Raise the basket, put in the food, lower gently into the fat and fry as individual recipes. Lift out and drain on absorbent paper.

● AVOID *Serving without draining.*

Rissoles

$\frac{3}{4}$ lb. cooked lean beef, corned beef, lean lamb or veal or a mixture of meats; 2 tablespoons butter or margarine; 4 tablespoons flour; $\frac{2}{3}$ cup brown stock or milk; $\frac{3}{4}$ cup soft bread crumbs; seasoning; pinch mixed herbs. *To coat:* 2 tablespoons flour; 1 egg; 3–4 tablespoons dry bread crumbs. *To fry:* vegetable oil.

Grind the meat, or chop very finely. Heat the butter or margarine in a saucepan, stir in the flour and cook over a low heat several minutes, stirring carefully. Gradually add the liquid. Bring to the boil and cook until thickened. Add the crumbs, ground meat, seasoning and herbs. Allow the mixture to cool; form into 8 round flat cakes. Coat in flour, then beaten egg, then in crumbs. For shallow frying, fry the cakes in a large pan until golden brown on either side and heated through. For deep frying, follow the Blue Print on this page, allow about 5 minutes and do not turn. Drain on absorbent paper and serve with the brown or tomato sauce given below.

Sauces for Fried Meats

Brown sauce Chop a medium-sized onion and sauté in 3 tablespoons fat until soft. Stir in 4 tablespoons flour and cook gently for a few minutes. Gradually add $1\frac{1}{3}$ cups brown stock, bring to the boil, cook until thickened and season well. Sieve or whirl in blender if wished.

Tomato sauce Use the recipe for brown sauce but substitute 4–5 large chopped tomatoes and 5–6 tablespoons water for the brown stock.

Steak au Poivre (Peppered steak)

Choose 4 club steaks.

Version 1: As Blue Print PLUS $\frac{1}{2}$–1 tablespoon crushed peppercorns.

Version 2: As Blue Print PLUS $\frac{1}{2}$–1 tablespoon crushed peppercorns, about $\frac{1}{2}$ cup heavy cream and $1\frac{1}{2}$–3 tablespoons brandy. Season the steaks with salt and press half the peppercorns into one side, then turn and repeat on the second side. Cook as the Blue Print. For the more luxurious version, prepare as above and pan broil as the Blue Print then add the cream and heat gently, with the meat, for 1–2 minutes. Add the brandy and ignite if wished. *Serves 4.*

Basic Hamburger

1 lb. ground beef (chuck, round or sirloin); salt and pepper; 1–2 tablespoons butter if sauteing round or sirlion; chuck may be pan broiled; all may be broiled.

Handle the beef as little as possible. Form lightly into four 1-inch thick round patties. Season. Melt the fat in a skillet. Add the hamburgers and cook on both sides as the Blue Print opposite. Lower the heat and continue cooking 2–6 minutes according to taste. Serve on toasted halved hamburger rolls with optional ketchup, relish or onion or tomato slices.

Plus Onions

Ingredients as above, PLUS 1 tablespoon minced onion.

Mix the seasonings and onions lightly into the beef. Cook and serve as Basic Hamburger.

Cheeseburger

Ingredients as above PLUS 4 slices Cheddar or processed cheese.

Cook the hamburgers. Put on top of halved toasted rolls, cover with the cheese and brown under the broiler. Top with slices of tomato and small pickled onions.

Hamburger Indienne

Ingredients as above, but add 1–2 teaspoons curry powder, seasoning and a little finely grated onion to the meat.

Cook as the Basic Hamburger. Top with rings of fried pineapple and a little chutney.

Nutty Hamburger

Ingredients as above, PLUS 3–4 tablespoons salted peanuts.

Cook as the Basic Hamburger, top with peanuts before serving. A few chopped nuts can be added to the Hamburger mixture.

Pimiento Hamburger

Ingredients as above, PLUS sliced rings red and/or green pepper.

Cook as the Basic Hamburger and top with the rings of fried pepper.

From the top:
Basic hamburger, Hamburger Indienne,
Cheeseburger, Nutty hamburger,
Pimiento hamburger

Never despise "boiled" meat for some of the most appetizing dishes are prepared by this method. The word "boiling" is really incorrect, for the liquid in the pan should simmer gently, *not* boil rapidly.

Normally one chooses fairly economical cuts for this purpose and it is ideal for cured meats, such as corned beef and tongue, although there is no reason why any meat cannot be cooked by this method if wished.

Allow minimum $\frac{3}{4}$–1 lb. fresh meat with bone; less without bone. Salted meats shrink during cooking, so allow minimum $\frac{1}{2}$ lb. without bone.

Blue Print Recipe
Boiling Meat

Choose a large pot so that the liquid surrounds the meat. If the meat fits too tightly into the pot, the outside tends to be dry and the meat does not cook as well as it should. Make sure the lid fits well so the liquid does not evaporate too quickly.

To prepare Wash and dry then tie the meat into a neat shape if necessary and prepare any vegetables.

To cook Start cured meats in cold water, fresh in boiling water. Put the meat with any vegetables into the pot. Add seasoning if required. Salted meat should have only a few peppercorns or pepper, no salt. Add herbs, other ingredients as the particular recipe and liquid, generally water. When boiling, remove any grey scum that may float to the top

Boiling Meat

and cover the pot tightly. Lower the heat and allow the liquid to simmer steadily for the time given in the table.

To serve Hot or cold, according to the individual recipes. If serving hot then serve some of the unthickened liquid with the meat and vegetables.

● **AVOID** *Cooking too quickly—the outside of the meat becomes overcooked before the center is tender; Cooking very salty meats before soaking.*
● **TO RECTIFY** *Reduce the heat when the liquid in the pan boils too quickly; If you should start to cook salted meats without soaking, pour away the original cooking liquid and fill up with fresh cold water. Add plenty of vegetables to help absorb the salt.*
● **TO REDUCERS** *A splendid way of cooking meat as no thickening is used in the liquid.*

Choice and Timing for Boiled Meat

BEEF
Cuts: Brisket, corned beef; short ribs; chuck; round; shank; fresh and smoked tongue.
Timing: 3–$3\frac{1}{2}$ hours. This is somewhat less for more expensive cuts.

Add: Vegetables or accompaniments such as horseradish sauce.

LAMB OR MUTTON
Cuts: Breast, riblets; shoulder; shank; head; tongue; leg (for special occasions and elaborately served).
Timing: $1\frac{1}{2}$–2 hours.
Add: Vegetables or accompaniments such as caper sauce.

PORK
Cuts: Smoked ham; butt; back ribs; salt pork, spare ribs, slab bacon; fresh and smoked hocks, smoked picnic; jowl bacon; pig's feet; sausage; head.
Timing: 2 hours.
Add: Vegetables to give flavor as the meat cooks; generally served cold.

VEAL
Cuts: Neck; heel of round; breast, riblets; brisket; shank; head, tongue, brains.
Timing: About $1\frac{1}{2}$ hours.
Add: Mixed vegetables; cream sauce; serve with parsley or brain sauce.

For Family Occasions

New England Boiled Dinner

Choose a 5–lb. corned beef brisket. Prepare and cook as the Blue Print, adding 1 clove crushed garlic and 6 peppercorns. Simmer $3\frac{1}{2}$ hours or until tender; $\frac{1}{2}$ hour before serving add 1 large yellow turnip (diced), 6 parsnips, 6 carrots, 6 medium pototoes, 12 small onions, head of green cabbage cut in wedges. Simmer until vegetables are tender. Lift the meat onto a platter and serve surrounded by vegetables. Leftover meat is excellent cold with salads or in sandwiches. *Serves 10–12.*

Corned Beef Hash

Allow $\frac{1}{2}$ cup chopped leftover corned beef, $\frac{1}{2}$ cup chopped cooked potato and 1 tablespoon chopped onion for each serving. Cook in skillet with shortening, turning until browned. Cover and cook over low heat until crust forms. If preferred, all ingredients may be ground, placed in a greased shallow dish and baked in a 425°F oven until crust forms, about 20–25 minutes. Serve with poached or fried eggs and ketchup.

Boiled Tongue

Although beef-tongue is cooked more often than others, the smaller lamb or calf tongues are excellent for small families. Smoked tongues have a better color, but either fresh or smoked are delicious. Prepare and cook as the Blue Print, adding herbs and a few strips lemon rind if wished. When the tongue or tongues are tender, allow to cool sufficiently to handle. Remove the skin, bones and gristle from the tongues. Reheat in the cooking liquid. Serve hot with raisin sauce opposite or cold with salad.

New England boiled dinner

Raisin or Currant Sauce

$\frac{1}{3}$ cup brown sugar; 1 tablespoon flour; $1\frac{1}{2}$ teaspoons dry mustard; $1\frac{1}{4}$ cups boiling water; $\frac{1}{4}$ cup vinegar; $\frac{1}{2}$ cup sherry; $\frac{1}{4}$ cup seedless raisins or currants; 1 tablespoon butter or margarine.

Soak raisins or currants in sherry while preparing sauce. Mix dry ingredients and add boiling water and vinegar slowly, stirring well. Cover and simmer 10 minutes. Add raisins or currants and sherry; simmer 5 minutes. Swirl in butter or margarine. *Makes about 2 cups.*

Irish Stew

Cover 3 lb. lamb (neck, breast, shoulder, shank) cut in 2-inch pieces with boiling water and cook as the Blue Print. Add diced potatoes, carrots, turnips, sliced onions and salt and pepper $\frac{1}{2}$ hour before finished; 20 minutes before finishing add dumplings below. Serve with broth and dumplings.

Dumplings

$1\frac{1}{2}$ cups flour; 3 teaspoons baking powder; $\frac{1}{2}$ teaspoon salt; 3 tablespoons shortening; about $\frac{3}{4}$ cup milk.

Put flour, baking powder and salt in a bowl and cut in shortening until mixture looks like meal. Stir in milk gradually. Dough should drop from spoon but not be runny. Drop by the spoonful onto the meat and cook 10 minutes. Cover and cook until dumplings are fluffy (about 10 minutes). Makes about 8 dumplings.

For Special Occasions

Pot-au-Feu

Approximately $3-3\frac{1}{2}$ lb. brisket, boned sirloin, bottom round, chuck or rump; about $3-3\frac{1}{2}$ lb. boned fresh pork; about $\frac{3}{4}$ lb. mixed root vegetables for soup (carrots, turnips, celeriac, small piece parsnip); seasoning; *bouquet garni; 1–2* small onions; carrots and turnips per person; 1 lb. garlic sausage; mayonnaise; tomato sauce; French mustard. Put the meats, the soup vegetables, seasoning and *bouquet garni* into a pot and cook as the Blue Print for about $1\frac{1}{2}$ hours. Add the rest of the vegetables, and the sausage and cook for a further $1-1\frac{1}{2}$ hours.

Slice the meats, arrange on a dish with the cooked vegetables round. Strain the liquid, serve in a sauce boat. Dishes of herbed mayonnaise, tomato sauce and Dijon mustard are generally served as well. *Serves 6–10.*

Storing and freezing *Uncooked fresh meat may be kept for several days in a refrigerator or some weeks in a home freezer. Cured meat, cooked or uncooked, keeps well in a refrigerator for some days but uncooked does not store as well in a home freezer as fresh meat. Cooked fresh meat freezes reasonably well but cooked cured meat, when frozen, should be used within 5–6 weeks.*

To use leftovers *See above. Boiled meats may be turned into rissoles, meat pies, etc.*

Braising Meat

Braising Meat

Braising is a method of cooking used to tenderize less tender cuts of meat, such as pot roasts and round or chuck steaks, and lean meats, such as veal steaks and chops and pork chops. The method differs from boiling in that the meat is first seared and browned and then covered and simmered either in its own juices or with a very little liquid added. Braising has the advantage of producing delicious economical dishes which need little attention and which, when the liquid used is wine, can be turned into gourmet fare.

Blue Print Recipe

Pot Roast

4 lb. top or bottom round, rump, chuck or brisket · 5–6 medium yellow onions · $\frac{1}{4}$ cup flour · seasoning · 3 tablespoons fat.

To make Pat the meat dry with paper towels; peel and slice the onions. Dredge the meat in the flour and seasoning and sear over high heat in a Dutch oven or heavy casserole. Pour off the excess fat. Add the sliced onions.

To cook Cover the pot tightly and simmer over low heat $2\frac{1}{2}$–3 hours or until tender. The moisture from the onions and the meat will make a good amount of gravy which may be thickened with 1–2 tablespoons flour (according to thickness wished) per cup of liquid.

To serve With boiled or mashed potatoes or buttered noodles and carrots. *All recipes based on this dish serve 6–8.*

Herbed pork chops

● **AVOID** *Adding water unless a rack is used. The onions provide plenty of moisture, but if omitted substitute water.*

● **SHORT CUT** *Use canned potatoes and carrots and add to meat 20 minutes before serving to heat through.*

For Family Occasions

Swiss Steak

Method as Blue Print but choose about $2-2\frac{1}{2}$ lb. rump, round or chuck steak, reduce onions to 1 and add 2 cups canned tomatoes. With the side of a thick plate, pound the flour and seasonings into both sides of meat. Add onion and tomatoes; continue as in Blue Print, cooking $2-2\frac{1}{2}$ hours. If desired, this may be cooked in a 300°F oven for the same amount of time, but bring the tomatoes to a boil on top of stove first.
Serve as the Blue Print.

For Special Occasions

Braised Herbed Pork or Veal Chops

Method as Blue Print but choose 6–8 thick pork or veal loin chops; OMIT onions but add 1 teaspoon dried basil to flour for pork or 1 teaspoon thyme for veal. Use olive oil for fat. Add $\frac{1}{2}$ cup Marsala wine at end.

Using a large skillet, cook as in Blue Print 45 minutes for pork, 20 minutes for veal, turning chops once. Remove chops to warm platter and add Marsala; cook over high heat, scraping pan, about 1 minute until wine is reduced by half.

Garnish meat with spiced apples and serve with rice and a green salad.

Curries of All Kinds

The spicy flavor of a good curry surely provides one of the most interesting meals. Do not imagine a good curry *must* be very hot; there are many versions of this dish and the Blue Print is for a moderately hot curry sauce only.

Blue Print Recipe

Beef Curry

2 medium-sized onions · 1–2 cloves garlic · $\frac{1}{4}$ cup butter or ghee* · 1 small eating apple · $\frac{1}{2}$–1 tablespoon curry powder · 1–2 teaspoons curry paste · 1 tablespoon flour · 2 cups beef broth · 1–2 tablespoons dried coconut or grated fresh coconut · 1–2 tablespoons white raisins · 1–2 tablespoons chutney · 1–1$\frac{1}{4}$ lb. uncooked beef (see method) · 1 teaspoon sugar · 1 teaspoon lemon juice or vinegar · seasoning. To accompany: 1 cup uncooked long grain rice · saffron powder (optional) · chutney · sliced peppers and tomatoes · popadams · Bombay duck · nuts · raisins · grated coconut · sliced banana · rings of raw onion or green onions.
*ghee is clarified butter.

To make Chop the peeled onions and crush the cloves of garlic. Toss in the hot fat. Peel and slice the apple, add to the onion mixture with the curry powder, paste and flour. Sauté gently for several minutes,

stirring well to prevent the mixture burning. Gradually blend in the broth and bring to the boil and cook until slightly thickened. Put the coconut, white raisins and chutney into the sauce, then add the diced meat. For special occasions, choose diced top round, rump, flank steak or brisket; for economy choose diced chuck.

To cook Simmer for about 1 hour in a tightly covered pan then add the sugar, lemon juice or vinegar and seasoning. Taste the sauce and add more sweetening or seasoning as desired. Cover the pan again and continue cooking for a further 1$\frac{1}{2}$–2 hours.

To cook the rice put this with about 2$\frac{1}{2}$ times the amount of cold water (i.e. to 1 cup use 2$\frac{1}{2}$ cups water). Add seasoning and a pinch saffron powder if desired. Bring to the boil, stir briskly, cover the pan tightly and allow to simmer for approximately 15 minutes or until the rice has absorbed the water and is tender.

To serve Arrange the curry in a border of saffron or plain rice or serve the rice in a separate dish. Arrange all the accompaniments in dishes so everyone may help themselves. The popadams should be fried in a very little fat until crisp. The Bombay duck (which is a dried fish) should be sprinkled over each portion of curry. *All recipes based on this dish serve 4–6.*

● **AVOID** *Cooking too quickly; one needs prolonged cooking for a true blending of flavors.*

● **TO RECTIFY** *Give yourself plenty of time to cook the sauce. If using cooked meat then allow the sauce to simmer for an hour or so before adding the meat. This prevents overcooking the meat.*

● **SHORT CUT** *Use a canned mulligatawny soup as a ready-made sauce or buy canned curry sauce and add your own flavorings.*

● **TO REDUCERS** *Do not thicken the sauce and have very small portions of cooked rice, chutney and the fattening accompaniments.*

For Family Occasions

Very hot curry As Blue Print PLUS 2–3 sliced red chili peppers, pinch cayenne pepper, little ground ginger or fresh ginger root.

Mild curry As Blue Print but OMIT the curry paste and use only half the amount of curry powder.

Sweet curry As Blue Print PLUS 1–2 grated carrots and 1 medium-sized can pineapple, guavas or mangoes. Add the carrots and most of the fruit to the onion and apple mixture, and use about 1$\frac{1}{3}$ cups only of broth and $\frac{2}{3}$ cup syrup from the can instead of the remainder of the broth. Garnish the curry with the remaining pieces of fruit just before serving.

Bhoona Goast

This is a very dry curry and can be made as the Blue Print, but reduce the amount of broth to a few tablespoons only. Cook gently until the meat is tender, stirring from time to time to stop the mixture from burning. Choose diced lean mutton instead of beef and omit the apple.

For Special Occasions

Eggplant Curry

Ingredients as Blue Print, but use only $\frac{1}{2}$ lb. meat, PLUS 4 thinly sliced eggplants and 1 or 2 lemons. The eggplants should be sprinkled with salt and left standing for about 15 minutes before adding to the curry sauce. Cook and serve as Blue Print, but garnish with thick wedges of lemon.

Lamb and Zucchini Curry

Method as Blue Print but use diced lamb (from leg or shoulder) in place of beef. Cook as Blue Print. Add 3–4 thinly sliced unpeeled zucchini about 30 minutes before the end of the cooking period. Serve as Blue Print. (Illustrated on page 19.)

Storing and freezing *Store cooked curry in the refrigerator for one or two days and reheat. Curry may be frozen, but it can destroy some of the flavor.*

Sweet curry

Bacon and ham provide a wide selection of dishes for various meals, ranging from a simple breakfast dish of bacon and egg to the more elaborate Ham en Croûte and Glazed Ham here.

Blue Print Recipe

Glazed Ham

Choose Boston butt or a ham for special occasions; picnic cut for medium quality; hock for family economy. Put the ham into a large pan, cover with cold water, or with cider, ginger beer or gingerale. Add vegetables if wished. Bring the liquid to the boil, lower the heat and simmer very gently for $\frac{2}{3}$ of the total cooking time (see below). Allow the ham to cool sufficiently to remove the skin. Score (cut) the fat at regular intervals; this allows the glaze to penetrate the fat and gives more flavor to the meat. Lift into the roasting pan. Spread the glaze, as the recipes below, over the ham and bake in the center of a moderately hot oven, 400°F, for the remainder of the cooking time.

Timing   Top quality ham. A wide roast that is not very thick cooks more quickly, so allow 20 minutes per lb. and 20 minutes over, while a thicker roast needs 25 minutes per lb. and 25 minutes over. More economical roasts need 30–35 minutes per lb. and 30–35 minutes over. Therefore a 4 lb. piece of shoulder would take either 4 × 20 plus 20 minutes or 4 × 25 plus 25 minutes, i.e. either a total of 1 hour and 40 minutes or 2 hours and 5 minutes.

To serve   Hot with vegetables, cold with salad. Some of the stock may be used for a clear sauce or for parsley sauce.

Baking Ham   If preferred the ham can be baked for all the cooking time. Soak as above and either fast roast (425–450°F for 15–20 minutes; 375–400°F for remainder) for 20–25 minutes per lb. and 20–25 minutes over or bake at constant temperature (325–350°F) for 30–35 minutes per lb. Forehock should be slow roasted, shoulder, ham or loin can be slow or fast roasted.

Glazes for Ham

These are sufficient to coat the fat on a piece of meat weighing about 4 lb. which will serve about 8.

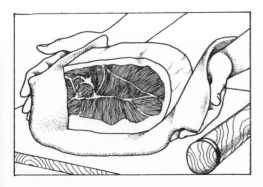

Glazed forehock of bacon

Honey Ginger Glaze

Blend 5 tablespoons thick honey, 2 teaspoons ground ginger and $2\frac{1}{2}$ tablespoons finely chopped preserved ginger together. Spread over the fat and roast as the Blue Print.

Pineapple Glaze

Blend 4 tablespoons brown sugar, 4 tablespoons syrup from canned pineapple and 1 teaspoon prepared mustard together.
Spread over the fat and roast as the Blue Print. Put the pineapple rings from the can round the joint and cook for about 10 minutes before serving.

Sugar and Spice Glaze

Blend 4 tablespoons brown sugar, $2\frac{1}{2}$–4 tablespoons soft bread crumbs (optional), 1–2 teaspoons mixed spice and 1 tablespoon corn syrup together.
Moisten to a spreading consistency with a very little stock from boiling the meat. Spread over the fat. Bake as the Blue Print, then serve hot with mixed vegetables as shown in the picture.

Ham en Croûte

Shoulder or ham about $3\frac{1}{2}$–4 lb.; 4 cups flour; pinch salt; 1 cup shortening; water to mix. *To glaze:* 1 egg.
Soak the shoulder or ham for 12 hours in cold water unless green or sweet-cure. If very salty, soak for 24 hours. Lift out of the water, dry thoroughly and cut away the skin. Sift the flour and salt, cut in the fat until the mixture is like fine bread crumbs. Mix with cold water to a rolling consistency. Roll out to about $\frac{1}{4}$-inch in thickness and cut off $\frac{2}{3}$ of the pastry. Place the shoulder or

ham on this, bring up the pastry to encase the sides of the meat, see Sketch. Roll out the remaining pastry for the lid and place over the meat. Cut away any surplus pastry, brush the edges with beaten egg and pinch together very firmly. Lift on to a baking sheet. Brush with beaten egg. Cut a slit in the top to allow the steam to escape and make small leaves of pastry. Press on top of the croûte and brush with beaten egg. Bake in the center of a moderate oven, 350–375°F, for 30 minutes, then reduce the heat to very moderate, 325–350°F, for the remainder of the time. Allow 25 minutes per lb. and 25 minutes over, so a 4-lb. piece will take 2 hours 5 minutes. Serve hot or cold, cut into thin slices. *Serves 8–10.*

Ham and Pâté en Croûte

Ingredients as Ham en Croûte PLUS about $\frac{1}{4}$ lb. pâté and $\frac{1}{2}$ lb. mushrooms. Roll out $\frac{2}{3}$ of the pastry as Ham en Croûte. Spread with most of the pâté and finely chopped mushrooms. Wrap round the ham. Spread the top of the ham with pâté and mushrooms, cover with the pastry lid and proceed as Ham en Croûte.

Ham and Corn Scallops

2 tablespoons butter or margarine; 4 tablespoons flour; $\frac{2}{3}$ cup milk; seasoning; $\frac{1}{2}$–1 teaspoon prepared mustard; $\frac{1}{2}$ lb. cooked ham; small can corn; 2 packages potato chips.
Make a thick sauce with the butter or margarine, flour and milk. Add the seasoning and mustard. Add the diced ham and corn (plus any liquid from the can). Put into 4 scallop or individual dishes. Crush the potato chips and sprinkle over the ham mixture. Heat for 15–20 minutes in the center of a very moderate oven, 325–350°F. *Serves 4.*

Ham en croûte

Specialty cuts are often called variety meats and the latter name is very appropriate, for there are many kinds of meat grouped under this heading and they can be cooked in an unlimited number of ways. The most popular specialty cuts are liver and kidneys.

LIVER

Liver is an excellent source of iron as well as protein, but can be spoiled by overcooking. Choose calf's liver for the best quality, lamb or pork liver for tender but less delicately flavored liver. The simplest way to cook tender liver is to slice it fairly thinly, coat lightly in seasoned flour and sauté for about 6–7 minutes in butter, oil or bacon fat until tender. Serve with fried or broiled bacon. Beef liver needs longer, slower cooking, as in the Ragout Sicilienne below.

Liver Ragout Sicilienne

1¼ lb. beef liver; ¼ cup flour; seasoning; 3 medium-sized onions; 1–2 cloves garlic; ¼ cup oil or fat; 1⅓ cups stock; 1⅓ cups cider or inexpensive red wine; a generous tablespoon red currant jelly; ½ teaspoon grated lemon rind; 3–4 tablespoons green olives.
Cut the liver into narrow strips. Mix the flour with seasoning; coat the liver in this. Cut the peeled onions into rings and crush the cloves of garlic. Heat the oil or fat in a pan, toss the liver in this, lift out and sauté the onion rings and garlic for a few minutes. Gradually blend in the stock and cider or wine, bring to the boil and cook until slightly thickened. Add the jelly and lemon rind. Replace the strips of liver, put a lid on the pan and simmer very slowly for about 2 hours. Add the olives just before serving. Serve with mashed potatoes, boiled rice or noodles. *Serves 4–5.*

Kidney Ragout Sicilienne

Use sliced beef kidney in place of liver.

Liver Kebabs with Orange Sauce

For the sauce: 2 oranges; 1⅓ cups beef broth; ¼ cup cornstarch; 2 tablespoons butter; seasoning; ½–1 teaspoon sugar. *For the kebabs:* 1 lb. calf's liver (cut in one piece about 1-inch thick); seasoning; pinch mixed dried herbs; about 12 mushrooms; 12 small cocktail onions; 4 slices bacon; ¼ cup melted butter. *To serve:* boiled rice.
Pare the rind very thinly from the oranges and simmer this in half the broth for about 5 minutes. Strain, return to the pan. Blend the cornstarch with the rest of the broth, add to the liquid in the pan with the juice of the oranges, the butter, seasoning and sugar. Bring to the boil, cook gently and stir until smooth and thickened. Meanwhile cut the liver into cubes, roll in seasoning and herbs; put onto 4 metal skewers with the mushrooms, onions and halved bacon slices in neat rolls. Brush with the melted butter and cook under a hot broiler for about 8 minutes. Turn several times during cooking so the

food cooks evenly. Serve on a bed of boiled rice with the orange sauce. *Serves 4.*
Note Extra orange segments can be added to the sauce, if liked.

Kidney Kebabs

Use 8–12 skinned whole or halved lamb kidneys in place of the calf's liver.

KIDNEYS

Kidney adds flavor to many dishes such as the steak and kidney pie on page 85 and the less expensive, but less tender, beef kidney can be used for this purpose. Lamb kidneys can be broiled or sautéed and form an important part of a mixed grill. They make a delicious dish for special occasions when cooked in red wine, as in the recipe below. Smaller quantities can be used as a filling for pancakes and omelettes or to serve on toast as a light snack.

Kidneys Bordelaise

About 20 lamb kidneys; 5 tablespoons flour; seasoning; good pinch grated nutmeg; 2 medium-sized onions; 2 slices bacon; 4–6 tablespoons oil or butter; 1 tablespoon chopped parsley; 1⅓ cups beef broth; ⅔ cup red wine. *To serve:* about 1½ lb. mashed potatoes. *To garnish:* parsley.
Skin the kidneys, halve for quicker cooking. Mix the flour, seasoning and nutmeg and coat the kidneys in the flour mixture. Peel and cut the onions into thin rings, cut the bacon into narrow strips. Heat the oil or butter in a pan, sauté the onion rings and bacon gently for a few minutes, then add the kidneys and cook gently for 5 minutes, stirring well. Add the parsley, mix thorough-

ly, then gradually blend in the broth and wine. Bring the sauce to the boil, stir and cook until thickened. Cover the pan and simmer for about 15 minutes. Meanwhile pipe the mashed potatoes onto a heat-proof serving dish; brown under the broiler. Spoon the kidney mixture into the center of the potatoes and garnish with parsley. Sliced pork kidneys may be used instead. *Serves 5–6.*

Kidneys Marengo

Recipe as above, but omit the potatoes. Top the kidney mixture with 5–6 fried or poached eggs and garnish with croutons.

BRAINS

All brains should be soaked about 4 hours in cold water, the membrane and blood clots removed and the brains simmered in water to cover (to which 1 tablespoon white vinegar and 1 teaspoon salt per quart of water has been added) 15 minutes for lamb brains, 20 minutes for calf or pork brains and 30 minutes for beef brains. Cool for 20 minutes in liquid, then refrigerate until ready to use.

Calf Brains in Black Butter

Slice 1½ lb. calf brains and roll in flour; sauté the brains in butter until brown, about 3–4 minutes on each side. Prepare the sauce. Set 10 tablespoons clarified butter over moderate heat until brown. Remove the butter and add ½ cup wine vinegar to the skillet. Boil until reduced by half. Add melted butter, stir, season to taste and pour over cooked brains. Sprinkle brains with 3 tablespoons capers and 1½ tablespoons chopped parsley. *Serves 6.*

Kidney kebabs with orange sauce (above)
Kidneys Bordelaise, Ox-tail stew with mustard dumplings,
Fricassée of sweetbreads and tripe—French style (right)

Cold Meat Dishes

All the dishes on this page have one thing in common: the meat is set in an aspic. This aspic is made from seasoned stock and gelatin, or from the natural setting qualities of the meat itself, as in the headcheese.

Blue Print Recipe

Ham and Chicken Mold

3 envelopes unflavored gelatin · 5½ cups well seasoned chicken broth · 2–3 hard boiled eggs · about 1–1¼ lb. cooked chicken · about 1–1¼ lb. cooked ham (make a total of 2¼ lb. meat in all) · few cooked peas · large can asparagus tips.

To make Dissolve the gelatin in the seasoned broth according to the directions on the package. Allow to cool. Pour a little into the bottom of a lightly oiled or rinsed 10 cup mold or bowl and leave this to set. Shell the eggs, slice, then arrange in a neat design on the aspic. Spoon a very little aspic over the egg slices and put into the refrigerator or stand over a bowl of ice. When the aspic is firm, put a layer of neatly diced meat and peas into the mold, cover with liquid aspic. Leave once again to set. Continue like this, using the *very well drained* asparagus for the final layer. Cover with the last of the aspic and leave until the mold is firmly set.

To serve Dip the mold for a few seconds in warm water. Invert on to the serving dish and serve with salad.

Serves about 8.
Naturally a smaller mold may be made with half the above quantity.

Storing and freezing *These jellied molds keep for several days in a refrigerator but tend to stiffen slightly. In a home freezer they keep well for 2–3 weeks but after this they dry out slightly.*
To use leftovers *Part of a mold looks rather unsightly so slice neatly before serving.*

For Family Occasions

Lemon-Flavored Lamb Headcheese

1 lamb's head; 1 or 2 extra lamb tongues; 1 lemon; 1–2 bay leaves; 1–2 onions; *bouquet garni*; 2 pig's feet; seasoning.
Wash the lamb's head in plenty of cold water. Put the head, the tongues, thin strip of lemon rind, bay leaves, whole onions, the *bouquet garni* (mixed fresh herbs tied in neat bunch or in muslin), the pig's feet and seasoning into a large pan. Cover with cold water. Bring slowly to the boil and remove any grey scum from the top of the liquid. Cover the pan and simmer slowly for about 2 hours, or until the meat on the head, tongues and feet is tender. If preferred, cook for about 45 minutes at 15 lb. pressure in pressure cooker; allow the pressure to drop at room temperature. Lift the head, tongues and feet from the liquid and when cool enough to handle cut all the meat from the bones and arrange in an 8-cup bowl or plain mold. Squeeze the lemon juice into the liquid in the pan and boil rapidly until you have about 2 cups. Strain over the meat in the bowl or mold and allow to set. Turn out and serve as the Blue Print. *Serves 8–12 according to the size of the head.*

Calf's or Pig's Headcheese

As instructions for Lamb Headcheese. Omit the extra tongues and pig's feet and instead use 1 lb. diced shin of beef or chuck steak and a small piece diced lean ham or bacon, if wished. Simmer for about 2½–3 hours then follow instructions above.

For Special Occasions

Ham and Tongue Mousse

1½ lb. cooked ham and tongue (adjust the proportions to personal taste); 2 teaspoons powdered gelatin or enough to set 1⅓ cups; ⅔ cup chicken broth; ⅔ cup heavy cream; 2 tablespoons dry sherry; seasoning.
Grind the ham and tongue finely and blend together. Soften the gelatin in a little of the cold stock, then dissolve in very hot stock as the aspic in the Blue Print. Blend the meats with this and allow to cool. Whip the cream lightly, add the sherry and whip again. Fold into the meat mixture, then season. Put into an oiled or rinsed 5-cup bowl or mold and allow to set. Turn out as instructions in the Blue Print. *Serves 4–5 as a main course or 8–10 as an hors d'oeuvre.*
To vary Use all ham or all tongue.
For family occasions, substitute corned beef for ham and tongue. Omit the sherry and add extra stock.

Lemon-flavored lamb headcheese

three

FISH AND POULTRY

This chapter covers three important groups of food—fish of all kinds, poultry, and game, together with the basic methods of cooking these and some new recipes and ideas.

Fish is not only an important protein food but a very adaptable one. There are so many different kinds of fish from which to choose and such a variety of ways in which fish may be cooked, that it should never be monotonous. If you are following a reducing diet, fish, if served without rich sauces or high-calorie garnishes, is relatively low in calories, particularly if you choose the white or shell variety. White fish (and by white fish I mean all the ocean fish with white flesh) is very easily digested, while shellfish and oily fish are not so easily digested.

Fish is a highly perishable food, so choose it wisely. Fresh white fish is firm in texture, with bright eyes and a pleasant smell. If it has a strong smell of ammonia, it is *stale*. Shellfish is of good quality when it has a firmlooking shell. The tails of lobster or shrimp should spring back again after being pulled out. (However, most of the shrimp you buy has been frozen first.) Both crab and lobster should feel heavy for their size. If they are surprisingly light it is because they are watery and are, therefore, not a good buy. Oily fish, such as mackerel and herring, should have bright silver scales and bright eyes. If the scales and eyes look dull, then be critical about buying the fish. All fish should have bright red gills. Store fish carefully; put it as near the freezing compartment in the refrigerator as possible and use quickly. Most fish freezes well and you can substitute frozen fish for fresh in many recipes, although the frozen will never have quite the same taste as the fresh.

From page 42 onwards are methods of cooking all kinds of poultry and game, with particular emphasis on chicken. Chickens are both plentiful and comparatively inexpensive.

Chicken can be cooked in many different ways, but choose the right kind of chicken for each cooking process. A large roasting chicken, when disjointed, would take too long to fry so could be overcooked on the outside before being cooked through to the center. Very young chickens are better cooked in a simple manner, such as frying and broiling, or poached and served in a cream sauce. This ensures that the delicate flavor is not lost and the young flesh does not become dry. Young chickens (often called broilers) have firm legs and plump breasts. The skin should be dry and firm looking.

Roasting chickens should have a flexible breastbone, firm, but not sinewy, looking legs and a really firm plump breast. A soup fowl should have a reasonable amount of fat, but do not buy if there is an excessive amount of pale creamy-yellow fat, for the bird will be wasteful.

A good turkey is broad-breasted with firm legs. Avoid turkeys where the legs seem deficient in flesh. Duck and goose rarely have very plump breasts, but check that there is a fairly generous amount of meat and not too much fat.

I hope you enjoy the many recipes in the pages of this section.

Fish dishes are often very underrated. They can be quite outstanding. It is, of course, very important to choose fresh fish and the points to look for are given on page 33. Careful cooking is essential.

Sometimes you will wish to bone the fish, unless the fish seller has done this for you. The pictures on this page show how to bone herring, but other fish, of a similar shape, can be dealt with in the same way. If you wish to fillet and skin flat fish, see the sketches on page 36.

Blue Print
To Cook Fish

The following points apply whichever method of cooking the fish is chosen.
1. Wash and dry the fish.
2. Season it lightly.
3. Choose any other flavoring desired. Remember most fish has a delicate flavor and this is easily lost if very strong tasting ingredients are added.
Fresh or dried herbs lemon thyme, dill, chervil, parsley, chives.
Fruits lemon, orange, apple (particularly with herring and mackerel), gooseberries (make a puree to serve with mackerel).
Vegetables tomatoes, mushrooms, peas and other green vegetables, onions (use sparingly), garlic (use sparingly), shallots.
Other flavorings horseradish (particularly with smoked fish), spices (particularly with oily fish), nutmeg, tomato ketchup or tomato paste, mustard (particularly with herring).

Successful Fish Cookery

Liquids milk, cream, wines of all kinds (but white are better), cider, vinegar.
Stuffings many stuffings blend well with fish and you will find a number of suggestions opposite.
4. Choose your method of cooking and prepare as the particular Blue Print or recipe.
5. Cook for the recommended time, but always test before serving since the thickness of fish fillets, steaks, etc., varies so much. The fish is cooked if it *just* flakes from the skin or bone when tested with the tip of a knife.
6. Have any sauces ready by the time the fish is cooked, unless you need the stock in which the fish has been cooked. Fish spoils if kept waiting for too long.
7. In order to enjoy a fish dish, choose the rest of your menu carefully. Do not precede a delicately flavored sole dish with a very strong flavored pâté or soup which would make the fish seem tasteless by comparison.

● **AVOID** *Handling the fish carelessly; support it with a pancake turner, for fish breaks easily and can be spoiled in appearance. Either under- or overcooking the fish. Serving fish that may not appear 100% fresh.*
● **TO RECTIFY** *If the fish does break, arrange neatly on the serving dish or plate and garnish or coat carefully with sauce to mask the broken pieces.*
● **SHORT CUTS** *Use frozen fish for quick dishes or make use of canned fish. Choose the quick cooking methods, i.e. broiling and frying.*
● **TO REDUCERS** *You are fortunate in that fish is low in calories; choose the methods that do not add extra calories the dish— broiling, baking (without fattening garnishes or sauces), poaching or steaming.*

Quantities

Allow per person:
1 medium-sized sole or similar fish, 1 medium-sized to large brook trout or similar fish.
4–6 oz. fish fillet, without bone or thick skin, rather more if there are large bones and heavy skin, as on fish steaks.
½ medium-sized or 1 small lobster.

1. Cut the head off the fish, remove the intestines and wash well. Save the roe to use with the fish. Wash in cold water.	on a wooden surface with the cut side downwards, run your fingers firmly along the back bone.
2. Split the fish along the belly.	4. Turn the fish over and you will find you can remove the bones very easily.
3. Open out and lay	

1 Dungeness or 4–5 blue claw crabs (if served in a sauce, lobster and crab can be used more economically).
1 pint mussels.
Minimum about 2 oz. shelled shrimp or 4 oz. with shells.
1 large or a pair of smaller smoked herring.
2–3 oz. roe for an appetizer, up to 6 oz. for a main dish.

Storing and freezing *In order to avoid continual repetition, the points here apply to most fish, but where there is a particular point of importance you will find this given on the relevant page.*
Store fresh fish with the greatest care. Even in a refrigerator they should be kept for the minimum period. Read your manufacturer's instructions about freezing fish and use within the suggested period.
Put the fish as near the freezing compartment as possible in the refrigerator. Often one can use ready-frozen fish to take the place of fresh fish in a recipe. The general recommendations about defrosting are as follows: You can cook from the frozen state if the pieces of fish are small, but when cooking large fish I find it better to let them defrost before cooking; otherwise the outside tends to become overcooked before the center is done.

To use leftovers *Cooked fish must be used quickly, unless you wish to freeze it. It can be put into fish pies, fish cakes, soups or salads. There are certain methods of cooking which enable you to make better use of cooked fish, i.e. poached and baked are better than fried or broiled fish.*

This is one of the most adaptable ways of cooking fish, for the fish can be placed into a suitable dish in the oven with a little margarine or butter, with milk, with vegetables or with a sauce and cooked until tender.

The fish may be stuffed before baking and recipes for stuffings, suitable for most fish, are given on this page.

Blue Print

To Bake Fish

This method is suitable for all white, oily, smoked and freshwater fish, but is less successful with shellfish, except in a sauce.

If Baking With No Additional Ingredients

Set the oven at moderate to moderately hot, 375–400°F. Rub the bottom of an oven-proof dish with a little butter or margarine. Put the prepared fish on this, top with a little more butter or margarine and seasoning to taste or any other flavoring, i.e. a little chopped parsley or dill, squeeze of lemon juice, etc.

If you wish the fish to have a slightly golden-colored look, *do not cover*. If you wish the fish to remain very moist, *cover* the dish with a lid, foil or other cooking wrap.

Unless stated to the contrary, put fillets of fish towards the top of the oven; thicker steaks or whole fish should be put in or near the center of the oven. This makes certain the outside of the fish is not overcooked before the center is done.

Timing

Thin fillets take about 12 minutes, or about 15 minutes if covered.

Folded fillets take about 16 minutes, or about 20 minutes if covered.

Whole flatfish, e.g. sole, thick steaks or very thick fillets take about 25 minutes, or about 30 minutes if covered.

Thick whole fish, e.g. trout, take about 30–35 minutes, or about 40 minutes if stuffed *or* covered, or a little longer if both stuffed and covered.

Baking with Additional Ingredients

Baking with liquid You can omit the butter or margarine, although this can be added. The cooking times are the same as above.

Baking with vegetables i.e. sliced tomatoes, mushrooms and onions. Always slice onions *very thinly* or chop finely, since they take longer to cook than most fish. The cooking times will be a little longer than those given above.

Wrapping in foil Allow an extra 5–10 minutes cooking time.

Quick Ways to Give Flavor to Baked Fish

Add a little cider or wine to the fish.

Put the fish on a bed of sliced tomatoes, season and top with sliced tomatoes; season well.

Blend a little sweet paprika with light cream, pour over the fish and bake.

Add tiny pieces of lemon flesh, chopped parsley and plenty of melted butter to the fish.

Sole and Lemon

4 small to medium-sized sole or other white fish; seasoning; 4 tablespoons butter or margarine; 2 small onions; 2 lemons. *To garnish:* parsley.

The fish may be cooked whole or divided into fillets for this dish. Season lightly. Cut 4 large pieces of aluminum foil, sufficient to wrap round the fish. Grease with half the butter or margarine and place the fish in the center. Peel the onions and cut into thin rings. Put over the fish. Slice the lemons thinly, remove any pits (which would give a bitter flavor to the fish). Put over the onions and top with the remaining butter. Wrap the foil around the fish, put on flat baking sheets and bake as the Blue Print. Open the foil and slide on to the hot serving dish or plates. Garnish with parsley. *Serves 4.*

Note Cooked lemons have a delicious but unusual flavor; obviously you may not like this, in which case add the lemons as garnish afterwards.

Some Stuffings for Fish

While you can use most stuffing recipes, the following are particularly suitable. The amounts below give enough stuffing for 4 generous portions.

Asparagus and onion Chop the stalks from a small can of asparagus or a small bunch of cooked asparagus (save the tips for garnishing the finished dish). Blend with $\frac{2}{3}$ cup soft bread crumbs, 1 small grated onion, seasoning and 4 tablespoons melted butter or margarine. This is suitable for most fish, but particularly fish with a delicate flavor.

Celery and apple Chop several sticks celery, blend with 2 peeled chopped eating apples, 2 teaspoons chopped onion, seasoning, 1 teaspoon sugar (optional) and 1 tablespoon raisins. This is a difficult stuffing to handle as it has no crumbs or binding, so is suitable for baking separately and serving with the fish or putting into whole fish. It can be varied by adding chopped parsley. This is suitable for mackerel and fairly strongly flavored fish.

Mushroom and tomato Chop $\frac{1}{4}$ lb. mushrooms, mix with 2 large peeled chopped tomatoes, a little chopped parsley, 2 tablespoons melted butter or margarine, and plenty of seasoning. This is suitable for all fish.

Sage and onion See page 43. This is suitable only for fish with a strong flavor.

Parsley and thyme See page 43. This is suitable for most fish.

Sole and lemon

The following fish dishes, although entirely different in flavor and appearance, are based on the process of baking fish described on page 35.

Fish in Cider

This is suitable for fish with a fairly good texture and flavor, such as trout, herring and mackerel.

4 portions or whole fish; 2–3 small onions; seasoning; 2 eating apples; about 1¼ cups cider; 2–3 bay leaves. *To garnish:* 1 lemon.
Wash and dry the fish. Peel and cut the onions into thin rings. Season the fish and put into an oven-proof dish with most of the onions, separated into rings, the peeled, finely chopped apples and the cider. Put the bay leaves into the liquid (the flavor of this herb is very strong, so add 1 leaf only if you are not fond of it). Top with the few remaining onion rings. Bake as the Blue Print on page 35. Garnish with the lemon and serve in the baking dish.

For Special Occasions

Sole with White Wine Sauce

4 large or 8 smaller fillets of sole (or use other white fish; whiting is excellent for this dish); seasoning; about 4 tablespoons butter; about 1¾ cups white wine; 4 tablespoons flour; ⅔ cup milk; 3–4 tablespoons heavy or light cream. *To garnish:* paprika; 1 lemon.
Roll or fold the fillets of fish, put into a baking dish and season lightly. Top with 2 tablespoons of the butter and the white wine. Cover the dish and bake in a moderate

Dishes Based on Baked Fish

oven, 350–375°F, for about 20 minutes or a little less, since the fish has to be kept waiting while finishing the sauce. Meanwhile heat the remainder of the butter in a saucepan, stir in the flour and continue stirring over a low heat for a few minutes. Gradually blend in the milk and bring to the boil, stir until a very thick sauce. Lift the fish on to a very hot serving dish, strain the liquid from cooking the fish gradually into the thick sauce, then stir gently until smooth. Stir in the cream and heat without boiling. Pour over the baked fish, top with paprika and garnish with sliced lemon.

To vary
Sole Véronique   Add a few pitted grapes (peel if wished) to the wine and fish. Garnish with more grapes and lemon.
Sole Sevilla   Place slices of orange under each rolled fillet when cooked and proceed as the recipe above. Garnish with pitted grapes; peel if wished.

1. Cut the fish down the center and round the edges.
2. Make a cut in the flesh at the tail end of the fish.
3. Hold the tail firmly with your left hand and insert the knife under the flesh and cut one fillet away from the bone, easing it gently as you cut the fish.
4. Lay the fillets with the skin underneath on a chopping board.
5. Make a cut across the tip of the fillet and gently cut the flesh away from the skin.

Sole Sevilla (above)
Trout in cider (below)

Broiling Fish

Broiling is not only a quick method of cooking fish, but a very wise one too. Fish that is broiled is more easily digested and certainly less fattening than fried fish.

Blue Print

To Broil Fish

This method is suitable for most fish except some smoked fish.

Heat the broiler before placing the fish under the heat, for it is important the fish is cooked quickly. Thin fillets do not need turning over, but thicker pieces of fish should be turned. Lift the fish carefully, for it can be easily broken.

Always brush the fish with melted butter or other fat before cooking so it does not become dry and baste with a little more butter or fat during cooking or when turning the fish; if cooking the fish on the broiling pan or rack, grease it or cover it with buttered foil so the fish does not stick.

Vegetables such as mushrooms or tomatoes may be cooked on the rack of the broiling pan or in the pan itself. Season the vegetables lightly and brush or coat with a little butter or fat.

Timing

Thin fillets take about 5 minutes.
Thicker fillets take about 8–9 minutes.
Thick steaks or whole fish take about 10 minutes.

Lift the fish from the broiling pan or rack with a turner and put on to a serving dish. There is no need to drain broiled fish on absorbent paper. Garnish with parsley and lemon or cooked tomatoes and mushrooms. Tartar sauce or other sauces may be served with the fish if desired.

● **AVOID** *Overcooking and cooking too slowly. Allowing the fish to dry.*
● **TO RECTIFY** *The broiler should be preheated and the heat may be lowered after browning the outside of the fish. keep well basted with melted butter.*

Storing and freezing *See page 34. Fish can be broiled from the frozen state.*

Quick Ways to Give Flavor to Broiled Fish

The following flavorings can be added to the melted butter, or other fat, used to brush the fish before broiling.
Grated lemon rind and lemon juice.
A little tomato ketchup or fresh or canned tomato paste.
A crushed clove garlic and seasoning.
A little curry powder and a few drops Worcestershire and/or Tabasco sauce.

The following toppings can be put on to the fish when it is nearly tender.
Fine soft bread crumbs blended with melted butter and seasoning.
Grated cheese blended with bread crumbs.
Slices of Cheddar cheese.
Cottage cheese mixed with chopped parsley and chopped chives.

For Special Occasions

Savory Broiled Bass

6 tablespoons butter; 1 tablespoon lemon juice; $\frac{1}{2}$–1 teaspoon paprika; seasoning; 4 bass steaks or other white fish. *To garnish:* parsley; lemon.
Heat the butter in a pan until it turns golden brown; this gives a delicious flavor to the fish but it is essential the butter does not become too dark. Add the lemon juice, paprika and seasoning. Brush one side of the fish with some of the butter mixture and put on the greased broiling rack or on buttered foil. Cook as the Blue Print, turning once. Serve with new potatoes and any hot butter; garnish with parsley and lemon. *Serves 4.*

Chablis Halibut

About 2 wine glasses Chablis or other dry white wine; 4 halibut steaks or other white fish; seasoning; 4 tablespoons ($\frac{1}{4}$ cup) butter. *To garnish:* cooked or canned corn; red pepper; parsley.
Put the wine in a shallow dish and leave the fish soaking in this for 1 hour. Turn the fish after 30 minutes. Lift the fish out of the wine, season lightly. Melt the butter, brush the fish with this and broil as the Blue Print, turning once. Serve with the hot corn, topped with red pepper and garnish with parsley. Heat any wine left in the dish and spoon over the fish before serving. *Serves 4.*

Broiled Lobster

Spilt lobster, remove the intestinal vein, and sac in head and crack the large claws. Combine the green liver and red coral in a bowl with $\frac{1}{4}$ cup soft bread crumbs, 2 tablespoons butter, $\frac{1}{2}$ teaspoon dried tarragon and 1 teaspoon chopped parsley for each lobster being filled. Replace liver-coral mixture in lobster, cover with foil and brush tails with well seasoned butter. Broil, starting with face-side up, with claws, (turning once) for about 15 minutes. Just before serving, remove foil and brown stuffing under flame.

Broiled Shrimp

Do not shell the shrimp. Naturally for this dish, they need to be jumbo shrimp. Lay the shrimp on foil on the broiling pan rack, brush with a little oil, then broil until the shells are brown. They also may be cooked over a barbecue fire. Serve with lemon and cayenne pepper.

Pacific Fish Steaks

Grill 4 portions of white fish as the Blue Print. Top with grated or sliced cheese and melt under the grill. Meanwhile toss $\frac{1}{8}$–$\frac{1}{4}$ lb. chopped shelled large Pacific shrimp or smaller shrimp in a little butter for 2–3 minutes, add 2 teaspoons lemon juice and a good shake of pepper. Spoon on top of the fish and serve at once. Garnish with wedges of lemon or whole unshelled shrimp. *Serves 4.*

Frying Fish

Frying is undoubtedly one of the, if not the, most popular forms of fish cookery. It is an excellent method, for the coating ensures that the moisture and flavor are sealed in the fish.

Blue Prints

1. To Fry Fish

Fish can be fried in two ways.
In shallow fat; this can be butter or margarine, cooking fat or oil.
In deep fat or oil.
Although fish can be, and often is fried without coating, (see Fish Meunière), it is frequently coated before frying. The coating gives a pleasant crispness to the outside as well as keeping the fish moist. There are several ways of coating fish.
1. With seasoned flour. Allow about $\frac{1}{2}$ tablespoon flour to each portion of fish.
2. With seasoned flour and then with beaten egg and dry bread crumbs (you can use fine soft crumbs if preferred). It is a good idea to coat the fish with a very thin layer of flour (about 1 teaspoon per portion) before the egg, as this helps the final coating to adhere to the fish. 1 egg plus about 1 cup dry bread crumbs should coat 4 portions.
3. With a batter; this is described opposite.
4. With more unusual coatings, such as oatmeal.

2. To Fry Fish in Shallow Fat

This method is suitable for all white and oily fish and some shellfish (such as shrimp), but is unsuitable for smoked fish and most shellfish.

It is excellent for fillets of fish, but deep frying is preferable for thick portions of fish for you have better overall browning; they *can*, however, be cooked in a small amount of fat.

Heat enough oil or cooking fat in a frying pan to give a depth of about $\frac{1}{4}$ inch, or preferably $\frac{1}{2}$ inch. Put in the prepared fish and fry quickly until crisp and brown on the underside, turn and fry on the second side, lower the heat and continue cooking until tender.

Timing

Thin fillets take about 4 minutes.
Thicker fillets take about 5–6 minutes.
Thick steaks or whole fish take about 10 minutes.

Lift the fish from the fat with a wide spatula and drain on absorbent paper before serving. Fried fish can be served without a sauce, just garnished with lemon and parsley, but tartar sauce is the usual accompaniment (see opposite).

● **AVOID** *Too cool fat which would make the fish greasy or too hot fat which would overcook the outside before the center is done.*

Quick Ways to Give Flavor to Fried Fish

Mix the juice of a small lemon with each egg used for coating the fish and blend the finely grated lemon rind with the crumbs. Add a small quantity of grated cheese to the crumbs used in coating the fish. *It is important that this cheese coating is used only on thin fillets.* Cheese is spoiled if overcooked and thicker portions of fish take too long to cook.
Add a little chopped parsley or chives to the crumbs used in coating the fish.

Mackerels in Oatmeal

Cut off the heads from mackerels, remove the intestines and clean. Remove the back bone (see pictures page 34.) Fillet if wished. Wash and dry the fish. Mix fine or medium oatmeal with a little seasoning and coat the fish in this. Fry as Blue Print 2 on this page.

For Special Occasions

Fish Meunière

Choose fillets of white fish, small whole white fish, trout or shelled shrimp.
4 portions fish or the equivalent in shrimp; seasoning; 6 tablespoons butter (even a little more if you like rather rich food); $1–2\frac{1}{2}$ tablespoons lemon juice; little chopped parsley; few capers (optional). *To garnish:* lemon.
Wash and dry the fish and season lightly. Heat the butter in a large pan and sauté the fish until just tender. Lift the fish onto a very hot dish. If there is very little butter left in the pan you will need to add more. Heat the butter until it turns golden brown, add the lemon juice, parsley and capers and pour over the fish. Garnish with sliced lemon and serve at once. *Serves 4.*

Fish Belle Meunière

Cook the fish as above, but omit the parsley and capers. Instead sauté a few soft roes and shrimp in the browned butter.

Trout with Shrimp

Although trout is shown in the picture, this recipe is suitable for most other fish. You will need about 1 stick plus 2 tablespoons butter for 4 portions fish or whole fish. Fry the fish, remove from the pan but do not allow the butter to turn too brown. Fry $\frac{1}{4}$ lb. sliced button mushrooms and a generous amount of shrimp in the butter, add 1–2 tablespoons lemon juice as the recipe above, together with extra seasoning. Spoon over the fish and garnish with parsley and lemon. *Serves 4.*

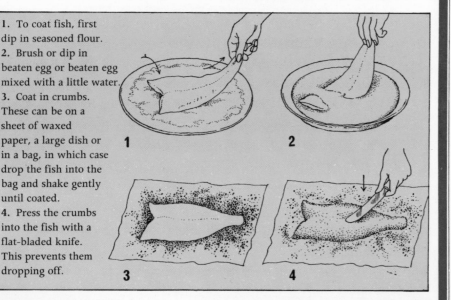

1. To coat fish, first dip in seasoned flour.
2. Brush or dip in beaten egg or beaten egg mixed with a little water.
3. Coat in crumbs. These can be on a sheet of waxed paper, a large dish or in a bag, in which case drop the fish into the bag and shake gently until coated.
4. Press the crumbs into the fish with a flat-bladed knife. This prevents them dropping off.

Trout with shrimp

Rolled Fillets of Fish

Roll skinless fillets of white fish and secure with toothpicks. Dip in the coating, remove picks before frying. Use an egg and bread crumb or batter coating, fry as the Blue Print on this page. If the fillets are rolled, they take slightly longer to cook.

Stuffed Rolled Fillets of Fish

Spread the fillets with a fairly firm stuffing, i.e. parsley and thyme (page 43), mushroom and tomato (page 35). Roll, then coat and fry.

Goujons (Ribbons) of Fish

This is a way of making the more expensive white fish, such as sole, go further. Divide the fish into neat strips, coat in egg and crumbs or batter and fry as the Blue Print. Small sprigs of raw or lightly cooked cauliflower (or broccoli or whole Brussels sprouts) can also be coated with batter and fried with the fish as in the picture. Garnish with lemon.

This is another advantage of deep frying: the flavors do not intermingle or impart flavor to the fat or oil. French fried potatoes or other vegetables, such as onion rings, can be fried immediately before the fish and kept hot. Batter-dipped fried fillets and French fries are illustrated on page 33.

Tartar Sauce

$\frac{2}{3}$ cup mayonnaise or Hollandaise sauce; 2 teaspoons each chopped parsley, chopped gherkins and capers; few drops tarragon vinegar (optional).

Mix all the ingredients together. If using mayonnaise as a basis for this sauce, you can make a large quantity and store the remainder in a screw topped bottle in the refrigerator.

Storing and freezing *Ready frozen fish may be used without waiting for it to thaw out, although it is difficult to coat frozen fish. Remember though you can buy ready-coated portions of frozen fish for shallow or deep frying. The cooking time is only a few minutes longer.*

To use leftovers *Fried fish is not very suitable for using in other ways. It could be frozen, ready to reheat, but take care it is not overcooked.*

Do not imagine that frying fish in deep fat (or oil) is more extravagant than shallow frying. If the temperature of the fat or oil is correct it is surprising just how *little is* absorbed by the fish coating.

Blue Print

To Fry Fish in Deep Fat

This method is suitable for white fish and for large shrimp. It is rarely used for oily fish and other shellfish and never for smoked fish. It is better to coat the fish when using this method of cooking. Choose either egg and crumbs, i.e. **2** on the Blue Print opposite or the batter coating below.

To make a batter to coat 4 portions of fish (or equivalent in scampi—jumbo shrimp), sift 1 cup flour, with a pinch salt. Add 1 egg and about 1 cup milk or milk and water. When coating in batter, dip the fish in seasoned flour first (allow about 1 teaspoon per portion); this encourages the batter to adhere to the fish. Dip in the batter. Allow any surplus batter to drop back into the basin so you do not have too thick a coating.

Make sure the pan of fat or oil is not over-filled, for naturally the level will rise when the fish is placed in the pan. *Test the temperature of the fat or oil;* it should be 365°F, or a cube of day-old bread should turn golden brown in under 1 minute. Place the frying basket into the hot fat or oil so it becomes coated, preventing the fish sticking to the mesh. Lift the warmed basket from the fat or oil, lower the coated fish into it.

Timing

Thin fillets take about 3 minutes.
Thicker fillets take about 4 minutes.
Thick steaks or whole fish take about 5–6 minutes.

Lift the fish from the fat or oil, allow the basket to remain over the top of the pan for a few seconds for any surplus fat to drop back into the pan. Drain on absorbent paper and serve. Deep fried fish can be served without a sauce, but a tartar sauce is the usual accompaniment.

● **AVOID** *Too hot fat or oil which will scorch the outside; Too cool fat or oil which will cause the coating to become greasy or even drop off the fish.*
● **TO RECTIFY** *Test the temperature of the fat before frying (see Blue Print).*

AVOID ANY DANGER OF FIRE—NEVER LEAVE A PAN OF FAT OR OIL UN-ATTENDED AND ALWAYS TURN THE HANDLE TOWARDS THE CENTER OF THE STOVE SO IT CANNOT BE KNOCK-ED AGAINST.

Goujons of fish (above left). Rolled fillets of fish (above).

I have used the term poach, rather than boil, for it describes the method that should be used for cooking fish. If fish really is boiled in liquid, it is cooked too rapidly and the outer flesh can, and probably will, break badly and become watery. Poaching means cooking gently in simmering liquid.

Blue Print

To Poach Fish

This is suitable for all kinds of fish including shellfish.

The liquid in which the fish is poached can be:

1. Seasoned water; when cooking crab, lobster, etc. many people like to use sea water.
2. Wine, cider or wine and water.
3. Milk or milk and light cream.
4. A court bouillon. This is made by using either fish stock (made by boiling the head, skins and bones of fish) or fish stock blended with white wine, a *bouquet garni* and seasoning.

The amount of liquid varies according to the thickness of the fish. Some people like to put the fish into cold liquid, bring the liquid to simmering point and continue; others like to put the fish into the simmering liquid. If putting into warmed liquid, shorten the cooking times below by about 2 minutes.

Timing

Thin fillets take about 7–8 minutes.
Thicker fillets, steaks or small whole fish take about 10–12 minutes.
Whole fish—allow 7–8 minutes per lb. or up to 10 minutes per lb. for solid type fish, i.e. salmon.
Wrap whole in cheesecloth and hang ends

over pan to facilitate removal. Lift fillets, steaks and small whole fish out of the liquid with a perforated wide turner, drain for a moment over the pan, then put on to a heated serving dish. If serving cold, allow to cool in the liquid; the cooking time should therefore be reduced by about 5 minutes.
Poached fish is generally served with a sauce; the easiest and simplest are on this page.

● **AVOID** *Overcooking; Failing to season the liquid which produces rather tasteless fish.*
● **TO REDUCERS** *An ideal method of cooking.*

SAUCES TO SERVE WITH POACHED FISH

White Sauce
2 tablespoons butter or margarine; 3 tablespoons flour; $1\frac{1}{2}$ cups milk or use half milk and half liquid from cooking the fish; seasoning.
Heat the butter or margarine in a saucepan. Stir in the flour and continue stirring over a low heat until the roux forms a dry mixture. Gradually add the milk or milk and other liquid, bring to the boil, cook until thickened, stirring all the time. Add seasoning to taste.
Anchovy sauce Use no salt in the sauce, add 1 teaspoon of anchovy paste.
Cheese sauce Add 4–5 tablespoons grated cheese to the thickened sauce, stir over a low heat; do not boil again. A little mustard can be added, if liked.
Cream sauce Add $2\frac{1}{2}$–4 tablespoons heavy cream to the thickened sauce, heat gently.
Lemon sauce Add the grated rind of 1 lemon to the flour. Add 1–$2\frac{1}{2}$ tablespoons lemon juice to the thickened sauce; do not boil again and heat very gently.
Parsley sauce Add 1–$2\frac{1}{2}$ tablespoons chopped parsley to the thickened sauce. Allow the parsley to cook for 2–3 minutes in the sauce for a milder flavor.
Shrimp sauce Add a few tablespoons whole or chopped shrimp to the sauce; heat gently so the shell fish is not toughened.

Haddock and mushroom scallops

On this page are a variety of fish dishes, including two other Blue Prints for simple methods of cooking fish.

Haddock and Mushroom Scallops

Little butter and cream; 2 cups mashed potatoes; about $\frac{1}{2}$ lb. fresh haddock; about $\frac{1}{2}$ lb. smoked haddock; $2\frac{1}{2}$ cups milk; 3 tablespoons butter; 4 tablespoons flour; $\frac{1}{4}$ lb. mushrooms; seasoning; 1 small can corn. To garnish: 4 tomatoes; parsley.
Blend a little butter and cream into the mashed potatoes. Put into a piping bag with a $\frac{1}{2}$-inch rose tip and pipe a border round the edge of 6 scallop shells or individual heatproof dishes. Brown gently under a very low broiler or in a very moderate to moderate oven while making the fish mixture. Put the fish into the milk with about one third of the butter. Simmer steadily until tender, i.e. about 10–12 minutes. Lift the fish out of the milk onto a flat dish; allow to cool slightly, then skin and flake. Meanwhile heat the remaining butter in a pan, stir in the flour and cook for several minutes, stirring all the time. Strain the milk used in cooking the fish into the roux. Bring gradually to the boil and cook until thickened, stirring all the time. Put in the whole mushrooms and simmer for about 5 minutes, then add the flaked fish. Season to taste and add some of the corn. Put the sauce mixture into the border of potatoes and top with hot corn. Garnish with wedges of tomato and parsley. *Serves 6.*
Note Other white and smoked fish can be used in this recipe.

Blue Prints

1. To Roast Fish

This method is suitable for white and oily fish.
It is similar to baking fish, as the instructions on page 35, but a more generous amount of butter or other fat is used. The fish is basted in the hot butter or fat as it cooks in a moderately hot to hot oven, 375–400°F, so the outside skin becomes crisp and brown. The cooking time is similar to that given for baking. It is very suitable for whole fish or thick pieces of cod, fresh haddock, etc.

2. To Steam Fish

This method is suitable for white fish, preferably whiting, sole, fluke and similar fish. It is an excellent way of cooking fish for small children, older people or invalids as it

Normandy herrings

is the most easily digested form of cooked fish.

The easiest method of steaming fish is to put the lightly seasoned fish on a buttered plate and top with a little butter. Sometimes this must be omitted if people are on a fat-free diet, but obviously it makes the fish more interesting. Top with a small quantity of milk. Put the plate over a pan of boiling water and cover with another plate, foil or a saucepan lid. Keep the water boiling and allow the following times.

Timing

Thin fillets take about 8–10 minutes.

Thicker fillets or thin steaks take about 12–15 minutes.

The liquid left on the plate can be added to a white, cheese or anchovy sauce (see opposite) to serve with the fish.

Fish Milanaise

4 portions white fish (preferably large fillets sole, whiting, flounder, etc.); seasoning; 2–3 tablespoons white wine; 4 tablespoons butter; about 6 oz. wide noodles; $\frac{1}{8}-\frac{1}{4}$ lb. button mushrooms; few cooked peas. *To garnish:* paprika; lemon.

Put the fish onto a large plate, add the seasoning, wine and about 1 tablespoon only of butter. Steam as the Blue Print. Meanwhile boil the noodles in plenty of well seasoned water and sauté the mushrooms in the remaining butter. Drain the noodles, return to the saucepan with the peas and mushrooms. Heat gently for a few minutes, then put on a hot dish. Lift the fish on top of the noodles and garnish with paprika and lemon. This can be served with any of the sauces opposite. *Serves 4.*

Normandy Herrings

4 large herrings; seasoning; 4 tablespoons flour; 6 tablespoons butter or margarine; 1 large onion; 2–3 eating apples; 1 tablespoon lemon juice. *To garnish:* parsley.

Remove the heads from the fish, clean and remove the back bone, if wished, as instruc-

Fish Milanaise

tions on page 34. Season the flour and roll the fish in this. Heat about 4 tablespoons of the butter or margarine in a large pan. Peel and chop the onion. Core the apples; slice 1 apple for garnish, as in the picture, and chop the remainder. Sauté the apples and onions in the pan until the apples are soft and the onion is transparent. Add the lemon juice. Put the chopped onions and apples into a hot serving dish and keep warm; keep the apple slices separate. Heat the remaining butter or margarine in the skillet and cook the fish until tender. Put on top of the mixture in the serving dish and garnish with the apple slices and parsley. *Serves 4.*
To vary Use shelled shrimp in place of the apples and onion. Fry the fish first; remove and keep warm, then fry the shrimp in the cleaned pan in a little extra butter. Add 1–2 tablespoons Chablis or Calvados and spoon over the fish.

In most families the traditional bird at Christmas time is a turkey, and indeed roasted poultry or game is an ideal choice for a celebration meal. The points about selecting poultry will be found on page 33. Choose quick roasting for prime birds and slower roasting for poorer quality, or when the bird has been frozen. *Always allow frozen poultry to thaw out before cooking. Read directions with turkey as it may take several days.*

Blue Print Recipes

1. To Roast Chicken and Turkey

A large roasting fowl or capon serves 6–8.
A medium-sized chicken can be cut into 4 portions and small spring chickens halved, or if very small, left whole as a portion for one. Rock Cornish hens are cooked and served as chicken. When buying turkey, remember there is a considerable weight of bone, so allow at least $\frac{3}{4}$ lb. per person, i.e. a 12 lb. bird (weight when trussed) would provide portions for 14–16 people.

These birds are dry-fleshed and must be kept moist during cooking, so cover the bird, particularly the breast, with a generous amount of butter or strips of fatty bacon. Put stuffing inside the bird as it helps to keep it moist but do not pack in. Baste the bird from time to time to keep it moist. The drumstick should be pliable and tender when cooked.

Timing

For quick roasting Set the oven to hot, 425–450°F; the heat may be reduced to moderately hot after 15 minutes if roasting

Roasting Poultry

a small chicken and 30 minutes for a larger bird.

Chicken 15 minutes per lb. and 15 minutes over.

Turkey Follow the directions on the wrapping—otherwise allow 15 minutes per lb. and 15 minutes over for a bird up to 12 lb. in weight. After this add an additional 12 minutes per lb. up to 21 lb., after this allow only 10 minutes for each additional 1 lb. If the bird is exceptionally broad breasted be a little generous with the cooking time.

For slower roasting Set the oven to 325°F for chilled stuffed capon or turkey. Set at 375–400°F for smaller, unstuffed birds. Allow an extra 15 minutes if stuffed.

Chicken 25–30 minutes per lb. up to 3 lb. then allow 15 minutes for each additional lb.
Turkey 30 minutes per lb. up to 15 lb. and 15 minutes for each additional lb. up to 20 lb., then 7–8 minutes for each additional lb. A roasting thermometer inserted in the inner thigh muscle (do not touch bone) will register 180°F when done. Let turkey sit 20 minutes before carving.

If using a covered roasting pan or foil, increase the oven temperature to 450°F and decrease total cooking time by 1 hour. Lift the lid of the pan or open the foil for about 30 minutes before the end of the cooking period so the skin may brown and crisp.

Accompaniments

The traditional accompaniments with both

these birds are: cranberry sauce with turkey; parsley and thyme stuffing and/or chestnut stuffing; thickened gravy. There are however more unusual accompaniments which may be served and these are given opposite.

To serve roasted chicken or turkey with sausages and bacons rolls, prepare the bird, i.e. put in stuffing, see the sketches. Heat the oven, cover the bird with butter or fat bacon. Cook for the time calculated. Add the sausages about 30 minutes before the end of the cooking time and the bacon rolls about 10–15 minutes before serving. Lift the bird on to the hot serving dish and use a little of the fat in the pan to add to the gravy. Hints on making gravy will be found on page 21.

1. Insert the stuffing under the skin of the neck.
2. Pull the skin right over the stuffing and

secure with a skewer.
3. Put any remaining stuffing (or if using two kinds, the second one) inside the bird.

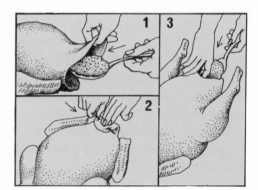

2. To Roast Duck and Goose

Duck and goose are birds that contain a high percentage of fat. I find I obtain a really fat-free bird, with deliciously crisp skin if I cook the bird for about 30 minutes then take the roasting pan out of the oven. Prick the skin carefully (do not prick too deeply) with a fine skewer and the excess fat spurts out. Do this once or twice for duck but at least twice more for a goose. Do not add extra fat when cooking duck or goose. The cooking times are the same as for chicken and turkey.

Quantities

A large duck can be cut into 4 pieces, but a small duckling should be halved.
Goose is a very extravagant bird, for it has very large bones and relatively little meat, so you should allow at least 1 lb. weight per person (after the bird is cleaned).

Accompaniments

The traditional accompaniments with both these birds are apple sauce and thickened gravy. Some less usual accompaniments are given opposite. Duckling always looks much more interesting if garnished with slices of orange.

Roast turkey

Young game can be roasted in the same way as poultry. Although it is not necessary to stuff game, I find that one can use some kind of stuffing for pheasant and grouse and suggestions are given below.

Blue Print

To Roast Game

Choose young pheasant, partridge, grouse or other young game birds, saddle (the back pieces) of hare or a whole leveret (a very young hare), rabbit (this must be very young and a tame rabbit is better than a wild one) or a roast of venison.

Quantities

A small bird is generally served to one person; a medium-sized grouse or other bird is halved, but there is a surprising amount of flesh on good pheasants and these can be carved like chicken.

Roast the bird as the Blue Print opposite for chicken and turkey. Game is also dry-fleshed, so must be covered with plenty of butter or fat bacon. The cooking times are the same as for chicken and turkey. Roast squabs are illustrated on page 33.

Accompaniments

Sauerkraut, sweet and sour red cabbage and pan roasted apples may be served with game birds. The gravy should not be too thick and can be flavored with wine. Garnish with watercress. Venison can be served with a wine sauce and chestnut puree and the gravy from hare or rabbit can be thickened with sour cream.

SOME INTERESTING STUFFINGS

Never make a stuffing too dry; it should be pleasantly moist. All stuffings given serve 5–6 if only one stuffing is made, but double that number if making two stuffings.

To Serve with Chicken, Turkey and Guinea Fowl

Parsley and thyme stuffing Blend together $1\frac{1}{4}$ cups soft bread crumbs, 1–2 tablespoons chopped parsley, 4 tablespoons shredded suet, or melted margarine or butter, or chicken or turkey fat, 1–2 teaspoons chopped fresh thyme or good pinch dried thyme, grated rind and juice of 1 lemon and 1 egg. Season well.

Forcemeat stuffing Blend $\frac{1}{4}$ lb. chopped lean ham with $\frac{1}{2}$ lb. bulk sausage, 1–2 teaspoons chopped parsley, grated rind 1 lemon, scant $\frac{1}{3}$ cup white raisins and 1 egg.

Liver stuffing Blend about $\frac{1}{2}$ lb. ground raw liver (this can be calf's liver, chicken livers, turkey or mixture) with 2 strips chopped bacon. Heat 4 tablespoons butter and toss the liver and bacon in this, then add 1 finely chopped onion; do not cook again. Blend with about 1 cup very smooth mashed potatoes, 2 eggs, 1 teaspoon freshly chopped mixed herbs or a pinch dried herbs and seasoning. This is also very good with duck, goose or pheasant.

Roasting Game

Giblet stuffing Cook the giblets until just tender. Remove all the flesh from the neck bone and chop this with the heart and liver. Blend with $\frac{2}{3}$ cup soft bread crumbs, 1 tablespoon chopped parsley, 1 tablespoon chopped nuts, $2\frac{1}{2}$ tablespoons raisins, seasoning and 1 egg. Finally chop a small onion, toss in 2 tablespoons butter or chicken fat and blend with the other ingredients. If using turkey giblets *double* all the other ingredients in this recipe. This is also good with duck or goose.

Chestnut stuffing Slit 1 lb. chestnuts on the flat side and boil in water for 5–10 minutes; remove the skins while still warm. Put the chestnuts into $1\frac{1}{4}$ cups chicken, ham or turkey stock and simmer until tender and nearly all the stock is absorbed, then chop or puree. Blend with $\frac{1}{4}$ lb. diced ham, $\frac{1}{2}$ lb. bulk pork sausage, seasoning and a little stock. If preferred, the chestnuts may be left whole and blended with the other ingredients.

To Serve With Duck and Goose

Sage and onion stuffing Peel, chop and cook 2–3 large onions for 10 minutes in $\frac{2}{3}$ cup water; season well. Strain, then blend with 1 cup soft bread crumbs, 1–2 teaspoons chopped fresh sage or $\frac{1}{2}$ teaspoon dried sage and $\frac{1}{4}$ cup melted butter or margarine. Bind with the onion stock and/or an egg.

Orange rice stuffing Grate the rind from 3 oranges and squeeze out the juice. Measure the juice and add enough water to give 2 cups liquid. Chop 1 large onion finely and toss in 4 tablespoons margarine or butter; then add $\frac{3}{4}$ cup long grain rice, the orange rind and juice and $\frac{1}{2}$ teaspoon chopped fresh sage. Simmer until the rice is nearly tender; season well, then add $\frac{1}{3}$ cup raisins. Do not overcook the rice; it becomes too solid when put into the bird and cooked again.

Celery and nut stuffing Chop the heart of a good-sized head of celery; do not use the outer sticks. Add the tender leaves, chopped finely. Mix with about 1 cup ($\frac{1}{4}$ lb.) chopped walnuts, about $\frac{2}{3}$ cup white raisins, $\frac{2}{3}$ cup soft bread crumbs (preferably brown), the grated rind and juice of 1 lemon or orange and $\frac{1}{4}$ cup melted butter or margarine. Season well.

To Serve with Game

Soak white grapes in a little red wine and put into the bird before roasting.

Blend cream cheese with a little brandy and put into the bird.

Blend 4 tablespoons butter with the cooked chopped liver of the game bird, season well and use as stuffing inside the bird.

Fried crumbs Make fairly coarse white bread crumbs. Fry in hot butter or margarine until crisp and golden brown. Drain on absorbent paper and serve with roasted game.

Potato chips Slice peeled potatoes thinly. Fry in very hot deep fat until crisp and brown. Drain on absorbent paper.

Storing and freezing *Roasted poultry and game should be stored in a refrigerator. If freezing poultry or game it is advisable to freeze the stuffing in separate containers.*

Roast pheasants

Frying & Broiling Chicken

I have headed this page as two methods of cooking chicken, for young chickens are very plentiful and inexpensive. Neither duck nor goose are suitable for frying or broiling and most turkey parts are too large. Certain recipes on these pages can be used with very young game.

Blue Print

1. To Fry Chicken

Choose young frying (broiler) chickens. If not ready-cut, then cut the chicken into neat pieces with a very sharp knife.
If the chickens are frozen, they can be cooked without defrosting, but I find I get a better coating if I allow the chickens to defrost, dry the pieces, then coat them.
Coat the chicken parts with seasoned flour, or egg and crumbs, or batter, in exactly the same way as described under frying fish on pages 38 and 39; the coating clings better if the skin is removed from the pieces.
The chicken parts may be cooked in shallow or deep fat.

Timing

The cooking times will be about 15 minutes in shallow fat, turning the parts regularly, or about 10–12 minutes in deep fat or oil.
Drain on absorbent paper and serve with salad or with cooked rice, as shown in the pictures, or with mixed vegetables.

● **AVOID** *Having the fat too hot or too cold. See the Blue Print on page 39.*

2. To Broil Chicken

Choose young chickens (broilers). Cut up as described under Blue Print 1. They may be broiled from the frozen state or defrosted, dried well then broiled.
Make sure the broiler is very hot before putting the chickens under the heat. Brush the rack of the broiling pan with melted butter, margarine or fat to prevent the pieces sticking.
Brush the chicken parts with melted fat of some kind; season if wished. Cook for approximately 15 minutes, turning several times and basting with the fat. When the outside of the chicken parts are brown and crisp, the heat may be reduced so the chicken will cook through to the center without charring. Mushrooms and tomatoes may be cooked on the rack of the broiling pan, or in the pan itself at the same time. Season the vegetables; brush with melted butter, margarine or oil before cooking so they do not dry out.

● **AVOID** *Cooking the chicken too slowly. Cooking the chicken without fat (unless counting calories), for it will become very dry.*
● **TO REDUCERS** *Broiling is an excellent method of cooking any food and young chicken is relatively low in calories. You can try basting the chicken with fruit juice or soy sauce rather than fat.*

Storing and freezing *Young chickens keep relatively well in a cool place or refrigerator. Frozen pieces may be stored in the freezing compartment of the refrigerator for the time stated on the package. You can freeze your own young chicken parts.*
To use leftovers *Use in salads or sandwiches. Do not cook again as the delicate flavor and texture will spoil.*

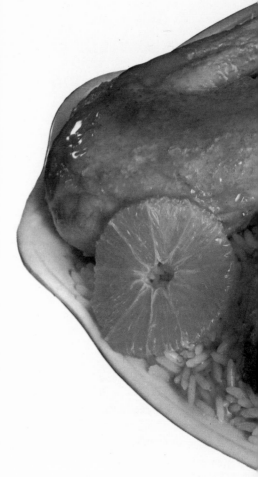

Fried chicken and oranges

For Family Occasions

Fried Chicken and Oranges

4 portions chicken; $\frac{1}{4}$ cup flour; seasoning; 4 tablespoons butter; 2 teaspoons oil; 3 large oranges.
Dry the portions of chicken and coat in seasoned flour. Heat the butter and oil in a pan. Fry the chicken as Blue Print 1 until nearly tender. Squeeze the juice from 2 oranges, pour over the chicken and finish cooking. Serve the chicken parts on a bed of boiled rice and garnish with the remaining orange, peeled and cut into rings. *Serves 4.*
To vary This is even more delicious if 3–4 tablespoons halved walnuts are added to the pan with the orange juice. The combination of crisp nuts and orange juice is very pleasant.

Fried Chicken Italienne

8 drumsticks of young chicken; 1 level tablespoon flour; seasoning; 1 or 2 eggs (depending upon the size); 1–1½ cups dry bread crumbs; 3 tablespoons grated Parmesan cheese. *To fry:* deep fat or oil. *For the rice*

Fried chicken Italienne

mixture: 4 tablespoons butter or margarine; 1 green and 1 red pepper; 1 cup long grain rice; $2\frac{1}{2}$ cups chicken stock or water and 1 or 2 bouillon cubes; seasoning; few cooked peas; little cooked or canned corn. *To garnish:* watercress or cooked spinach or other green vegetable.

Coat the drumsticks with the flour mixed with seasoning, the beaten egg, then the crumbs blended with the cheese. If possible chill for a while so the coating sets well. Meanwhile heat the butter or margarine in a pan. Dice the peppers, removing the cores and seeds, and toss in the butter for a few minutes. Add the rice and mix with the butter and peppers. Put the stock or water and bouillon cubes into the pan, bring to the boil, stir, season well and cook until the rice is nearly tender. Add the peas and corn and continue cooking until the rice is tender and the liquid absorbed. Meanwhile deep fry the drumsticks as Blue Print 1; take particular care that the fat or oil is not too hot, otherwise the cheese will scorch. Drain on absorbent paper. Pile the rice mixture on a very hot dish. Arrange the drumsticks around and garnish with the watercress or alternative. *Serves 4.*

Stuffed Chicken Breasts

2 whole chicken breasts; $\frac{1}{2}$ lb. bulk sausage; 1 tablespoon chopped parsley; $\frac{1}{8}$ lb. ($\frac{1}{2}$ cup) mushrooms; butter or chicken fat for frying or broiling. *To garnish:* cooked tomatoes.
Remove the bones from the chicken breasts and cut in half. Blend the sausage, parsley and finely chopped mushrooms together. Divide this mixture into 4 portions and press each portion against the chicken breasts. Do this on the underside where the bones were removed. Fry or broil the breasts as Blue Prints 1 or 2, frying in or basting with the butter or chicken fat. Serve with fried or broiled tomatoes. *Serves 4.*

For Special Occasions

Broiled Halves of Chicken

4 1-lb. squab chickens or 2 2-lb. chickens; seasoning; 4 tablespoons butter; grated rind 1 lemon. *To garnish:* watercress; lemon.
Split the chickens right down the backbone, so they open out quite flat, see the sketches. Mix the seasoning with the melted butter, add the lemon rind. Broil the chickens as described under Blue Print 2, basting with the

butter as they cook. Garnish with watercress and sliced lemon. *Serves 4.*

To vary Squabs or young partridges may be cooked in the same way. Omit the lemon if wished and flavor the butter with a few drops Worcesterhsire sauce and a pinch curry powder.

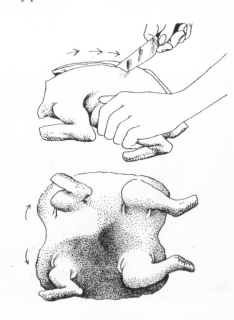

Using Cooked Poultry and Game

The recipes on this page make good use of cooked poultry and game. Read the points outlined in the Blue Print before preparing the recipes.

Blue Print

Using Cooked Poultry and Game

Never waste the carcass of a bird; simmer in water to give a good stock, flavor the liquid with herbs and vegetables and season well. Choose recipes where the meats are given the minimum heating time. Both poultry and game (with the exception of duck and goose) tend to have a dry flesh which will be spoiled by a second long cooking. Remember a certain amount of flavor is lost when food is cooked a second time, so compensate for this by adding herbs, cooking fresh vegetables in the sauce or using spices. Serve the dish as soon as possible after cooking and make sure the accompaniments are interesting and freshly cooked; crisp salads are splendid with any of these dishes.

Creamed turkey duchesse

Creamed Turkey Duchesse

$2-2\frac{1}{2}$ cups riced potatoes; 2 eggs or 2 egg yolks; 4 tablespoons butter or margarine; seasoning; $\frac{1}{4}$ lb. (1 cup) button mushrooms; 1 green pepper; $1\frac{1}{4}$ cups turkey stock (made by simmering the carcass or giblets); 4 tablespoons flour; $\frac{3}{4}$ cup milk; few drops Tabasco sauce; about 1 lb. diced cooked turkey plus any small pieces of stuffing (optional); 3–4 tablespoons light cream. *To garnish:* parsley. Blend the riced potatoes with 1 egg or egg yolk and half the butter or margarine; season well. Form into a border round the edge of an oven-proof dish. Brush with the second egg or egg yolk, diluted with a few drops of water and brown in a moderate oven, 350–375°F. Meanwhile simmer the mushrooms and diced green pepper (discard the core and seeds) in the stock for 10 minutes. Strain the liquid from the mushrooms and pepper; put this on one side for the sauce. Heat the remainder of the butter or margarine in a saucepan; stir in the flour, cook for several minutes stirring all the time; add the milk gradually, then the stock. Bring to the boil, and cook until thickened, stirring briskly; season well. Flavor with the Tabasco. Taste and add a little more Tabasco, if desired. Put the vegetables and turkey into the sauce and heat gently for a few minutes. Add the stuffing and cream towards the end of the heating period. Bring the dish out of the oven. Pile the turkey mixture into the center and garnish with parsley. *Serves 4–6.*
To vary Cooked pheasant or chicken may be used instead of turkey. If using pheasant, simmer 1–2 diced onions in the stock to give more flavor.

Chicken Pilau

2 onions; 1 clove garlic (optional); 2 tablespoons chicken fat or oil; 1 cup long grain rice; $2\frac{1}{2}$ cups chicken stock (made by simmering chicken carcass or giblets); $\frac{1}{3}$ cup white raisins; few pine or other nuts (optional); $\frac{3}{4}$ lb. diced chicken; seasoning. *To garnish:* few nuts or dry bread crumbs. Peel and chop the onions, crush the garlic. Sauté in the hot fat or oil for a few minutes, then add the rice, turn in the fat or oil. Add the stock, bring to the boil, stir, then simmer in an open pan for about 10 minutes. Add the rest of the ingredients and cook for a further 10–15 minutes until the liquid has just been absorbed. Pile on a hot dish and top with the nuts or crumbs. *Serves 4–5.*

Duck and Chestnuts

$\frac{1}{2}$–1 lb. chestnuts; about 12 small onions or shallots; 4 tablespoons rendered duck fat or margarine; 4 tablespoons flour; $1\frac{1}{4}$ cups duck stock (made by simmering the carcass or giblets); $\frac{3}{4}$ cup red wine; seasoning; 1 small eating apple; $\frac{1}{2}$–$\frac{3}{4}$ lb. diced cooked duck plus any skin; little fat to fry the skin. *To garnish:* 1 eating apple; little lemon juice. Slit the chestnuts, boil for 5–10 minutes, remove the skins while warm. Peel the onions. Toss the onions in the hot duck fat or margarine until golden. Lift out of the pan, stir in the flour and cook the roux for several minutes. Add the duck stock gradually, bring to the boil; cook until thickened, stirring all the time. Add the wine. Put the chestnuts and onions into the sauce; season well. Cover the pan, simmer for 20–25 minutes. Peel, core and dice the apple, put into the sauce with the duck and heat for a few minutes. To many people the skin of a duck is almost the most delicious part, so cut any pieces of skin left into neat dice. Put a little fat in a small skillet, heat and sauté the diced skin until very crisp. Put the duck mixture into a hot serving dish. Garnish with rings of apple, dipped in lemon juice and top these with the very hot crisp skin. *Serves 4–5.*

four
VEGETABLES AND MEALS WITHOUT MEAT

In this chapter you will find a great number of dishes using vegetables. Some of the recipes treat them as an accompaniment to the main dish, in others the vegetables themselves are the basis of the meal.

With modern freezing, canning and dehydrating, it is now possible to obtain almost every vegetable at any time during the year. Frozen vegetables are always very young and tender, so do not overcook them; follow the directions on the package carefully.

Canned vegetables have been cooked in the process of canning, so should be heated only. Prolonged cooking spoils much of their flavor and texture. Dehydrated vegetables are of two types: Firstly the modern freeze dried variety (i.e. the type that are first frozen and then dried); these need very little soaking and a short cooking time. Secondly there are the more traditional dehydrated vegetables which should be soaked well and/or given a long cooking period.

It is surprising how often beautifully fresh vegetables are spoiled by overcooking and this applies particularly to green vegetables. They contain essential mineral salts and Vitamin C (the vitamin that helps to build up resistance to colds and give a clear healthy skin). Unfortu-

nately this vitamin is lost if the vegetables are stale (so shop critically), or if the vegetables are overcooked. Page 48 gives the correct *modern* method of cooking green vegetables, used to preserve valuable minerals and vitamins. Please do not consider this only as a method of cooking to preserve food values. It also ensures you have vegetables that are full of flavor, a good color and an interesting texture.

Most people, young and old, are fond

of fried potatoes—but how often are these disappointing? The perfect fried potato should be dry, not greasy, crisp, not soggy and an even golden brown in color. Page 51 deals with the 8 secrets of successful fried potatoes and gives some new ways of shaping and presenting fried potatoes too. Instructions for pan roasting potatoes are on page 22.

The usual protein foods,—meat, fish and poultry—are expensive and there may be times when you wish to serve a sustaining meal without using them. You will find a number of the dishes, give a really good meal, based upon vegetables.

The body's utilization of vegetable protein is always increased with the addition of a small amount of animal protein. Therefore the addition of a small amount of salt pork bacon, sausage, ham bone or cheese to dried bean dishes not only adds a zest to the dish but improves its nutritional value.

Vegetables lose any watery flavor and taste better when "dried out". Return drained vegetables to the pan in which they were cooked and shake over low heat until excess moisture evaporates.

I think you will find this section packed with information to provide interesting and nutritious meals for all the family.

Although the list of green vegetables is very long and cooking times vary, the basic principles of cooking practically every variety are covered in the Blue Print.

Buying Green Vegetables

In order to ensure you have the very *best* green vegetables available, check on the following points when buying.

Broccoli—green or purple—should have very green leaves (if they have the slightest yellow tinge, they are stale); the flower should be firm.

Avoid cabbage or greens with slightly yellow leaves; these indicate a stale vegetable. Feel the vegetables; they should be heavy for their size. If surprisingly light this indicates there is little heart to the cabbage.

The outer leaves of cauliflower should be green and firm looking and the flower firm and white.

If spinach or greens look limp do not buy if possible—they could revive when put into cold water, but they may be too stale to be good.

Storing Green Vegetables

Unpack as soon as possible. If you have a very large refrigerator you can pack the vegetables into covered containers, but lacking that, this is the way to store:

Keep as much air circulation as possible around the vegetables.

Store away from bright light if possible.

Cooking Green Vegetables

Keep in the coolest place possible.

If storing cabbage, sprouts and firm greens for more than a day, sprinkle lightly with cold water.

If storing spinach, greens or broccoli for more than a day (which is not advisable), then keep dry; if sprinkled with water they are inclined to become slimy.

Preparing Green Vegetables

Do not wash, soak, cut or shred the vegetables until ready to cook. Mineral salts are soluble in water and will be lost by soaking. Vitamin C is destroyed by leaving cut surfaces exposed to the air.

Wash the vegetables in cold water; leave in the water for the shortest time possible.

If you add a little salt to the water it makes sure that tiny insects, often found in green vegetables, will be drawn out.

Cabbage and Similar Green Vegetables

Shred as finely as possible with a sharp knife to shorten cooking time.

Sprouts Remove only the very outer leaves; all too often much of each sprout is wasted by excess removal of leaves. Make a cross at the base of each sprout; this helps to shorten cooking time.

Cauliflower The stems and green leaves

are delicious, so remove these and trim ready for cooking. Discard only the imperfect outer stems and leaves. You can trim the thick part of the stems, but if these are placed into the boiling water a few minutes *before* the flower, they become tender when ready to dish up the vegetable.

Spinach When preparing spinach just break away any surplus stalks at the base. The coarse vein in larger leaves can be peeled off with the fingers.

Beetgreens Pull the green leaves away from the stems, then trim the stems and cook as a separate vegetable. These are delicious when cooked in boiling salted water, strained and topped with melted butter and chopped chives or parsley.

Broccoli Remove the very outer leaves. Keep the flower heads and the small leaves surrounding these intact. Separate the stalks and scrape. Choose a large saucepan so the flowers and stalks may be laid flat in the boiling salted water in the pan.

Blue Print
The Modern Method of Cooking

1. Prepare the vegetables as this page.
2. Put only enough water into the pan to give a depth of $1-1\frac{1}{2}$ inches—except for cauliflower and spinach, see below. Add a good pinch salt.
3. Make sure the saucepan has a tightly fitting lid.
4. Bring the water to the boil.
5. Remove the vegetables from the water in which they were washed, drain—except for spinach, see below.
6. Take the prepared vegetables over to the pan in a colander or bowl.
7. Add the vegetables *gradually* to the boiling water. This is important for the water should continue to boil and it will do this if the vegetables are added steadily, rather than all at once.
8. When all the vegetables have been added to the water, put on the lid and time the cooking.

Shredded Cabbage can be ready in 2–3 minutes, tougher types of cabbage take a minute or so longer.

Brussels Sprouts, if small, will take only 5–6 minutes.

Broccoli about 8–10 minutes.

Cauliflower As this vegetable does take longer to cook than cabbage, allow about 3 inches of water. Follow points 1–7 above, place the flower or flowerets downwards in the boiling salted water.

Allow about 15–20 minutes for a whole cauliflower, 10–15 minutes for separated cauliflower, until the stems are just tender but the flower unbroken.

Cauliflower with brown sauce topping

Cabbage pancakes

Spinach and beet greens These contain a high percentage of water, so wash well (often spinach has a lot of sand and soil sticking to the leaves, so may need washing in 2–3 changes of cold water); do not drain. Simply put into the pan with *no extra water*, just the water adhering to the leaves. Add a little salt. Cook steadily for 2–3 minutes, so the water runs off the leaves, then raise the heat slightly and continue cooking until tender.

The very young small leafed spinach takes only about 5–6 minutes. The beet greens rather more. If you are worried about the spinach sticking to the pan, put in $\frac{1}{2}$ inch water, bring to the boil, then add the damp vegetable.

9. Drain the vegetables *as soon as they are cooked*, top with a little butter or margarine and serve as quickly as possible.

Use the vegetable water if possible to add to gravy, soups and stews. Some people like to drink it, but that, I must confess, is an acquired taste.

Toppings for Green Vegetables

Sprinkle the vegetables with freshly chopped herbs.

Top broccoli, cauliflower or cooked spinach with Hollandaise sauce (page 88), white or cheese sauce (see pages 16–17). Always incorporate some of the vegetable liquid into the sauce.

Use a tomato sauce or a brown sauce. Spoon over cooked cauliflower and top with chopped parsley.

● **AVOID** *Overcooking green vegetables, or keeping them for any length of time before serving.*

● **TO RECTIFY** *Although you cannot revive overcooked vegetables, some of the toppings on this page give additional flavor.*

● **SHORT CUT** *The smaller the pieces of vegetable, the quicker the cooking time.*

● **TO REDUCERS** *All green vegetables are low in calories, so when you are planning diet meals serve as great a variety of green vegetables as possible.*

Storing and freezing *Details of storing are given opposite. Raw spinach, cauliflower and broccoli freeze very well; cabbage is less successful.*

To use leftovers *Page 52 gives many suggestions for using these.*

New Ways with Green Vegetables

Remember that firm green cabbage (excellent as the basis for coleslaw), savoy cabbage (green with curly leaves) or red cabbage (often considered only for pickling) can be used in any of the recipes. As the leaves of savoy cabbage are firmer than those of a tender green cabbage, allow 3–4 minutes longer cooking time than that given in the Blue Print. It is usual to cook red cabbage until quite tender and this can take a minimum of 30 minutes. You may, however, prefer its very firm (rather than crisp) texture if cooked for a shorter time.

Cabbage Pancakes

1 very small green cabbage, or use the *tender* outer leaves of a large cabbage and save the heart for another occasion; seasoning. *For the batter:* 1 cup flour; pinch salt; 1 egg; $1\frac{1}{3}$ cups milk and water. *For frying:* oil or fat. Shred the cabbage and cook *very lightly* as in the Blue Print opposite, season well. Meanwhile make a pancake batter with the flour, salt, egg and milk and water. Drain the cabbage and mix with the batter. Heat a little oil or fat in a pan, pour enough of the mixture into the pan to give a thin coating. Cook until golden brown on the under side, turn and cook on the second side. Continue to make the rest of the pancakes. Serve topped with broiled or sautéed mushrooms. *Serves 4–6.*

Vichy Cabbage

1 small cabbage; 1–2 onions; at least 1 tablespoon chopped parsley; about 2 tablespoons margarine; $\frac{2}{3}$ cup beef or chicken stock; seasoning.
Shred the cabbage and chop the onion. Mix the onion and parsley together. Heat the margarine in a pan, toss the onion and parsley in this. Add the stock, bring to the boil, put in the cabbage gradually, as described in the Blue Print opposite. Cover the pan and cook for 2–3 minutes, lift the lid of the pan, add seasoning to taste, turn the cabbage round in the stock and allow this to boil for another 1–2 minutes until the mixture is still crisp and the liquid evaporated. This makes a pleasant alternative to the more usual way of cooking. (Illustrated on page 47) *Serves 4–6.*

Sweet and Sour Cabbage

1 small red, green or savoy cabbage; seasoning; 2–4 teaspoons sugar (preferably brown); 4 tablespoons butter; 1 small apple; $1\frac{1}{3}$ cups chicken stock or water and 1 bouillon cube; 1 tablespoon vinegar; 1 tablespoon flour.
Shred the cabbage finely, season lightly. Put the sugar and butter into a large saucepan and stir over a low heat. Continue cooking

until the mixture turns golden brown, taking care it does not burn; stir once or twice. Add the peeled chopped apple and nearly all the stock or water and bouillon cube. Bring to the boil. Add the cabbage gradually, so the liquid continues to boil, then stir in the vinegar. Cook for about 5–6 minutes with green cabbage, 10–15 minutes with savoy cabbage and 30 minutes with red cabbage. The vegetable should just be slightly crisp. Blend the flour with the rest of the liquid, stir into the cabbage, stir very well and continue stirring until the mixture thickens slightly. Test the cabbage and if sufficiently cooked serve; otherwise continue cooking for a few more minutes, adding a little extra stock or water if necessary. *Serves 4–6.*

Cauliflower Fritters

1 medium-sized cauliflower; salt. *For the batter:* 1 cup flour; pinch salt; 2 eggs; $\frac{2}{3}$ cup water; 5 tablespoons milk. *For frying:* oil or fat.
Separate the cauliflower and cook in boiling salted water as the Blue Print opposite; take particular care that the vegetable *is not overcooked*. Sift the flour and salt, add the egg yolks, water and milk, then fold in the stiffly beaten egg whites Drain the cauliflower carefully so the flowerets are not broken. Heat the oil or fat. While you can fry these fritters in shallow fat, it is easier and better to use deep fat. Dip the sprigs into the batter and fry for 1–2 minutes only in the hot fat. Drain on absorbent paper.
To make a light supper dish, toss in grated Cheddar, Gruyère or Parmesan cheese. *Serves 4–8.*

To vary Brussels sprouts or broccoli can be used instead of cauliflower.
Yoghurt fritters Use yoghurt or sour cream instead of water and milk.
Tomato and cauliflower fritters Use tomato juice instead of water and milk.

Cauliflower Pancake Gâteau

Pancake batter (see Cabbage Pancakes). *For frying:* oil or fat. *For the filling:* 1 cauliflower; salt; little butter and heavy cream; chopped chives and chopped parsley (optional). *To serve:* melted butter.
Make a pancake batter as the recipe for Cabbage Pancakes. Cook the pancakes in hot oil or fat. Keep hot while the cauliflowerets are cooked in salted water, as the Blue Print. Strain the cauliflower, put into a hot bowl and mash roughly with a fork. Blend with a little melted butter and cream. Spread each pancake with this mixture; pile one on top of the other. Top the pile with the chopped chives and parsley, if liked. Pour a little melted butter on top and serve at once. Serve with poached or shirred eggs. *Serves 4–6.*

To vary Cooked creamed spinach or even creamed broccoli can be used instead of cauliflower, or spinach and cauliflower can be used alternately. (Illustrated on page 47.)

Cooking Root Vegetables

Root vegetables are not only an excellent addition to soups and stews and a splendid basis for Russian salad, but they are well worth cooking in various ways to serve with fish and meat, or as a dish by themselves. Potatoes are covered on page 51.

Blue Print

To Cook Root Vegetables by Boiling

1. Prepare the vegetables as this page.
2. Since most root vegetables take longer to cook than green vegetables, put about 3 inches of water into the pan.
3. Bring the water to the boil, add salt to taste.
4. Add the vegetables steadily (see the Blue Print on page 48) and cook until tender. This will vary according to the size but an indication is given below.
Artichokes—Jerusalem 25 minutes; add 2 teaspoons lemon juice to the water.

Beet   Allow 35 to 45 minutes, according to size. Do not add salt.
Carrots   Young whole baby carrots, 15 minutes. Sliced older carrots, 20–30 minutes. Whole old carrots, 45 minutes.
Celeriac (celery root)   As turnips; add 2 teaspoons lemon juice to the water.
Celery, Fennel and Oyster Plant   Diced will take 10–15 minutes.
Endive   As celery; add 2 teaspoons lemon juice to the water.
Parsnips, Rutabagas and Turnips   If young and sliced, about 15 minutes. If old and diced into $\frac{1}{2}-\frac{3}{4}$-inch cubes, 20 minutes. If sliced, about 30 minutes.
5. Cook the vegetables until tender; boil steadily but *not* too rapidly; otherwise the vegetables often break on the outside.
6. Drain, then return to the pan with a little butter or margarine and toss in the pan as the fat melts.
7. Add chopped fresh herbs if desired, then serve.

● **AVOID** *Overcooking these vegetables. Naturally they must be tender when served hot, but they must retain a little of their firm texture to be interesting.*
● **TO RECTIFY** *If overcooked, mash the vegetables as potatoes (see page 51).*
● **TO REDUCERS** *Although some of the vegetables in this group are higher in calories than green vegetables, i.e. rutabagas and turnips, small portions will be allowed in most reducing diets. Celery and chicory are very low in calories.*

Chinese style vegetable soup

Preparing Root Vegetables
These vary in character a great deal.
Artichokes   Scrape or peel. Keep in cold water with a little lemon juice until ready to cook as they darken in color.
Beets   Remove stalks and leaves. Wash. Do not cut; otherwise the vegetable bleeds.
Carrots, Turnips, Rutabagas, Parsnips   Remove stalks and leaves. If very young, scrub well or scrape gently. If old, peel thinly.
Celeriac (celery root)   Peel and slice or dice. Treat as artichokes before cooking.
Celery and Oyster Plant   Wash in cold water and divide into neat pieces.
Endive   Needs just the outer leaves removed.
Fennel   Remove the leaves; these can be chopped and added to white or other sauces instead of parsley. Wash and slice the root.

Buying Root Vegetables

Check to see they are unblemished. If you buy ready washed root vegetables, use fairly quickly as the soil adhering to vegetables acts as a protection.

New Ways to Cook and Flavor Root Vegetables

Cook in chicken stock instead of water. Use only enough stock to keep the vegetables from burning. Lift the lid of the pan for the last few minutes so the excess liquid evaporates. This method is excellent with *all* root vegetables.
Cook the vegetables as the Blue Print, then toss in butter or margarine, mixed with a very *little sugar*; excellent with carrots, turnips, parsnips and rutabagas.
Mash some root vegetables as potatoes, see page 51.
Roast or fry some root vegetables as potatoes, see page 51. The most successful to roast are parsnips and rutabagas. Parsnips should be parboiled for 10–15 minutes before roasting. The most successful to fry are artichokes, carrots, parsnips and rutabagas.

Chinese Style Vegetable Soup

1 tablespoon corn or olive oil; 4 tablespoons long grain rice; 5 cups chicken stock, or water and 5 chicken bouillon cubes; seasoning; 1 small carrot; 1 small turnip; small piece rutabaga; 1–2 sticks celery. *To garnish:* chopped parsley.
Heat the oil in a saucepan. Add the rice and turn in the oil for several minutes. Pour the stock into the pan, or the water and bouillon cubes; bring to the boil. Stir briskly, add seasoning. Lower the heat and cover the pan. Simmer gently for 20 minutes, until the rice is *just* tender. Grate the vegetables finely or coarsely according to personal taste, add to the soup and heat for a few minutes only so the vegetables retain their firm texture. Add extra seasoning if required. Serve topped with parsley. *Serves 4–6.*
To vary   Add yoghurt to the soup just before serving.

Cooking Potatoes

Potatoes may be cooked and served in dozens of ways, but however interesting and unusual the recipe, it is based on the methods outlined on these pages.

Blue Print
To Fry Potatoes

Although it is possible to fry raw potatoes in shallow fat, a better result is obtained by cooking in a deep pan of oil or fat.

To make   Peel the potatoes, cut into the required shape, i.e. strips, slices, etc. Keep in cold water until ready to cook; then dry thoroughly in a cloth.

To cook   Heat the oil or fat to 365°F. To test this, drop in one slice; it should start to cook at once. If it drops to the bottom of the oil or fat, the oil is not sufficiently hot. Put the basket into the hot oil or fat (this makes sure the potatoes do not stick). Lift the basket from the oil. Put some of the prepared potatoes into this, lower into the hot oil or fat and cook until tender. Lift out of the pan. Continue cooking all the potatoes until tender. Reheat the oil or fat, then fry the potatoes very quickly until golden brown; this takes approximately 2 minutes for each batch.

To serve   Drain on absorbent paper and serve as soon as possible. The potatoes may be sprinkled with salt just before serving.

For perfect fried potatoes remember:

1. Dry the potatoes well.
2. Test the temperature of the oil or fat.
3. Heat the frying basket so they do not stick.
4. Do not cook too many potatoes at one time.
5. Cook until tender only.
6. Reheat the oil or fat.
7. Fry very quickly for the second time.
8. Drain on absorbent paper and serve.

To vary   New potatoes may be washed, but not peeled, dried then fried as the Blue Print.

Ribbon potatoes   Cut ribbons from the potatoes and fry as the Blue Print.

Allumette potatoes (matchsticks)   Cut very thin strips and fry as the Blue Print.

Potato balls   Make balls with a vegetable scoop and fry as the Blue Print.

To Boil Potatoes

If you have never boiled potatoes with the skins left on, you are missing much of their good flavor. The skins may be removed after cooking and they pull off quite easily. This is an excellent method of cooking potatoes that tend to break in boiling.

If you wish to peel before cooking, cut away the peel from old potatoes, scrape away the skin from new potatoes. Keep in cold water until ready to cook so the potatoes do not discolor. Put the potatoes into boiling salted water; lower the heat so the potatoes cook steadily, rather than rapidly. Allow from 20–30 minutes according to size. Flavor new potatoes with a sprig of fresh mint during cooking; remove this before serving. Drain the potatoes and return to the pan with melted butter and chopped parsley.

To Scallop Potatoes

4 cups sliced potatoes; 3 tablespoons butter; 3 tablespoons flour; $1\frac{1}{2}$ cups milk; seasoning; $\frac{1}{4}$ lb. (1 cup) grated Cheddar or Gruyère cheese.

Melt the butter and add the flour, stirring for about 2 minutes. Add the milk gradually and stir until the sauce thickens. Season and add the cheese; stir until the cheese is melted. Place the potatoes and sauce in alternate layers in a greased oven-proof casserole. Bake covered in a moderate, 350°F, oven $1\frac{1}{2}$ hours. Remove the cover after about $\frac{1}{2}$ hour. *Serves 6–8.*

To vary   Omit the sauce and dredge the layers with flour and dot with butter. Cover with 2 cups hot milk and cook as above.

To Steam Potatoes

Put well washed or peeled potatoes into a steamer over a pan of boiling water. Sprinkle with a little salt and cook but allow an extra 5–10 m.. time.

To Bake Potatoes

Old potatoes bake better than new potatoes for they have a delicious floury texture, but I have baked new potatoes. Of course, Idahos are the classic baking potato. Wash and dry large potatoes. If you like a crisp skin, brush this with a little melted butter or margarine. Prick the potatoes with a fork so the skins will not burst. For large potatoes, allow 1 hour in the center of a moderate to moderately hot oven, 375–400°F, or $1\frac{1}{4}$–$1\frac{1}{2}$ hours in a very moderate oven. Lift the potatoes from the oven. Mark a cross on top and serve with butter.

Mashed Potatoes

Boil old potatoes as the method above. Drain, return to the pan and break with a masher or electric beater until quite smooth. If you need *perfectly* smooth mashed potatoes, then put through a food mill and return to the pan. Add *hot* milk plus 2 tablespoons of butter or margarine and seasoning. Beat hard with a wooden spoon until very white. Pile into a hot dish and fork into shape.

Duchesse Potatoes

Put cooked and drained boiled potatoes through a food mill. Add about 4 tablespoons butter or margarine and 1–2 egg yolks to each 1 lb. potatoes. As you wish the potatoes to hold a shape, omit the milk used in mashed potatoes. Duchesse potatoes are used for forming a border round a dish or to make a nest shape. Put the potatoes into a cloth piping bag with a $\frac{1}{2}$–1-inch potato rose tip. Pipe into the required shape and brown in a moderately hot·oven, 400°F.

Cheese and potato ring

There is no great point in cooking more vegetables than you need for they *should* be freshly cooked for each meal. However, the following dishes provide interesting ways to use small amounts of leftover vegetables.

Cabbage and Tomato Casserole

1 onion; 4 tablespoons margarine; 1 small apple; 4 large tomatoes; $\frac{2}{3}$ cup water; seasoning; about $\frac{1}{2}$ a small cooked cabbage; 3–4 oz. (1 cup) grated Cheddar cheese; 1 cup dry bread crumbs.

Grate the onion. Toss in the hot margarine with the peeled and grated apple and peeled tomatoes. Add the water and seasoning. Simmer until a thick puree. Add the cooked shredded cabbage. Heat for a few minutes only. Put into a hot heat-proof dish. Top with the cheese and crumbs. Brown under the broiler. *Serves 4.*

To vary Cauliflower, thickly sliced potatoes, etc. may be used in place of cabbage.

Camp Fire Corn

3–4 slices fairly fat bacon; about 1 cup leftover cooked or canned corn; 4 eggs; seasoning; little butter or margarine; 4 slices bread or toast. *To garnish:* parsley or green pepper.

Chop the bacon in small pieces. Heat in a skillet until crisp. Lower the heat, add the corn and stir the bacon and corn for a few minutes. Beat the eggs with seasoning. Pour into the pan. Scramble lightly. Serve on the buttered bread or toast and top with parsley or rings of green pepper. *Serves 4.*

Leftover Vegetables

Zucchini Bake

Approximately $\frac{1}{2}$ lb. cooked zucchini; 2 tablespoons margarine; 1 tablespoon chopped chives or green onion; 2 eggs; $\frac{2}{3}$ cup milk; seasoning; little grated nutmeg.

Mash the zucchini with the softened margarine and chives or onion. Add the beaten eggs and warm milk. Season well. Pour into a pie plate and top with grated nutmeg. Bake in the center of a very moderate oven, 325–350°F, for 40 minutes, until just set. This is excellent with toast as a supper dish.

Succotash

Combine 1 cup each cooked or canned corn and lima beans with $\frac{3}{4}$ cup light cream, $1\frac{1}{2}$ tablespoons butter and seasoning. Heat gently. *Serves 4.*

Spinach Soup

Chop finely or puree in blender 1 cup cooked spinach. Combine with 1 can frozen or condensed potato soup, adding milk as directed. Heat and serve garnished with paprika. *Serves 2–3.*

Quick Ways to Use Leftover Vegetables

Leftover mashed potato can be shaped into patties and sautéed. Heat cooked diced vegetables in a little butter, add to well seasoned eggs and make Vegetable Scramble or a Vegetable Omelette. Blend cooked vegetables with a sauce and use as a filling for pancakes or omelettes.

Vegetable Pudding Make a pancake batter with 1 cup flour, pinch salt, 1 egg and $1\frac{1}{3}$ cups milk. Heat 4 tablespoons margarine or fat in an 8-inch square pan. Add leftover vegetables, turn in the hot fat, then heat for a few minutes. Pour the batter over the hot vegetables. Bake for approximately 30 minutes above the center of a hot oven. Lift out of the pan, top with freshly chopped herbs and/or grated cheese and serve. *This makes an excellent supper dish for 4.*

Storing and freezing *Leftover vegetables spoil quickly. Use as soon as possible. You can freeze leftover vegetables but use the quickest method of reheating after you remove them from the freezer; otherwise they have little, if any, flavor.*

Cabbage and tomato casserole

five
SOUPS, SALADS AND SNACKS

At the start of this chapter of family cooking, you will find a selection of interesting sandwiches of all kinds. It is recorded that the word "sandwich" was added to our language in memory of the 4th Earl of Sandwich (who lived in the 18th century) and who once spent 24 hours without a pause at the gaming tables, with no other food than beef between slices of bread.

The traditional American-type sandwich is still two slices of bread with a filling in the center. This can be meat, fish, salads, etc., but whatever the filling, it is important that the bread is fresh, generously spread with butter or mayonnaise and the filling kept moist, so the sandwich is never dry and hard to eat. On the other hand, if the sandwich is to be kept before eating, it is important that the bread does not become soggy. In this case, when using mayonnaise spread the bread with a thin coating of butter first.

The most colorful looking sandwiches in the world originated in Denmark, but you will be offered these delicious open sandwiches in other parts of Scandinavia too. They can be sufficiently sustaining to serve with a knife and fork for a light meal

or small and elegant enough to eat with your fingers at a cocktail party.

Toasted sandwiches provide the quick and easy snack for cold weather and there are few things more appetizing than a freshly cooked bacon and egg or bacon and cheese toasted sandwich.

It is a mistake to think that salads are just for hot weather. With the wide variety of ingredients available from which to create good salads, they can be served throughout the year. Often one can serve a crisp green or mixed salad with a hot dish as a change from cooked vegetables. A fresh salad blends well with

a spicy hot dish.

I am a great lover of homemade soups. I find if I am very tired that a bowl of interesting hot soup is a wonderful light meal. The soup is easy to digest and gives one a feeling of warmth and well being. Because so many of us are calorie conscious these days I have also included some soups for reducers. Many soups can provide a meal in a bowl; others are more suitable for the start of a meal. Do not forget that soups are excellent in hot weather, when they can be served cold, iced or jellied.

Making soups today need not be a long and tiresome job. If you have a pressure cooker, use this for making stocks and soups and reduce the cooking time to a matter of minutes. If you possess a blender, then puree the soup in this to give a smooth texture. It takes almost no time at all to produce a smooth puree, and saves the tiresome chore of sieving.

I feel this particular part covers so many recipes we need today when time is precious. From here you will be able to select a complete light meal on a tray to give your family while they watch television or picnic in the garden.

A plate of sandwiches can be prepared very quickly, but, if properly made, and if the fillings are chosen with a thought to food values, the sandwiches can be as nutritious as a cooked meal. If your family need to take sandwiches regularly to work or school, make sure they have protein foods plus raw vegetables in the fillings to give the nutritional balance needed.

Blue Print

To Make Perfect Sandwiches

Make sure the bread is reasonably fresh.
Cut the bread with a really sharp knife (unless using ready-sliced bread).
Make sure the butter or margarine is sufficiently soft to spread without breaking the bread. If you leave the butter or margarine at room temperature for a short time it should be soft; choose a flat-bladed knife for spreading on the bread. If using mayonnaise, spread bread with a thin coating of butter first.
If the filling is very moist in texture, lay lettuce leaves on the bread before adding the filling, so preventing the filling making the bread and butter too soft.
Wrap sandwiches or cover as soon as they are made. This prevents them from becoming dry. Use paper towels, foil, waxed paper or polyethylene wrappings.
Cut the crusts off the bread for dainty-sized sandwiches, but if they are to take the place of a meal, then you can leave the crusts on the bread.

A NEW LOOK TO THE BREAD IN SANDWICHES

Make sandwiches with one slice of white and one slice of brown bread and arrange as the picture on this page.
Use very fresh bread, remove the crusts, spread with the filling and roll.
Make double-decker sandwiches, i.e. a slice of buttered bread, then filling, then a slice of bread, buttered on both sides, more filling and a final slice of buttered bread—just the thing for hungry children. You can either use the same filling or have two different fillings.
Ribbon sandwiches are made by preparing double-decker sandwiches as above, or even having four slices of bread—use white and brown breads alternately. Cut into narrow fingers.
Have a change of breads; wholewheat, rye and fruit breads of all kinds can be used in sandwiches with appropriate fillings, so can some of the interesting crisp breads available. Use firm fillings for crisp breads, so they remain firm and crisp.

SOME INTERESTING SANDWICH FILLINGS

Here are a few of my favorite sandwich fillings, but obviously it is very easy to plan an infinite variety.

With Cheese

Blend cream or cottage cheese with:
Chopped green pepper and mayonnaise.
Mashed banana.
Chopped well drained pineapple and/or pineapple and nuts. Or top the cream cheese with pineapple as in the French loaf.
Seedless raisins and nuts.
Chopped eating apple.
Grated raw carrots and a little mayonnaise.
Little red currant or other jelly.
Blend grated Cheddar or other cheese with:
A little mayonnaise to soften.
Any of the fillings above.
Chopped or sliced cucumber.
Chopped or sliced tomato and watercress.
Chopped lean ham or other meats.
Flaked cooked fish or chopped shellfish.
Fish pâtés or pastes (spread the pâtés or pastes over the bread and butter, then add the cheese filling).
Shredded lettuce and chopped celery.

With Egg

The eggs may be soft boiled for a moist filling, hard boiled or scrambled. Hard boiled or scrambled eggs can be blended with mayonnaise for extra flavor. If you chop hard boiled eggs instead of slicing, they are easier to eat in a sandwich.
Blend the cooked eggs with:
Chopped or sliced smoked salmon and/or a little caviar as in the French loaf.
Chopped ham, salami, other meat or chicken.
Flaked cooked fish or chopped shellfish.
Chopped stuffed olives and/or chopped gherkins or cucumber.
Chopped green pepper by itself or with chopped tomato and watercress as in the French loaf.

With Fish

Flaked white fish, mixed with chopped cucumber, shredded lettuce and mayonnaise.
Chopped shellfish mixed with plain or curry flavored mayonnaise and lettuce as in the French loaf.
Mashed cooked cod's roe blended with chopped crisply fried bacon.
Smoked cod's roe mixed with a very little prepared horseradish and lettuce. Use other smoked fish with the same ingredients.

With Meat

Mix chopped cooked ham with:
Well drained pineapple and lettuce.
Peanuts, and spread the bread with peanut butter.

Checkerboard and double-decker sandwiches

Finely chopped mustard pickle and watercress.

Top sliced ham with:
Very thick apple sauce or apple jelly, lettuce or watercress and some chopped eating apple as in the French loaf.

Mix chopped cooked beef or tongue with:
Prepared horseradish and lettuce.
Cooked halved prunes and watercress.

Mix chopped cooked lamb with:
Lettuce and mint jelly.
Halved grapes, sweet chutney and lettuce.

Mix chopped cooked chicken with:
Mayonnaise, chopped pepper and lettuce.
Chopped almonds, shredded lettuce and mayonnaise.
Sliced cooked mushrooms, mayonnaise and watercress.

Top sliced cooked chicken with:
Pâté and a little lemon juice.

Storing and freezing *Wrap the sandwiches well and store in the refrigerator as far away from the freezing compartment as possible. Sandwiches freeze well; wrap and allow time for them to thaw out before serving. Avoid freezing sandwiches containing boiled eggs (scrambled eggs are reasonably good), mayonnaise, lettuce and other crisp salad ingredients.*

To use leftovers *Wrap and store or freeze, or fry the sandwiches in hot butter.*

Toasted Sandwiches

These sandwiches are excellent for a hot snack and allow you to blend hot toast with cold ingredients or with cooked food, whichever is available.

Blue Print

To Make Toasted Sandwiches

Do not be too conservative in your selection of bread; most breads toast well. Choose brown, white, whole grain and fruit bread, as well as large soft and hard rolls.

If the filling is to be hot, prepare this before toasting the bread, for the fresher the toast,

Triple-decker sandwich of bacon and mustard, eggs and cheese fingers and flaked fish and mushrooms

the better the sandwich.
Put the hot sandwiches on a very hot plate so they do not cool too quickly.

Cold Fillings

Raw mushrooms, sliced, mixed with cream cheese and shredded lettuce.
Flaked cooked or canned salmon or tuna blended with cucumber and mayonnaise.
Scrambled egg mixed with chopped anchovy fillets (this can also be served hot).
Mashed sardines blended with a little lemon

juice and finely chopped gherkins and pickled onions to taste.
Flaked crab mixed with a little mayonnaise, curry powder and capers (other shellfish can be substituted).

Hot Fillings: With Cheese

In order to heat the cheese, make the toast, put the cheese filling on one piece of buttered toast, heat under the broiler for a minute then top with the second slice of toast. Choose a good cooking cheese: Cheddar, Gruyère, Emmental, Dutch Edam or Gouda.
Sliced cheese, topped with anchovy fillets.
Grated cheese, blended with little mustard, cream and chopped pickled onions.
Grated cheese and pickled walnuts.
Sliced cheese, grilled until melted then topped with sliced banana and toast.

With Egg

Cook the egg so it is ready at the same time as the toast.
Scrambled egg mixed with minced ham and chopped red pepper.
Scrambled egg blended with asparagus tips.
Scrambled egg and fingers of cheese (shown in the middle layer of the sandwich on this page).
Fried eggs and crisply fried or broiled bacon slices.
Fried egg and fried tomatoes.
Fried egg and sliced or broiled sausages.
Fried egg and sliced fried mushrooms.

With Meat

Have bacon fried or broiled, other meats boiled, roasted or broiled.
Bacon and prepared mustard (shown in the top layer of the sandwich on this page).
Bacon and fried apple rings.
Bacon and fried bananas.
Bacon and hot pineapple rings.
Bacon and hot prunes.
Corned beef and pickled onions.
Corned beef, crisp lettuce and prepared horseradish.
Boiled tongue and cranberry sauce or red currant jelly.
Boiled ham, chopped and mixed with chopped hard boiled egg and cream cheese, heated for about 1 minute on the toast, then covered with more toast.
Diced chicken blended with a thick white sauce, cheese sauce or curry sauce.

With Fish

Chopped smoked salmon or smoked trout, blended with very hot scrambled egg and watercress.
Flaked broiled herrings mixed with mustard and chopped cucumber.
Flaked white fish blended with fried mushrooms (shown in the bottom layer of the sandwich on this page); do not overcook mushrooms.
Fried scampi (large shrimp), blended with tartar sauce.
Fried fillets of fish topped with tartar sauce.

Open Sandwiches

While it is very quick and easy to place food on top of buttered bread, it takes time, practice and a real appreciation of color and garnish to produce professional looking open sandwiches.

Blue Print

To Make Open Sandwiches

Choose a firm type of bread; this can be white, brown, rye or crisp bread.

Cut it fairly thinly and spread generously with butter or margarine.

Select the toppings with an eye to color as well as flavor and food value. Learn to make your garnishes stand-up as in the pictures (the sketches show how this is done).

Keep the sandwiches very fresh until ready to serve. Lay light weight polyethylene wrapping over the top of the sandwiches; heavy paper or foil can crush the toppings. If you wish to pack open sandwiches for picnics, choose toppings that do not spoil by covering. Lay a square of waxed or greaseproof paper over the top of each sandwich (instead of a second slice of bread and butter, as in an ordinary sandwich).

The following hints apply to all sandwiches:

● **AVOID** *Having too much filling or topping, so the sandwiches look untidy. Using "tired" looking ingredients; all fillings and toppings must be fresh and retain their texture. Keeping sandwiches exposed to the air for too long before serving.*

● **TO RECTIFY** *Cover fillings before they are used. Cover the sandwiches and keep in a cool place.*

● **SHORT CUTS** *Buy ready-sliced bread. Cut loaves lengthwise if you are slicing the bread; this gives a large strip of bread to be buttered and covered with filling and topping. Halve soft rolls or long French loaves, spread with butter and filling or topping and make a large sandwich, rather than a number of small individual sandwiches.*

● **TO REDUCERS** *Use low calorie breads and crisp breads instead of ordinary breads and choose the less fattening fillings or toppings.*

SOME TOPPINGS FOR OPEN SANDWICHES

Because a number of varying ingredients are used in the true Danish open sandwich it is a little difficult to group them under a basic food. However, I *have* done this and have given the food used more plentifully than any other on the sandwich. The choice of bread is a personal one, most of the toppings are improved by being put on crisp lettuce.

With Cheese

Sliced Flora Danica cheese topped with fruit; this can be halved apricots, rings or segments of orange (fresh or mandarin oranges), prunes or nuts. Garnish with a glacé cherry, lettuce and parsley. Other cheeses can be used.

Sliced Danish Blue cheese, topped with grapes and slices of radish. This cheese is also excellent with mayonnaise and nuts; with twists of cucumber and tomato; crisply fried or broiled twists of bacon and/or frankfurters; ham rolls and potato salad. Other cheeses can be used.

Sliced Camembert with fresh or canned fruit and mayonnaise.

Sliced Danish Samsoe topped with sliced hard boiled egg, twists of tomato and mixed vegetable salad.

Sliced Flora Danica cheese on sliced cucumber or lettuce and thick mayonnaise, topped with grated raw carrot.

With Egg

Scrambled egg, topped with twists of smoked salmon and twists of lemon and tomato. Add a little prepared horseradish if wished. Other smoked fish can be used with the scrambled egg.

Scrambled egg, topped with fingers of thinly sliced Danish Havarti or Esrom cheese, sliced olives and radish roses.

Sliced hard boiled egg, mayonnaise and twists of crisp bacon.

Sliced hard boiled egg, pâté and potato salad.

With Fish

Small fried fillets of fish, with thick mayonnaise, mustard flavored mayonnaise or tartar sauce and topped with twists of cucumber, lemon and tomato.

Shelled shrimp, topped with thick mayonnaise, parsley and lemon and/or cucumber twists.

Bismarck or other herring. (There is a wide variety of flavorings given to herrings in Scandinavia, some sweet, some savory, which you can buy in cans. These are splendid for open sandwiches.) Top with single rings of raw onion, parsley and slices of tomato. Also excellent topped with scrambled egg or served with slices of apple dipped in lemon juice or mayonnaise.

With Meat

Luncheon meat slices or rolls, topped with slices of cucumber and tomato and twists of lemon; or add potato salad or cottage cheese, cooked well-drained prunes and orange twists to the meat. Other meats blend well with these accompaniments.

Liver pâté topped with crisply fried bacon, tomato and parsley; or add fried sliced mush-

rooms, bacon, gherkins and sliced tomato to the pâté.

Cooked ham topped with fingers of cheese or scrambled egg, chopped chives, twists of cucumber and tomato. Thinly sliced smoked pork loin is an even more delicious topping for these open sandwiches. Ham or smoked pork blends well with prunes, potato salad and raw onion rings, or with prunes, potato salad and orange twists.

Slices of salami, laid flat, or rolled, then topped with scrambled egg and chopped gherkins or a gherkin fan, or just with raw onion rings. The rolls of salami (or cooked ham) can be filled with potato or mixed vegetable salad or soft cream cheese.

Steak Tartare: blend minced raw fillet steak with seasoning, very finely chopped onions, gherkins and capers. Form into a neat round, put on buttered bread topped with lettuce. Place an egg yolk in half an egg shell on top of the meat.

Serve hot or cold portions of fried chicken on buttered bread and lettuce. Garnish with crisply fried bacon or pâté, twists of cucumber and tomato and more lettuce or watercress.

Storing and freezing *See comments under other sandwiches. It is less simple to store or freeze this particular type of sandwich.*

Two selections of Danish open sandwiches

Some Garnishes for Open Sandwiches

Twists

1. Making lemon, orange, cucumber and tomato twists. Cut slices of fruit, tomato or cucumber; these should be fairly thin, but sufficiently thick to stand upright.
2. Make a cut at one side.
3. Twist so the garnish stands upright.

Gherkin fans

4. Slice a gherkin several times.
5. Open to form a fan.

Radish roses

4. Cut the radish from the base downwards.
7. Put into ice cold water to open out.

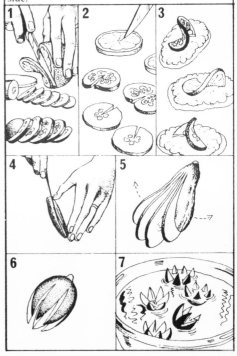

57

Take a pride in making interesting and varied salads. All too often a salad consists of the same mixture of vegetables; be adventurous and add fruits and nuts. We are told that "salads are good for you". That is true, but they are also capable of being some of the most delicious dishes.

Blue Print

To Prepare Some Salad Ingredients

Beets Peel and dice or slice cooked beets. Put in seasoned vinegar. Grated raw beets make a change.

Cabbage and similiar greens Wash and shred finely.

Celery, Belgian endive and Seakale Wash, discard the very outer leaves or sticks. Chop neatly or as the particular recipe.

Cucumber Slice thinly, peel if wished, leave for a while sprinkled with salt and weighted down. Pour off excess water and marinate in seasoned vinegar or lemon juice, or oil and vinegar or lemon juice.

Fruit Wash and slice if necessary. If adding the fruits that discolor easily (apples, peaches, avocados, etc.), then toss in lemon juice or well seasoned oil and vinegar or coat with mayonnaise.

Green Vegetables—Lettuce, Curly Endive and Watercress Wash lettuce and similar vegetables, pull apart gently and then pat dry in a cloth or shake in a cloth or salad shaker. Use ice cold water for washing them. Tear apart or use the leaves whole. Watercress is sprigged and washed.

Green and Red Sweet Peppers Cut the pulp or flesh into rings or dice. Discard cores and seeds. Some people like to blanch peppers for a few minutes in boiling, salted water to soften slightly. Drain well.

Potatoes and Root Vegetables Cook in skins where possible and do not overcook. Peel when cooked, dice and toss in dressing while warm if possible so the vegetables absorb the flavor. Add other ingredients to the salad while warm, but leave fresh herb garnishes and any crisp additions, such as celery, until cold.

Radishes Wash, discard the green stalk, slice or cut into shapes as page 57.

Rice Boil long grain rice, rinse well if sticky; if boiled carefully this should not be necessary. I like to toss the *warm* rice in mayonnaise or oil and vinegar so it absorbs the flavorings.

Tomatoes Peel if wished, slice or quarter or cut into "water lilies."

AVOID *Adding dressings to most green vegetables too early; they lose their crispness. The more robust cabbage, used in coleslaw, is not spoiled by being coated with mayonnaise or oil and vinegar and left for some time before serving.*

Green Salad

Choose a selection of green ingredients only. These can be lettuce, endive, chicory, green pepper, celery, cucumber and watercress. Prepare the vegetables; it makes the salad more interesting if you mix more than one type of lettuce, then toss in well seasoned oil and vinegar. This is an ideal salad to serve with steaks and other cooked meats or fish.

Mixed Salad

You can use as many and varying ingredients in this salad as wished.

Choose a lettuce or other similar green vegetable. Add sliced or diced cucumber, sliced tomatoes, radishes (whole or sliced), green or red pepper, cut into strips or dice, chopped celery or leaves of chicory, green onions and sliced hard boiled egg. To make the mixed salad more interesting, add chopped nuts, diced apples and cooked whole corn kernels. Avoid too many solid vegetables, such as potatoes, if the salad is being served with a fairly substantial dish. Obviously you can change the emphasis of the mixed salad according to the type of food with which it is being served. If serving with fish, I would be very generous with cucumber and use chopped fresh dill in the dressing.

Quantities to Allow

Obviously the quantities allowed depend upon the quantity of other vegetables used, but this may be a guide to buying salads.

Beets Allow $\frac{1}{2}$ medium beet per person (unless being served by itself, when a whole one should be served for each person.)

Cabbage—a small cabbage cuts up to make coleslaw for about 6–8 people.

Celery—a bunch serves about 6. A **Belgian endive** serves 1–2.

Cucumber—a medium-sized one is enough for about 6.

Green or red pepper—serves 4–6.

Lettuce or other green vegetable—allow 1 small to medium-sized lettuce for 4–6.

Potatoes and other root vegetables—allow about $\frac{1}{4}$ lb. for each person.

Radishes—2–3 per person.

Rice—allow about $\frac{1}{4}$ cup rice before cooking for each person.

Tomatoes—1 medium-sized per person.

Storing and freezing *Unfortunately salads do not store particularly well when once prepared. The salad ingredients keep well in covered containers in the refrigerator, but as soon as they are mixed together, particularly with dressing, they lose their crispness. Salads do not freeze.*

Curly endive or chicory

Belgian endive

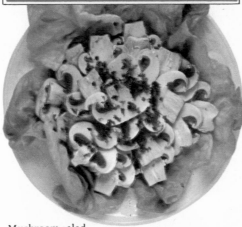

Emphasis on Vegetables

Mushroom salad

The recipes for two basic salads are given on the left, but remember you can serve one vegetable alone for a salad, or mix two or three. These simple salads are excellent as an hors d'oeuvre as well as an accompaniment to hot or cold meats.

For Family Occasions

Belgian Endive and Pepper Salad

There is often confusion about the word "endive." In the U.S. this means the white vegetable which looks like a delicate head of celery and has a slightly bitter flavor. In many countries this is called "chicory" but here chicory (or curly endive) means the vegetable that looks like a curly lettuce, (see sketches).

Wash and separate the endive leaves. Cut a raw red pepper into narrow strips. Wash and slice a few button mushrooms. Toss the pepper and mushrooms in a little oil and vinegar dressing, put into a bowl and arrange the endive leaves round. Serve this salad with cold meats or cheese.

Coleslaw

This salad is based on shredded cabbage. Choose green cabbage or use the heart of cabbage, not the tougher outer leaves. Wash and shred the cabbage very finely. Blend with mayonnaise.

This is a very basic coleslaw. It can be varied by adding grated raw carrots, chopped celery, chopped apple, raisins, green and/or red pepper and chopped nuts. It can be tossed in sour cream or oil and vinegar rather than mayonnaise. Serve this with cold meats, cheese or with broiled meats and fish.

Mushroom Salad

Raw mushrooms are delicious in a salad. Choose firm small button mushrooms, wash and trim the stalks but do not peel. Slice neatly and season or toss in an oil and vinegar dressing. Put onto crisp lettuce and top with chopped parsley or a mixture of fresh herbs. Serve this salad with hard boiled eggs or cheese, or as part of a mixed hors d'oeuvre.

For Special Occasions

American Salad

The salad illustrated on this page is typically an American one, for it has a colorful and delicious variety of garden ingredients, including corn.

Mix cooked green beans, cooked or canned corn, finely diced red pepper, sliced raw mushrooms, sliced firm tomatoes, and black olives. Toss in oil and vinegar. Put into a dish and top with rings of raw Bermuda onion. Serve this salad with cold chicken or turkey.

Oil and Vinegar (French) Dressing

The proportions of oil and vinegar can be varied according to personal taste, but the classic ingredients are salt, pepper and 3 parts oil to 1 of vinegar. I prefer the following·

Put a little salt, pepper, pinch dry mustard or little prepared or Dijon mustard and a pinch sugar onto a plate. Gradually blend in 2 tablespoons olive or other first-class salad oil. Add 1 tablespoon white wine, white cider, red wine or brown cider vinegar. The choice of vinegar can be varied according to the type of salad. You can add chopped herbs or part of a crushed clove of garlic if wished.

It is sensible to make up large quantities of this dressing (mix in the blender), then store it in screw-topped jars. Shake just before use.

Storing and freezing *See comments about storing on the left. I find peppers freeze well. Freeze without wrapping, wrap when very hard. Use in salads when only just defrosted.*

To use leftovers *Cover, store in a refrigerator or cool place and use as soon as possible.*

American salad

Fruit blends with most other ingredients. You can use fresh, canned or defrosted frozen fruit. Choose citrus fruits to serve with rich foods, for example orange with duck, grapefruit with boiled ham. Fruit blends well with all types of cheese salads, but particularly with cottage cheese. Dried prunes are an excellent accompaniment to cold beef, pork or duck, so add these with raw apple to a green salad.

Emphasis on Fruit

For All Occasions

Orange Salad

Lettuce; large oranges; oil and vinegar dressing; chopped parsley.
Arrange the lettuce on a dish, cut away the peel from the oranges and cut into segments. Moisten with dressing and top with chopped parsley if wished. Serve with duck, pork or goose.

You can add a little chopped green pepper, endive or celery, but do not make this salad too elaborate, as the oranges are very important to counteract the richness of the meat.

Carrot and Apple Salad

Top prepared lettuce and watercress or other green salad vegetable with coarsely grated carrot, as shown in the picture. Arrange segments of apple, dipped in oil and vinegar dressing, as a garnish. This salad can be made more interesting if finely chopped apple and chopped nuts are mixed with the carrot. Serve with cooked sausages, pork, goose or other fairly rich meats or with cheese.

Chicken peach salad (top)
Carrot and apple salad (below)

For Special Occasions

Avocado Salad

2 avocados; oil and vinegar dressing; lettuce; 1–2 oranges; 2 tomatoes; cucumber. Halve the avocados, remove the pits, then peel away the skin from the pears. Slice and put into the dressing immediately so the fruit does not discolor. Arrange a bed of lettuce on a dish. Cut the peel from the oranges, then cut into segments, and slice the tomatoes. Arrange the pears, oranges and tomatoes on the lettuce. Garnish with twists of cucumber. Serve this salad with cold poultry or meat or with hot roasts. (Illustrated on page 53.) *Serves 4–6.*

Chicken Peach Salad

Cooked chicken has a very delicate flavor and a salad has to complement this. The salad shown on this page is an ideal blending of flavors. Arrange the prepared lettuce, watercress and endive in a bowl. Top with neatly diced pieces of cooked chicken, sliced fresh pear, dipped in oil and vinegar dressing, sliced canned peaches and fresh or dried dates. Serve with mayonnaise or oil and vinegar dressing and garnish with lemon.

Storing and freezing *Store as other salads. Frozen chicken can be used, but do not freeze the completed salad. Ripe avocados freeze well, but use immediately when they are defrosted.*
To use leftovers *Cover, store in a refrigerator and use as soon as possible.*

Practically every kind of cheese can be served in a salad. The cheese may be sliced, diced, grated or cut into neat wedges. Cottage cheese should be piled neatly on the bed of greens, or used as a filling for ham (or salami), as in the pictures on this page.

Eggs are generally hard boiled for salads, but scrambled egg mixed with mayonnaise and finely chopped chives or other fresh herbs is delicious. The scrambled egg can be put on top of the salad ingredients or used as a filling for tomato shells or tiny boat shapes of well seasoned cucumber (see the sketches).

Hawaiian Salad

1 lettuce; 1–2 heads endive; about 8 oz. cottage cheese; fresh or canned pineapple rings; 2–3 oranges; 1 apple; piece cucumber; oil and vinegar dressing.

Prepare the lettuce, put on a flat dish. Wash and separate the endive leaves, arrange at either end of the dish. Spoon the cottage cheese into the center of the lettuce, garnish with halved pineapple rings, orange segments, apple and cucumber slices (both dipped in oil and vinegar). *Serves 4.*

Note About 2 tablespoons mayonnaise can be blended into the cheese if wished.

Californian Cottage Cheese Salad

Arrange lettuce on individual plates. Top with cottage cheese, halved walnuts, cooked, well drained prunes and radish slices.

This salad can be served on buttered bread or crisp bread as an open sandwich.

Stuffed Ham Rolls

1 lettuce; 6 large slices lean ham or mortadella; about 8 oz. cottage cheese; 1–2 tablespoons chopped nuts; 1–2 tablespoons chopped gherkins. *To garnish:* 4–6 slices of cucumber.

Prepare the lettuce and arrange on 4 or 6 small dishes. Halve the ham or mortadella slices. Blend the cottage cheese with the nuts and gherkins, spread over the ham and roll neatly. Put 2–3 rolls on each plate, garnish

Hawaiian salad (right)
Californian cottage cheese salad, Stuffed ham rolls and Cheese and mushroom salad (below)

Cheese and Eggs in Salads

with watercress and twists of cucumber. *Serves 4–6.*

This salad can be served on buttered bread or crisp bread as an open sandwich.

Cheese and Mushroom Salad

Arrange slices of cucumber on a dish, top with cottage cheese, then arrange sliced raw mushrooms over the cheese. Garnish with parsley.

This salad can be served on buttered bread or crisp bread as an open sandwich.

Egg and Carrot Salad

3 hard boiled eggs; 2 medium-sized carrots; 4–5 tablespoons salted peanuts; 2 teaspoons chopped parsley; mayonnaise; lettuce.

Chop the eggs coarsely, peel and grate the carrots. Mix with the peanuts, chopped parsley and mayonnaise to moisten. Use the larger lettuce leaves as cups and spoon some of the egg mixture into the center of each cup. Serve the lettuce heart in the middle of the dish of filled lettuce leaves. *Serves 4.*

To vary

Egg and Shrimp Salad Use shelled shrimp instead of peanuts.

Egg and Potato Salad Use diced cooked new potatoes instead of grated carrots, add chopped chives and chopped parsley.

Egg and Corn Salad Omit the nuts and use cooked corn in the salad.

Storing and freezing *See comments on other salads. Cottage cheese can be stored for several days in a refrigerator or for a limited time in a freezer—it tends to dry out if kept for too long.*

To use leftovers *Cover, store in a refrigerator and use as quickly as possible..*

1. Use scrambled egg in salads to fill tomato cases.

2. Scrambled egg also makes an interesting filling for cucumber boats.

One of the most appetizing ways to serve cold meat and fish is mixed with other ingredients in a salad, rather than just having sliced meat or a piece of fish on a plate.

By mixing the meat or fish with other foods you make it look more appetizing; often it gives added moistness and it can make the meat or fish go further. Serve these cold salads with hot biscuits or popovers.

Ways to Serve Meat in Salads

Cut the meat into neat pieces (as the chicken on page 60) and mix with the salad. Cut the meat thinly, roll round a stuffing and serve on a bed of salad.

Beef Rolls

Mix prepared grated horseradish with cream cheese or mayonnaise. Spread on slices of cooked beef and roll. Or blend chopped mustard pickle and a little mayonnaise, spread over the beef and roll.

Pork or Ham Rolls

Cottage cheese is an excellent filling for these meats since it is not too rich. Flavor the cheese with a little chopped onion and freshly chopped sage. Spread over the meat and roll.

Cover the pork or ham with diced raw apple, mixed with diced cooked prunes, roll firmly. Blend cottage or cream cheese with a little curry powder. Spread on the meat and roll firmly.

Tongue Rolls

Blend mayonnaise with chopped gherkins and capers. Spread over the tongue and roll. A sweet chutney also blends well with tongue. Spread thinly, top with chopped cucumber and roll.

Some meats, lamb and veal for example, have the wrong texture to roll neatly.

Meat and Fish Salads

Ham and Pâté Cones

8 good-shaped slices ham; 8 cooked or canned asparagus tips; about 4 tablespoons coleslaw (see page 59); approximately $\frac{1}{2}$ cup canned or homemade pâté; stuffed olives. To garnish: lettuce; radishes.

Spread a slice of ham on a board and lay an asparagus tip diagonally on the meat. Add the coleslaw. Roll into a cone. Put the pâté into a piping bag with a $\frac{1}{4}$- or $\frac{1}{2}$-inch rose tip. Press out rosettes at the top of each ham cone and top with a slice of sutffed olive. Serve on a bed of lettuce and garnish with radishes. Serves 4.

Note   If the pâté is rather firm, blend with a little mayonnaise or cream.

Mixed Meat Rolls

A good mixture of meats to serve would be salami filled with chive cream cheese, mortadella filled with coleslaw (see page 59) and the ham and pâté cones above.

Ways to Serve Fish in Salads

Flaked fish with white flesh or shellfish may be mixed with other ingredients in a salad. The fish and potato salad below is a good basic recipe that can be varied in many ways.

Paella salad

Fish and Potato Salad

About $1–1\frac{1}{4}$ lb. white-fleshed fish; about 1 lb. potatoes, preferably new; seasoning; piece cucumber; few radishes; few capers; 1 apple (optional); mayonnaise. To garnish: lettuce; tomatoes; 1 lemon.

Cook the fish and the potatoes in well seasoned water. Dice the potatoes neatly when cooked and flake the fish. Blend with the diced cucumber, sliced radishes, capers and diced apple. Add just enough mayonnaise to bind, about 5–6 tablespoons. Put into a plain mold or bowl and leave until ready to serve. Turn out onto a bed of lettuce and garnish with sliced tomatoes and lemon. Serves 4–6. To vary   Chopped hard boiled eggs can be added to the above ingredients and white and shellfish can be mixed together. It is particularly good with mussels.

Paella Salad

$\frac{3}{4}$ cup long grain rice; pinch saffron; $1\frac{3}{4}$ cups water; seasoning; 5–6 tablespoons oil and vinegar dressing; about $\frac{1}{2}$ lb. shelled cook shrimp; about $1\frac{1}{4}–1\frac{1}{2}$ cups diced cooked chicken; 1 avocado; 2 tomatoes; watercress; stuffed green olives.

Put the rice, dissolved saffron, water and seasoning into a saucepan. Bring the water to the boil, stir briskly, cover the pan, lower the heat and cook for 15 minutes. By this time the liquid should have evaporated and the rice cooked without being sticky. Toss the rice in dressing while hot. Cool and add the shrimp and chicken. Put the salad in a bowl with the peeled sliced avocado around two sides and the tomato wedges around the other two sides. Insert the watercress at the edges. Garnish with the stuffed green olives. Serves 4–6.

Storing and freezing   *Although meat and fish may be frozen or stored, the salad ingredients on this page, including rice, do not freeze well.*
To use leftovers   *Cover, store in the refrigerator and use as quickly as possible.*

Ways to Serve Poultry in Salads

As a general rule, allow about $\frac{3}{4}$ cup total ingredients for each serving.

Chicken or Turkey Salad

Cut the chicken or turkey into dice. If planning to use the salad for sandwiches, make the dice small; if serving as a salad, make the dice larger. To each cup of diced turkey or chicken, add $\frac{1}{4}$ cup diced celery and $\frac{1}{4}$ cup diced cucumber. Moisten the mixture with mayonnaise or, if you are a reducer, with jelly made from the cooked down broth. Serve chilled on a bed of lettuce; in a ripe, peeled tomato cup garnished with capers and halved hard boiled eggs; or in half an avocado garnished with lemon or lime.

Chicken Salad Véronique with Tongue

For each cup of diced cooked chicken, use $\frac{1}{2}$ cup of halved seedless grapes and two thick slices of tongue. Mix the chicken and grapes together and moisten with lemon mayonnaise (see page 18). Arrange the tongue slices pointing inwards around the edge of a serving dish and put the salad in the center on a bed of lettuce.

Chinese Chicken Salad

1 whole chicken breast; 1 can bean sprouts; soy sauce; vinegar; peanut or corn oil; salt; sugar; monosodium glutamate.
Shred the cooked skinned and boned chicken breast. Rinse the bean sprouts well and soak in cold water. Make a dressing out of the rest of the ingredients, using the salt sparingly (soy sauce is salty) and using only a dash of monosodium glutamate. Combine the chicken breasts with the bean sprouts and toss with the dressing. Serve this well chilled.
This is an excellent salad for reducers.

Duck and Orange Salad

1 roasted duck; 2–3 oranges; 1 small can pitted black olives; 1 head lettuce; lemon mayonnaise (page 18).
Remove the skin and fat and cut the duck into bite-sized pieces. Peel and section the orange, being sure to remove all the white pith. Wash and thoroughly dry the lettuce. Line a salad bowl with the lettuce. Toss the duck and orange sections together in a bowl. Moisten with lemon mayonnaise. Add the mixture to the salad bowl and garnish with black olives and wafer-thin slices of orange if wished. *Serves 4–6.*

Chicken Salad Véronique with tongue

Molded Salads

Molded salads make beautiful buffet fare, are welcome summer eating and complement heavy dishes perfectly. On page 32 you will find molded meat salads, which are a meal in themselves.

Blue Print Recipe

Tomato Aspic

$4\frac{1}{2}$ cups tomato juice · 3 slices onion · seasoning · 1 bay leaf · 4 cloves · $\frac{3}{4}$ teaspoon celery seeds · 2 tablespoons lemon juice · 2 envelopes unflavored gelatin · $\frac{1}{2}$ cup cold tomato juice · lemon mayonnaise.

To make   In a saucepan combine the 4 cups tomato juice, onion, seasoning, bay leaf, cloves, celery seeds and lemon juice and simmer 30 minutes. Strain and add water to make $3\frac{1}{2}$ cups. Soften the gelatin in the $\frac{1}{2}$ cup tomato juice. Dissolve in the hot tomato juice mixture. Pour into a 6-cup mold that has been rinsed out with cold water. Chill until firm.
To serve   Dip the mold for a few seconds in warm water. Invert onto the serving dish. Serve with lemon mayonnaise (page 18). If a circular mold has been used, the center may be filled with fish, chicken or vegetable salad.

● AVOID   *Adding solids to the gelatin mixture before it has begun to thicken: they will either sink to the bottom or float on top. Letting the gelatin become too firm if adding solids.*
TO RECTIFY   *If the gelatin becomes too firm to work with, reheat it.*

● **SHORT CUT**   *Place the gelatin in the freezing compartment of the refrigerator or place in a bowl of ice to hasten the thickening.*
● **TO REDUCERS**   *This is an ideal salad with few calories.*

Storing and freezing   *All the dishes based on this recipe keep for 2–3 days in the refrigerator and freeze well.*
To use leftovers   *Slice and serve individually on a bed of lettuce.*

Tomato-Avocado Mold

Ingredients as Blue Print PLUS 1 avocado. Make as Blue Print. When the gelatin has begun to thicken and becomes the consistency of unbeaten eggs, prepare the avocado. Cut it in half lengthwise, peel it and cut into long crescent slices. Line the bottom and sides of a 6-cup mold with the avocado and gently pour in the thickened gelatin. Chill and serve as the Blue Print.

Tomato-Egg Mold

Ingredients as Blue Print PLUS 6 hard boiled eggs. Make as Blue Print and when the gelatin has begun to thicken, line the bottom of a 6-cup mold with the peeled eggs halved lengthwise. Place eggs white-side-down. Pour in the thickened gelatin and chill until firm. Unmold and serve as Blue Print.
To vary   Add 2 cups mixed vegetables or diced chicken to the thickened gelatin instead of the avocado or eggs.

Sunburst Salad

Dissolve 1 package lemon-flavored gelatin in 1 cup boiling water. Add $\frac{1}{2}$ cup cold water and a pinch of salt. Chill until the gelatin is slightly thickened and add $1\frac{1}{2}$ cups shredded carrots. Pour into a 4-cup mold and chill until firm. Unmold as Blue Print. *Serves 6.*
To vary   Follow the above recipe, but use only half the amount of shredded carrots and add $\frac{3}{4}$ cup shredded cabbage.

Making Soups

Meat soups, some of which are covered on this page, are among the easiest to make. Meat has such a pronounced flavor, that it not only gives an excellent stock, but makes a complete soup with few additional ingredients (see Blue Print 2, Consommé). Of course there are many meat soups where other ingredients are added to give a more filling dish.

Blue Print Recipes

1. To Make Stock

The term "stock" is used when making many soups, also in stews and other such dishes.

A brown stock is made from beef or game bones. A marrow bone gives the finest stock of all.

A white stock is made from veal, chicken or turkey bones. If you add the giblets of the poultry, you darken the stock although you do give additional flavor.

To make Cover the washed bones with cold water.

To cook Bring the water to the boil, remove any grey scum if this has formed. Add seasoning, a *bouquet garni* of herbs and simmer in a tightly covered pan for 2–3 hours, or allow at least 40 minutes at 15 lb. in a pressure cooker.

Various vegetables can be added to give flavor, but remember that a stock that has had vegetables in it does not keep as well as one without.

- **AVOID** *Adding too much liquid;* otherwise the stock has little flavor.
- **TO RECTIFY** *If the stock is lacking in flavor, remove the saucepan lid and let the liquid evaporate and become more concentrated.*
- **SHORT CUT** *Use stock cubes instead of making stock.*
- **TO REDUCERS** *Good clear, unthickened stocks are ideal for low calorie soups.*

2. Consommé

1 lb. shin of beef · 6½ cups beef stock (see Blue Print 1) · carrot (optional) · 1 onion (optional) · bay leaf · seasoning · 2 egg whites plus shells · sherry to taste. To garnish: as individual recipes.

To make Cut the meat into neat pieces. Put into the pan with the stock.

To cook Bring to the boil. Add the whole vegetables (if the stock is well flavored these should not be necessary). Put in the bay leaf and a little seasoning. Simmer steadily for about 1½ hours. Strain the consommé, return to the pan, add the egg whites and shells and simmer very gently for about 10 minutes. The egg whites and shells gather up any tiny particles of meat or other matter and give a perfectly clear soup. Strain through a damp cloth and add a little sherry before serving.

To serve Hot, lightly frozen or jellied. The consommé may set lightly without gelatin, but if it will not, then dissolve about 1 teaspoon softened gelatin in each 2½ cups warm consommé. Allow to set lightly, whisk and serve in chilled soup cups. *All recipes based on this serve 4–6.*

Garnishes for Consommé

The garnish gives the name to the particular consomme. Add tiny cubes of cooked vegetables, the soup is then **Consommé Jardinière**; add matchstick shapes of cooked vegetables for **Consommé Julienne**.

Here are some more versions of consomme. **Consommé à l'Africaine** Garnish with cooked rice; flavor with curry powder and sliced canned or cooked artichoke hearts. **Consommé Epicurien** Garnish with shredded blanched almonds and chopped chervil. **Consommé Nouilles** Garnish with noodles. This may be made more interesting by adding clear, very well sieved, tomato pulp or a little tomato paste.

Argentine Beef Soup

2 tablespoons olive or other oil; 2 large onions; 2–3 slices fatty bacon; 4 tablespoons flour; about 4 large peeled tomatoes plus 3–4 tablespoons water or medium-sized can tomatoes; 4 cups beef stock (see Blue Print 1); ½ lb. chuck steak; about ¾ cup fresh or frozen peas; 2–3 large carrots; *bouquet garni*; seasoning.

Argentine beef soup

Heat the oil in a large pan; sauté the peeled chopped onions for several minutes, add the chopped bacon and cook for a further few minutes. Stir in the flour; cook until a thickened roux. Stir well. Add the chopped fresh tomatoes and water, or the canned tomatoes, and the stock. Bring to the boil. Add the diced beef, peas, peeled diced carrots, *bouquet garni* and a little seasoning. Cover the pan and simmer gently for about 2 hours. Serve with hot toast. *Serves 6.*

A little pasta can be added to the soup 30 minutes before the end of the cooking time.

Storing and freezing *Stock is a highly perishable liquid so store in the refrigerator. Even so it will need boiling every 2–3 days. You can freeze stock. Remember the container should not be too full as the stock will expand in freezing. Leave about ¾-inch headroom. Treat consommé in the same way, but try to freeze without the sherry and add this when defrosted. The reason is that alcohol loses flavor in freezing.*

To use leftovers *Never waste good stock; add it to a gravy, stew or casserole.*

Making stock

Poultry and Game Soups

These soups can be extremely economical, for the basis of many poultry or game soups is the carcass. Do not discard poultry or game bones. There is a great deal of flavor to be obtained by simmering these. The giblets should be used for this purpose also, although you may like to omit the liver as it tends to give a bitter taste. Naturally, less meaty parts of a chicken or a less tender game bird could be used instead of the carcass. This produces a stock with more flavor and the flesh of the poultry may be pureed or chopped and added to the soup.

Blue Print Recipe

Chicken Soup

The carcass of a chicken · about 6–8 cups water to cover · seasoning · 1–2 onions · 1–2 carrots · *bouquet garni* **· 4 tablespoons flour. To garnish: fried croutons (see page 125).**

To make Put the chicken carcass plus the giblets (less the liver), if available, into a saucepan. Cover with water, add seasoning, vegetables and herbs.

To cook Bring the liquid to the boil, cover the pan and simmer for at least 2 hours; or allow about 40 minutes at 15 lb. pressure. Strain the stock. Any small pieces of chicken can be chopped or pureed and added to the stock. Blend the flour with a little stock, put into the pan with the remainder of the stock and cook until slightly thickened, stirring well.

To serve Hot topped with croutons. *All recipes based on this serve 5–6.*

● **AVOID** *Using too much liquid; otherwise the soup lacks flavor.*
● **TO RECTIFY** *If too much liquid has been added, lift the lid of the pan so the liquid evaporates.*
● **SHORT CUT** *Shorten the cooking time and add 1–2 chicken stock cubes to taste.*
● **TO REDUCERS** *Do not thicken.*

Storing and freezing *Keep for 2–3 days only in the refrigerator. All these soups freeze well, with the exception of the noodle variety; pasta in a soup is oversoftened and is spoiled by freezing.*
To use leftovers *Heat as the recipe. Avoid boiling the soup when cream and egg yolks are already added.*

Tomato Chicken Soup

Ingredients as Blue Print PLUS 3–4 tablespoons tomato paste.
Make the soup as the Blue Print, add the tomato paste gradually. Taste after adding some of the paste to check that the flavor is not too strong.

Chicken Noodle Soup

Ingredients as Blue Print PLUS 4–5 tablespoons shell noodles.
Make the soup as the Blue Print, add the noodles and cook steadily for about 15 minutes or until tender.

To vary Add about 2 tablespoons tomato paste to the soup, blend thoroughly, *then* add the noodles. If desired diced carrots, chopped onions and peas may be added to the soup *with* the noodles.

Cream of Chicken Soup

Ingredients as Blue Print PLUS $\frac{2}{3}$–$1\frac{1}{4}$ cups light or heavy cream and 1–2 egg yolks.
Make the soup as the Blue Print. When thickened, draw the pan on one side so the soup is no longer boiling. Blend the cream and egg yolks and whisk into the soup. A little dry sherry or white wine can be added for extra flavor.
Garnishes Top the soup with lightly browned almonds, asparagus tips, parsley, paprika and/or croutons (see page 67).

Game Soup

Method as Blue Print but use the carcass of a small hare or 1–2 pheasants or other game birds, such as partridge, grouse, quail or wild duck in place of chicken.
Flavor the completed soup with a little red wine and 1 tablespoon red currant jelly.

Chicken noodle soup

Chicken Broth

Ingredients as Blue Print PLUS about $1\frac{1}{2}$–2 cups diced vegetables.
Make the soup as the Blue Print. Add the vegetables to the strained stock *before* thickening and cook for about 15 minutes. Thicken as the Blue Print or thicken and *then* add a little cream or cream and egg yolks, as the Cream of Chicken Soup.
To vary Add 2 tablespoons rice or pearl barley. Add a few cooked prunes.

Fish Soups

It is surprising just how rarely one is given fish soup in a private home, although many restaurants specialize in this. Fish soups are so varied, ranging from delicate creamy flavors to highly spiced soups and the luxurious shellfish bisques. In many cases you need fish stock for the soup and the Blue Print deals with making this.

Blue Print Recipe

Fish Stock

To make Use the skins and bones from fish or, if insufficient to give a good flavored stock, buy a fish head too. When using lobster or similar shellfish, simmer the shells in liquid. This produces a very delicate pale pink stock which enhances the color of the soup.

To cook Put the bones, skin, head or shells into a pan. Cover with cold water, or use partially water and partially white wine. Add seasoning and a *bouquet garni*. Bring the liquid to the boil, remove any grey scum, simmer steadily for about 30–40 minutes in a covered pan, or allow about 10–15 minutes at 15 lb. in a pressure cooker. Sliced onions, carrots and celery may be added. Strain the stock carefully.

- **AVOID** *Overcooking fish stock; it does not improve the flavor.*
- **SHORT CUT** *It may sound unusual, but chicken stock, or water and a chicken bouillon cube can be used in fish soups, or use bottled clam juice.*
- **TO REDUCERS** *Fish is a low calorie food and some of the un-thickened fish soups would be a very wise choice.*

Creamed Fish Soup

About $\frac{1}{2}-\frac{3}{4}$ lb. bass or other white-fleshed fish; 4 cups fish stock (see Blue Print); 4 tablespoons cornstarch; 2–4 tablespoons butter; seasoning; grated rind 1 lemon; $\frac{2}{3}$ cup milk; $\frac{2}{3}$ cup heavy cream. *To garnish:* chopped parsley or dill and/or cooked peas; paprika.

Put the fish into about $1\frac{1}{3}$ cups of the fish stock. Simmer gently until just tender. Strain the fish from the liquid and put the stock into a saucepan. Blend the rest of the fish stock with the cornstarch, put into the saucepan, add the butter, a little more seasoning if required and the lemon rind. Bring to the boil; cook until slightly thickened, stirring well. Add the milk and cream and the flaked fish. Heat for a few minutes only, *without boiling*. Top with the garnish and serve. *Serves 4–6.*

To vary To make a thicker soup, either decrease the amount of fish stock (which gives a creamier result) or increase the amount of cornstarch, not to exceed $\frac{1}{2}$ cup.

Creamed shellfish soup Use prepared or canned mussels, shelled shrimp or flaked crab meat instead of the fish.

Reducer's Soup Cook the fish as above. Add to *well flavored* fish stock, blend in a little yoghurt instead of milk and cream.

Spiced Fish Soup

2 tablespoons oil; 1–2 cloves garlic; 1 large onion; 3 large tomatoes; 4 cups fish stock (see Blue Print); $\frac{1}{2}$ teaspoon paprika; pinch allspice; good pinch saffron*; pinch turmeric; about $\frac{3}{4}$ lb. bass or other white-fleshed fish; seasoning. *To garnish:* croutons or garlic croutons (see page 67); parsley.

*If using a few saffron strands instead of saffron powder, infuse this in the stock for about 30 minutes, then strain and use the stock.

Heat the oil in a pan, fry the crushed garlic, the chopped onion and skinned chopped tomatoes until a thick puree. Blend the fish stock with all the flavorings, add to the puree, together with the finely diced, skinned raw fish. Simmer until the fish is tender. Season to taste and garnish with the croutons and parsley just before serving. *Serves 4–6.*

Genoese Fish Soup

Follow the recipe for the Spiced Fish Soup and add a few shelled shrimp and mussels just before serving.

Crab Bisque

8 medium-sized cooked blue claw crabs; 2 cups fish stock (see Blue Print) or water; 1 lemon; seasoning; *bouquet garni*; 1 onion; $\frac{1}{2}$ cup mushrooms; 4 tablespoons butter; $1\frac{1}{4}$ cups light cream; 2 egg yolks; 2 tablespoons sherry.

Remove all the meat from the crabs, and put on one side. Put the crab shells into a pan with the stock or water, the pared lemon rind, a little lemon juice, seasoning and *bouquet garni*. Cover the pan tightly and simmer for about 30 minutes. Chop the onion, slice the mushrooms and toss in the hot butter. Add the strained crab stock and crab meat and heat gently. Blend the cream with the egg yolks, add to the crab mixture and heat, *without boiling*. Stir in the sherry, heat for 1–2 minutes and serve. (Illustrated on page 53.) *Serves 4–5.*

Lobster Bisque

1 medium-sized cooked lobster; 2 cups water; 1 onion; 1 lemon; small piece celery; seasoning; $1\frac{1}{3}$ cups light cream; 2 egg yolks; 2–3 tablespoons dry sherry or brandy.

Remove all flesh from the lobster and put on one side. Put the crushed shell into a pan with the water, chopped onion, pared lemon rind and a little juice and chopped celery. Season, cover the pan tightly and simmer for 30 minutes. Strain the lobster stock into a pan, add the flaked lobster and the cream, blended with the egg yolks, and heat *without boiling*. Add the sherry or brandy, heat for about 2 minutes and serve. Garnish with the tiny side claws. *Serves 4–6.*

To vary Shrimp, scallops or oysters may be used instead of lobster. Scallops need cooking, so slice or dice and simmer in the strained fish stock for about 4 minutes before adding the cream.

Storing and freezing *Fish is highly perishable so do not store any of these soups. Frozen fish may be used in making the soup, but I find the flavor of fish rather disappointing if frozen.*

Clam chowder

Chowders

The term Chowder is used to describe a really thick soup, usually with a milk base and generally containing fish or shellfish and vegetables. Notable exceptions to this definition are the famous Manhattan Chowder, made with a tomato base, and Corn Chowder, made with vegetables only. Pilot crackers are traditionally served with chowders.

Blue Print Recipe

New England Clam Chowder

24 chowder clams · $\frac{1}{4}$ lb. salt pork · 1 large onion · 2 large potatoes · seasoning · $\frac{1}{4}$ teaspoon thyme · 2 cups light cream. To garnish: chopped parsley · paprika.

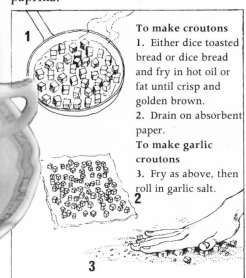

To make croutons
1. Either dice toasted bread or dice bread and fry in hot oil or fat until crisp and golden brown.
2. Drain on absorbent paper.
To make garlic croutons
3. Fry as above, then roll in garlic salt.

Corn chowder

To cook Scrub clams and place in a deep kettle with 1 quart cold water. Cover and simmer 5–8 minutes or until clams open. Remove clams from shells and chop finely; set aside. Strain broth and reserve 2 cups. Place diced salt pork in a deep saucepan and sauté slowly over low heat until brown but not crisp; remove from pan and reserve. Sauté the chopped onion until limp but not browned. Return the salt pork to the pan and add 1 cup boiling water, the 2 cups clam broth, diced potatoes, seasoning and thyme. Cover and simmer until potatoes are tender but not soft. Add chopped clams and heat *without boiling*. Serve immediately garnished with chopped parsley and paprika. *All recipes based on this serve 6–8.*

● **AVOID** *Overcooking clams; they become tough.*
● **SHORT CUT** *Use canned minced clams and bottled clam juice.*
● **TO REDUCERS** *Substitute milk for the cream or make Manhattan Chowder instead.*

Fish Chowder

As Blue Print but use $\frac{3}{4}$ lb. boned haddock in place of the clams and 2 cups Fish Stock (see Blue Print page 66) in place of the clam broth. Add the haddock to the stock the last 10 minutes of cooking. Continue as Blue Print.

Corn Chowder

As Blue Print but use 3 cups cooked or canned corn for the clams and water for the clam broth. Continue as Blue Print.

Manhattan Clam Chowder

As Blue Print but add $\frac{1}{2}$ cup each chopped green pepper and celery when sautéing onions. Use 2 cups tomato juice instead of the cream.

Storing and freezing *Store in the refrigerator and reheat gently; avoid overcooking. These chowders freeze well but should be used within several weeks.*

A cold soup should be refreshing in flavor so it sharpens one's appetite for the rest of the meal.

A cucumber soup is excellent cold, and ideal when these vegetables are plentiful and inexpensive, see Blue Print 1.

Fruit soups are popular in several European countries. These are unusual, but very suitable for the first course of a meal providing a sharp-flavored fruit is chosen and it is not oversweetened in cooking.

Blue Print Recipes

1. Cucumber Soup

2 small or 1 large cucumber · 1 onion · 4 tablespoons butter · 4 cups white stock · seasoning · $\frac{2}{3}$ cup heavy cream

To make Peel, seed and chop nearly all the cucumber. Put a small piece on one side to slice for garnish and retain a small portion of the peel to give color and additional flavor to the soup; too much peel gives a bitter taste. Peel and chop the onion.

To cook Toss the vegetables in the hot butter for a few minutes; take care they do not brown. Add the stock, the piece of cucumber peel and a little seasoning. Simmer for 20 minutes, then puree in a blender or put through a food mill. Cool, then blend in the cream.

Cold Soups

To serve Chill well and top with sliced cucumber. *All recipes based on this serve 4–6.*

To vary Add a pinch curry powder to the soup.
Use a little white wine in place of some of the stock.
Blend $\frac{1}{2}-\frac{3}{4}$ cup grated Cheddar cheese with the hot cucumber mixture immediately after pureeing. Cool and continue as the Blue Print.
Use 2–3 large leeks instead of the cucumber.
Use 4 onions stead of the cucumber.
Use 1 lb. tomatoes and 1 large old potato instead of the cucumber.

2. Savory Apple Soup

2$\frac{1}{4}$ cups water · 1 lemon · $\frac{1}{4}$ cup sugar · 1 lb. cooking apples · 1–2 pickled gherkins · $\frac{2}{3}$ cup cider or white wine · $\frac{2}{3}$ cup light cream. To garnish: little cream cheese or sour cream · paprika · watercress.

To make Put the water, sliced lemon and sugar into a pan.

To cook Bring the liquid to the boil. Peel and core the apples, add to the liquid then simmer for 15 minutes or until tender. Remove the lemon and puree the apples in a blender or put through a food mill. Add the sliced gherkins to the warm soup with the cider or wine. Allow to cool and blend in the cream. Remove the gherkins if wished.

To serve Garnish with the cream cheese or sour cream, paprika and watercress. *All recipes based on this serve 4–6.*

To vary Remove several apple slices before the fruit becomes a pulp and use as a garnish.
Add a generous $\frac{1}{2}$ cup white or black raisins to the apples as they cook.
Use a little more water and thicken the soup with a few tablespoons wholewheat or rye bread crumbs.
Use sharp plums or cooking cherries instead of apples.

Storing and freezing *Keep for 1–2 days in the refrigerator. The soups freeze well; add wine and cream after defrosting if possible.*

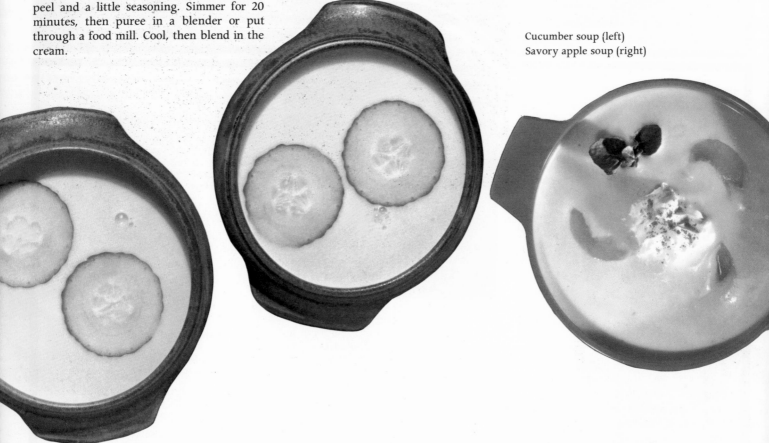

Cucumber soup (left)
Savory apple soup (right)

six

EGGS AND SAVORY PIES AND FLANS

This chapter covers a variety of cookery skills and dishes. Pages 70–75 and page 88 deal with eggs in cooking. An egg is probably the most versatile ingredient in cooking. It forms the basis of main dishes that can be served at all meals of the day, it gives light cakes, puddings, soufflés, omelettes and it is the thickening agent in many classic sauces. If you consider the price of an egg, it is still very inexpensive compared to other foods. Remember eggs are not only invaluable in cooking, they also have a very high food value.

One often hears the expression, (describing a not very talented cook), she (or he) ''cannot boil an egg.'' You know boiling eggs cannot be said to be difficult, but they do need care in timing. You will therefore find the Blue Print on the next page deals with the right way to boil an egg so the white is light and not tough. The page also gives some new ways of serving boiled eggs.

The rest of the egg cookery section covers pancakes, soufflés and some very interesting egg dishes (such as the French classic, Piperade). If you have never made Hollandaise sauce, fearing it is too difficult, may I suggest you follow the Blue Print on page 88. It is a surprisingly simple sauce—and quite delicious. Here you will also find the Italian classic dessert Zabaglione.

Page 80 commences the section on savory pies and flans. These can be served hot or cold for main meals, quick family or party snacks. The fillings for flans can be of cheese, fish, meat or colorful vegetables.

Some of the best known tarts and flans for tea have been popular for several centuries. The recipe on page 86 is for the *real* Maid of Honour, which has been known since Tudor times. There is a more modern recipe that I find very popular on the same page.

During the past years the Italian Pizza, which is a savory yeast flan or tart, has grown in popularity. This can be a very inexpensive or quite luxurious dish, according to the topping selected. If you do not wish to make the yeast dough (which is very simple), then try the other variations on page 83.

Can you make perfect puff pastry? The Blue Print on page 86 gives the do's and don'ts for success. Of course if you do not have the time to spare you can make all the recipes with frozen puff paste patty shells; defrost and reroll.

Puff pastry is not confined to desserts alone and on page 86 you will also find a delightful recipe for a delicious hors d'oeuvre or cocktail appetizer.

I hope you enjoy this chapter, it is so varied that I am confident there will be many dishes for you to try.

Boiling an Egg

The flavor of an egg, when boiled, is very pronounced and therefore one should be ultra-fussy that the eggs are very fresh.

Blue Print Recipe

To Boil an Egg

Regular boiling of eggs can darken a pan slightly, so you may like to keep a small pan specially for this purpose. There are two ways in which you can boil an egg. Method 1 gives a lighter texture to the egg white and is therefore ideal for small children and invalids.

Method 1 Put the eggs carefully in enough *cold* water to cover. Bring the water to the boil *as quickly as possible*, and time the cooking from the moment the water is boiling. Since the egg cooks slightly *as the water heats*, the cooking time is shorter than that for method 2.

Method 2 Lower the eggs into boiling water and time the cooking.

Timing	Method 1	Method 2
Lightly set egg	$2\frac{1}{2}$–3 min.	$3\frac{1}{2}$–4 min.
Firmly set egg	4 min.	5 min.
Hard boiled egg	8–9 min.	10 min.

● **AVOID** *Boiling any eggs that have even the finest cracks, for these could develop into larger cracks and some of the egg could be wasted. Overcooking eggs when you wish them to be hard boiled; if overcooked they develop a dark ring round the yolk and an unpleasantly strong flavor.*

● **TO RECTIFY** *Put a teaspoon vinegar in the water if you have to boil a slightly cracked egg; this helps the egg white to stop spreading into the pan. Put hard boiled eggs into cold water as soon as they are set, then crack the shells. This cools the eggs quickly, stops continued cooking and should prevent the dark line round the yolk (unless the egg has been cooked for too long a period).*

● **TO REDUCERS** *A boiled egg is very low in calories as there is no added fat or sauces and so is ideal for a diet meal.*

Storing and freezing *Boiled eggs do not store well and they are one of the few things that do not freeze, they become like rubber.*

For Family Occasions

Eggs Mornay

4 eggs; 2 tablespoons butter or margarine; 4 tablespoons flour; $1\frac{1}{3}$ cups milk; seasoning; $\frac{1}{4}$ lb. (1 cup) grated Cheddar cheese.

Boil the eggs; these can be firmly set or hard boiled, according to personal taste. Plunge into cold water to cool, crack the shells, then remove these. Heat the butter or margarine in a pan, stir in the flour and cook for several minutes. Gradually blend in the milk and bring to the boil, then cook until the sauce has thickened. Season well, stir in the grated cheese. Do not continue cooking after the cheese has melted. Arrange the whole or halved eggs in a dish, top with the cheese sauce and serve at once. *Serves 4 as an hors d'oeuvre or 2 as a main dish.*

Eggs Florentine

Ingredients as above (or use poached eggs if preferred). Put on a bed of cooked spinach, coat with the sauce as above.

Eggs au Gratin

These are the same as Eggs Mornay, but topped with a layer of fine bread crumbs and grated cheese so you have a crisp topping. If the sauce is hot the dish may just be browned under the grill. If the sauce and eggs have become cold, then heat and brown in a moderately hot oven for about 15–20 minutes.

Scotch Eggs

4 eggs; little flour; seasoning; $\frac{3}{4}$–1 lb. sausage meat. *To coat:* 1 egg; 3–4 tablespoons crisp bread crumbs. *To fry:* fat or oil.

Hard boil the eggs and cool, as the Blue Print. Coat each egg in a little seasoned flour; this makes the sausage meat adhere to the egg better. Divide the sausage meat into four portions; press out into neat squares on a floured board. Wrap round the eggs, then seal the ends and roll until neat shapes. Coat in beaten egg and crumbs.

These may be fried in deep fat or oil, in which case turn once to brown and fry for about 5–6 minutes. If using shallow fat or oil, then turn several times and cook for about 10–12 minutes. Remember it is essential to ensure that the sausage meat is thoroughly cooked. If preferred, bake for about 25 minutes in the center of a moderate to moderately hot oven, 375–400°F. Serve hot or cold. *Serves 4.*

For Special Occasions

STUFFED EGGS

These can be used for a main dish with salad or as an hors d'oeuvre.

Cold stuffed eggs

The quantities of filling are enough for 4 hard boiled eggs.

Hard boil, cool and shell the eggs as the Blue Print, remove the egg yolks, mash or sieve and continue as the suggestions below. In each case the yolks are put back into the whites.

For Hot Stuffed Eggs

Creamed eggs Mix the yolks with 3–4 tablespoons heavy cream and seasoning. Top with fine crumbs and melted butter, brown under the broiler.

Cheese eggs Mix the yolks with 3 oz. ($\frac{3}{4}$ cup) grated Cheddar or Parmesan cheese and 1–2 tablespoons heavy cream. Top with fine crumbs and brown under the broiler.

Curried eggs (good cold as well as hot). Blend the yolks with 2 tablespoons mayonnaise, 2–3 teaspoons chutney and 1–2 teaspoons curry powder. Top with fine crumbs and brown under the broiler.

For Cold Stuffed Eggs

Anchovy eggs Blend the yolks with a little mayonnaise and anchovy paste to taste if wished. Top with rolled anchovy fillets or with anchovy stuffed olives.

Corn eggs Blend the yolks with well drained canned corn, seasoning and a little mayonnaise (grated cheese can be added if wished). Top with strips of fresh sweet red pepper or canned pimiento.

Crab meat eggs Blend the yolks with flaked crab meat; use some of the dark as well as the light flesh. Moisten with a little cream or mayonnaise and lemon juice; season well. Top with paprika and piped rosettes of really thick mayonnaise if desired.

Seafood eggs Flavor the yolks with anchovy paste and a few drops soy sauce if wished. Add chopped shrimp or other fish if wished, then top with shelled shrimp.

Other fillings can be caviar, mashed sardines, diced ham and tongue or flaked salmon. Always use a moist filling or moisten with mayonnaise or a little heavy cream. Season well.

Cover with foil or waxed paper so the eggs do not dry.

Scotch eggs

A perfect omelette should be moist in texture, very light and served piping hot. In order to achieve this, cook the mixture quickly so the eggs set in a short time; too slow cooking toughens them. Never keep omelettes waiting; they should be cooked *as required* then served immediately. This means all fillings and garnishes should be prepared before you start to cook the omelette. Omelettes are suitable for serving either as an hors d'oeuvre or as a main dish.

● **AVOID** *Putting too many eggs into the pan; this slows up the cooking. A 5–6-inch omelette pan should be used for a 2–3 egg omelette. Using too large a pan for the number of eggs for this means you have a wafer thin layer which becomes dry. Washing the pan after use; it is the main reason why omelettes stick.*

● **TO RECTIFY** *Make several small omelettes if you have only a small pan. This does mean the first omelettes are kept waiting; unless you can persuade your family to eat them as they are cooked rather than serving them together. If you make a lot of omelettes, it is worth while investing in two omelette pans so you can cook two omelettes simultaneously. If the only pan you have is*

To Make an Omelette

really too big for the number of eggs, then work on half the pan, Sketches 4, 5 and 6 illustrate this. Treat an omelette pan with great respect; season it when new, see Sketch 1, and wipe out with soft paper or a soft cloth after use.

Blue Print Recipe

To Make a Plain Omelette

2 or 3 eggs · seasoning · 1 tablespoon water · 2 tablespoons butter · filling or flavoring (see individual recipes) · garnish as recipes.

To make Beat the eggs, seasoning and water lightly. I use a fork only for a plain omelette like this, for I find overbeating gives a less moist result.
To cook Heat the butter in the omelette pan. Make quite sure it is hot, but do not let

it darken in color, or it will spoil the look of the omelette. Pour the eggs into the hot butter then *wait $\frac{1}{2}$–1 minute until the eggs have set in a thin film at the bottom. Hold the handle of the omelette pan quite firmly in one hand, then loosen the egg mixture from the sides of the pan with a knife and tilt the pan slightly (it should be kept over the heat all this time). This is known as "working" the omelette and it allows the liquid egg from the top of the mixture to flow to the sides of the pan and cook quickly. Continue tilting the pan, loosening the sides and moving the mixture until it is as set *as you like*. People vary considerably in the way they like their omelettes cooked; some prefer them just set, others fairly liquid in the center. Add any filling mentioned in the recipe.
To serve Fold or roll the omelette away from the handle of the pan, see Sketch 2. Hold the pan firmly by the handle, then tip the cooked omelette on to the very hot serving dish or plate, see Sketch 3. Garnish as the recipe and serve at once. *All recipes based on this serve 1 person as a main course or 2 people as an hors d'oeuvre unless stated otherwise.*
Storing and freezing *Omelettes cannot be stored or frozen.*

1. To season a new omelette pan. Sprinkle with a thick layer of salt. Heat gently for some minutes, pour out the salt then rub with oil.

2. Folding or rolling the omelette.

3. Tipping the omelette onto the dish.

4. To make an omelette in a too large pan. Heat the butter as the Blue Print.

5. Pour in the eggs and before they have had time to set tilt the pan so they run back and cover half the pan only.

6. Continue cooking as Blue Print working the omelette but using only half the pan.

SOME FLAVORINGS AND FILLINGS FOR OMELETTES

Omelette aux Fines Herbes

Ingredients as Blue Print PLUS 1–2 teaspoons freshly chopped herbs or $\frac{1}{4}$–$\frac{1}{2}$ teaspoon dried herbs. Mix the herbs with the beaten eggs. Cook and serve as the Blue Print. Garnish with freshly chopped herbs.

Bacon Filled Omelette

Ingredients as Blue Print PLUS 2 slices of bacon and 1 tomato. Chop and fry the bacon; keep hot. Cook the omelette as the Blue Print, add the bacon then fold or roll. Serve as the Blue Print, garnished with cooked or raw tomato slices.

Cheese Omelette

Ingredients as Blue Print PLUS 1–2 oz. ($\frac{1}{4}$–$\frac{1}{2}$ cup) grated cheese. Cook the omelette as the Blue Print but add the cheese just before it is completely set. Fold or roll and serve as the Blue Print. Garnish with a little more grated cheese and parsley.

Ham Omelette

Ingredients as Blue Print PLUS $\frac{1}{4}$ cup diced cooked ham. Mix the ham with the beaten eggs. Cook as the Blue Print.

Mushroom Omelette

Ingredients as Blue Print PLUS $\frac{1}{4}$–$\frac{1}{2}$ cup chopped fresh mushrooms and a little extra butter. Cook the mushrooms in some of the butter. Mix with the beaten eggs. Cook as the Blue Print. Garnish with more mushrooms or parsley.

Shrimp Omelette

Ingredients as Blue Print PLUS $\frac{1}{4}$ cup chopped shelled shrimp. Mix the shrimp with the beaten eggs. Cook as the Blue Print. Garnish with a thick slice of lemon.

Pastel de Tortillas (Omelette Cake)

8 eggs; seasoning; 4 tablespoons water; about 4 tablespoons butter. *For the sauce:* $1\frac{1}{2}$–2 lb. (4–6) tomatoes; $\frac{1}{4}$ cup ground raw beef; 1 clove garlic; 1 onion; seasoning; good pinch dried or fresh basil. *Layer one:* about 1 cup mixed cooked vegetables; little butter. *Layer two:* $\frac{1}{4}$ lb. (1 cup) mushrooms; 2–4 tablespoons butter. *Layer three:* $\frac{1}{4}$ lb. (about 1 cup) cooked shrimp or other shellfish; little butter.

This is an unusual variation of the Spanish omelette or Tortilla.

The omelettes are made just as the Blue Print, but do not cook these until all the fillings and sauce are ready. To make the sauce, chop the tomatoes, put into a pan and simmer until the juice flows, then add the beef, crushed garlic, chopped onion, seasoning and herbs. Simmer for about 30 minutes, puree if wished, then reheat. The sauce must be fairly stiff, so allow any surplus liquid to evaporate in an uncovered pan.

Heat the vegetables in the minimum of butter (they must not be greasy). Slice or chop the mushrooms, simmer in the butter. Toss the shrimp or shellfish in butter.

Make four omelettes as the Blue Print. Put the first omelette on a hot dish, cover with the vegetable layer, then add the second omelette and the mushroom layer, the third omelette and the shellfish and the final omelette to cover. Top with some of the sauce and serve the rest separately. *Serves 4–5 as a main course, 8–10 as an hors d'oeuvre.*

Emergency Shelf Omelette

Ingredients as Blue Print (using 3 eggs) PLUS can asparagus spears, can diced potatoes, little extra butter or use 1–2 tablespoons oil, $\frac{1}{4}$ cup diced Cheddar cheese and parsley. Open the cans, cut the tips from the asparagus spears. Chop the stalks. Heat the tips and put on one side for garnish. Sauté the drained diced potatoes in hot butter or oil until golden; drain. Mix the chopped asparagus stalks, sautéed potatoes and cheese. Make the omelette as the Blue Print but add the potato mixture while it is still fairly soft. Fold. Slide out of the pan (as you have a very generous filling) on to a hot dish. Garnish with hot asparagus tips and parsley. *Serves 2 as a main dish.*

Bacon filled omelette (opposite)
Pastel de Tortillas (Omelette Cake), below left
Emergency shelf omelette (below)

Poached and Scrambled Eggs

All too often a poached or scrambled egg is spoiled by overcooking. This produces a tough hard poached egg or a dry scrambled egg, or one that curdles and becomes watery due to too much heat.

Blue Print Recipes

1. Poached Eggs

METHOD 1. To make Half fill a shallow pan or skillet with water. Add a good pinch salt and bring to boiling point. Pour in 1–2 teaspoons vinegar if wished; this helps to prevent the white spreading in the water but does give a faint vinegar taste to the eggs. Break the first egg into a cup or saucer, slide into the water. Continue like this, adding the number of eggs required.

To cook Lower the heat once the eggs have been added so the water bubbles very gently. Move the water round the eggs in a whirling movement. This, like the vinegar, assists in giving the eggs a good shape. Cook for 2–3 minutes only until set.

To serve Lift each egg out with a slotted pancake turner or perforated spoon; allow to drain over the water. Serve on hot buttered toast or as the suggestions below.

METHOD 2. To make Put water into the base of an egg poacher. Add a teaspoon of butter or margarine to each small metal cup and allow to melt as the water boils. Break an egg into each cup; season lightly if wished.

To cook Until just set; be careful they do not become too firm.
To serve As above.

● **AVOID** *Boiling the water too rapidly; this produces a very badly shaped egg and one where the white breaks away.*
● **TO RECTIFY** *If this has started to happen, reduce the heat at once and gather the white together with a metal spoon or spatula.*
● **TO REDUCERS** *Choose Method 1 for poaching the eggs.*

2. Scrambled Eggs

3 or 4 eggs · seasoning · 1–2 tablespoons milk or light cream (see method) · 2 tablespoons margarine or butter.

To make Beat the eggs with seasoning and the milk or cream. It is not essential to add milk or cream, although this gives a lighter scrambled egg.

To cook Melt the margarine or butter in a saucepan. Add the eggs, make sure the heat is low then leave the eggs for about 1 minute. Stir gently with a wooden spoon until lightly set.

To serve Spoon on to hot buttered toast or fried bread or serve as the suggestions below. Scrambled eggs make a light meal served with broiled or fried bacon. *All recipes based on this serve 2–3.*

● **AVOID** *Leaving the eggs too long without stirring; they then set too firmly.*
● **TO RECTIFY** *If the eggs have become rather firm, add either another raw, seasoned egg, or a little milk or cream and blend gently with the firm egg.*
● **TO REDUCERS** *Omit the cream.*

For Special Occasions

Eggs Benedict

Make Hollandaise sauce as page 88. Poach 6 eggs as Blue Print 1, put on toasted buttered English muffins which have been topped with a piece of broiled ham. Coat with the Hollandaise sauce. Top with paprika. *Serves 3 as a main dish or 6 as an hors d'oeuvre.*

Oeufs en Matelote

Poach the eggs as Blue Print 1, but use meat stock instead of salted water. Top with a thick, well seasoned onion puree and serve on rounds of toast. Garnish with anchovy fillets. The mixture of meat and fish in this particular recipe is most interesting and a very pleasant combination.

Piperade

2–4 tablespoons butter or use half butter and half olive oil; 1 green pepper; 1 red pepper (optional—or use half a green and half a red pepper); 1–2 onions: 1–2 tomatoes; 1 clove garlic; 6 eggs; seasoning.
Heat the butter or butter and oil in a pan. Add the prepared peppers, either diced or cut into thin rings, (discard the seeds and core), the peeled sliced or chopped onions and tomatoes and the crushed clove of garlic. Cook gently until tender, then add the beaten seasoned eggs and scramble as Blue Print 2; *do not add milk or cream*. Serve with crusty French bread or with crisp toast. *Serves 2–3 as a main dish or 6 as a light hors d'oeuvre.*

Eggs with Asparagus

Heat the tips of canned or cooked asparagus in butter or margarine, then add the eggs, beaten with cream or milk, and scramble as Blue Print 2.
To vary Add diced ham or cooked chicken or shrimp in place of asparagus.

Storing and freezing *You can store the cooked, scrambled eggs for sandwich fillings and they can be frozen, although they do become slightly tough. Poached eggs are quite unsuitable for freezing; they can however be stored then chopped to add to sauces etc. in place of hard boiled eggs. Naturally they must be poached until firm for this purpose.*

Piperade

Scrambled eggs

Fried bacon and eggs

Fried Eggs Hussarde

4 small slices bread; 4 tablespoons fat; 2 slices cooked ham; 1–2 tomatoes; seasoning; 4 eggs.

Cut the bread into neat rounds. Heat most of the fat, fry the bread until crisp and golden brown on both sides. Lift out of the pan on to a hot oven-proof dish. Top with chopped ham, thickly sliced tomatoes and seasoning. Put into the oven to soften the tomatoes while frying the eggs. Heat the remainder of the fat in the pan. Fry the eggs as Blue Print 1, put on top of the tomato slices and serve at once. *Serves 2 as a main dish, 4 as a snack.*

Snow Eggs

4 thick slices Gruyère or Cheddar cheese; little prepared mustard; 4 slices cooked ham; 4 eggs; seasoning. *To garnish:* paprika; chopped parsley.

Put the cheese into a shallow oven-proof dish. Spread with the mustard and top with the ham. Put into a moderate to moderately hot oven, 375–400°F, for about 10 minutes. Meanwhile, separate the egg yolks and whites. Beat the yolks with seasoning, pour over the ham and cheese. Bake for 5 minutes. Beat the egg whites until very stiff, add seasoning and pile over the egg yolk mixture. Return to the oven, lower the heat to very moderate and leave for about 10–15 minutes. Garnish with paprika and chopped parsley. *Serves 4.*

Fried Eggs Turque

4–6 chicken livers; 4 tablespoons butter; $\frac{1}{2}$ tablespoon chopped parsley; 4 large tomatoes; seasoning; 4 eggs; French bread.

Slice the chicken livers and sauté in half the hot butter until tender. Add the chopped parsley and arrange in the center of a hot dish. While the livers are cooking, heat the peeled chopped tomatoes with seasoning until a thick puree. Spoon over the livers. Fry the eggs in the remaining hot butter as Blue Print 1 and arrange round the tomato and liver mixture. Serve with hot French bread. *Serves 4.*

Storing and freezing *None of these dishes store or freeze.*

Perfectly fried eggs with broiled or fried bacon are one of the best and quickest dishes to serve at breakfast time, or any other meal of the day. The soft yolk of the egg gives moistness to broiled meat or fish. I enjoy hot fried eggs on thick slices of cold boiled ham or as a topping on Welsh Rarebit (instead of poached eggs).

Shirred eggs are equally good for a light main dish or an hors d'oeuvre. They can be varied in many ways. As shirred eggs are generally served in the cooking utensil, it is worth while investing in interesting oven-proof dishes if you serve them frequently.

Blue Print Recipes

1. Fried Eggs

To cook If you have fried bacon or sausages there may be enough fat left in the pan; if insufficient then heat a scant tablespoon of fat; check it is not too hot. Break the first egg into a cup or saucer or directly into the hot fat. Tilt the pan for a few seconds to encourage the white to set in a neat shape. Add the second egg, tilt the pan, then continue like this. If very fussy about the shape, you can put an old round metal cookie cutter into the pan and heat this as you heat the fat, then break the egg into it. When set, lift away the cutter and use for each egg.

Lift the eggs from the pan with a slotted pancake turner so they are drained of any surplus fat.

Some people like the yolk covered with a layer of white; to do this, spoon the fat over the yolk as its sets.

To serve As soon as possible after cooking.

●**AVOID** *Overcooking; fried eggs cook very quickly. Too hot fat; if you dislike a crisp skin at the bottom of the eggs. Too cool fat; this allows the white to spread over the pan and give the egg an irregular*

Fried and Shirred Eggs

shape, making it difficult to dish-up. Too cool fat also produces a greasy egg.
● **TO RECTIFY** *Check cooking progress carefully and dish-up as soon as the eggs are set. Remember they continue cooking if kept warm for any length of time.*
● **TO REDUCERS** *Choose a non-stick pan so you need the minimum of fat.*

2. Shirred Eggs

1–2 tablespoons butter or margarine
2 eggs · seasoning.

To make Put half the butter or margarine into one or two individual baking dishes (use one dish for a main dish, two for hors d'oeuvre).

To cook Heat the butter or margarine for a few minutes in a moderate to moderately hot oven, 375–400°F. Break the eggs over the hot butter or margarine, add a little seasoning, then the rest of the fat in one or two small knobs. Bake for just over 10 minutes towards the top of the oven.

To serve With a teaspoon, while still very hot. *All recipes based on this serve 2 as an hors d'oeuvre or 1 as a main meal.*

To vary This is a very basic way of baking the eggs, you can:
Put cottage or mashed cream cheese into the dish or dishes with the butter or margarine. Heat this for a few minutes, then add the egg or eggs, seasoning, a little grated sharp cheese and butter or margarine. Cook as Blue Print 2.
Put a layer of light or heavy cream over the hot butter or margarine, then add the egg or eggs, seasoning, another layer of cream and the remaining butter or margarine. Cook as Blue Print 2.
Add chopped ham, chicken, shrimp or asparagus tips to the butter or margarine, heat, then add the egg or eggs, seasoning and the rest of the butter or margarine. Cook as Blue Print 2.
All these variations make excellent light dishes.

●**AVOID** *Cooking the eggs too slowly; they become leathery.*
●**TO RECTIFY** *Check on the cooking after about 6–7 minutes; the egg whites should be setting. If they are still very transparent raise the oven temperature.*
●**TO REDUCERS** *Use as little butter as possible and choose low calorie flavorings.*

...shed tradition in many ... thin crepes, served ...on, on Shrove Tuesday, ... excellent as the base for many ... uvre, entrées and desserts throughout th... year.

Blue Print Recipe

To Make Crepes

1 cup flour · pinch salt · 1 egg · 1⅓ cups milk or milk and water. For frying: oil or fat (see method).

To make Sift the flour and salt, add the egg and a little milk or milk and water. Beat or whisk thoroughly to give a smooth thick batter. Gradually beat in the rest of the liquid.

To cook For each crepe you cook, put about 2 teaspoons oil or a knob of fat the size of an unshelled almond into the pan. If using a non-stick pan then brush with oil or melted fat before cooking each crepe. This is essential if you want really crisp crepes. Heat the oil or fat until a *faint* blue haze is seen coming from the pan. Pour or spoon in a little batter, then move the pan so the batter flows over the bottom; it should give a paper thin layer, see Sketches 1 and 2. Cook fairly quickly until set on the bottom. This takes about 1½–2 minutes. To test if ready to toss or turn, shake the pan and the crepe should move easily if cooked on the under surface. Toss or turn carefully as directions given with the sketches. Cook for about the same time on the second side.

To serve Lift or slide the crepe out of the pan. Keep hot (see below) while cooking the rest of the crepes. *This batter should give*

1. Spoon or pour a little thin batter from a jug.

2. Immediately turn and tilt the pan to allow the batter to coat the bottom of the pan in a paper-thin layer.

3. To turn the crepe, slip a pancake turner under the crepe and turn carefully.

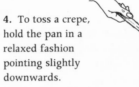

4. To toss a crepe, hold the pan in a relaxed fashion pointing slightly downwards.

5. Flick the wrist very briskly upwards so the crepe lifts from the pan, turns and drops back again.

enough crepes for 4 people; but you may be able to serve a greater number if using a substantial filling, as in the Savory Crepe Boat and Orange Crepe Gâteau opposite.

To keep crepes hot Either put a large plate over a pan of boiling water and place each cooked crepe on this or keep hot on an uncovered dish in a 180°F oven.

● **AVOID** *Making the batter too thick. Insufficient heating of the oil or fat before cooking each crepe. Pouring too much mixture into the pan. Trying to turn or toss before the crepe is properly set. Washing the pan after use.*

● **TO RECTIFY** *Follow the proportions in the Blue Print. This gives a very thin batter. Always whisk the batter just before cooking as it tends to separate slightly as it stands, and the batter at the bottom of the bowl is slightly thicker than at the top. Check the heat of the oil or fat very carefully. Learn the knack of pouring a little batter into the pan, see the sketches. Shake the crepe well before trying to toss or turn; if it does not move easily it is not ready. Wipe the used pan with soft paper immediately after use.*

● **SHORT CUTS** *There are commercial crepe mixes, or blend the ingredients in the blender. Blend the liquid and egg first, then add the flour and salt. In this way you prevent the flour sticking round the sides of the blender.*

Storing and freezing *The uncooked batter may be stored for several days in a refrigerator and can be frozen for a few weeks. Wrap cooked unfilled crepes in aluminium foil (separate each crepe with squares of waxed paper). Store for several days in a refrigerator or 10–12 weeks in a freezer. Most filled crepes can be frozen.*

Savory crepe boat

Red Currant Crepes

Ingredients as Blue Print opposite PLUS red currant jelly and superfine sugar.
Make the crepes as the Blue Print. Fill with hot red currant jelly and top with sugar. *Serves 4–6.*
To vary Use hot jam or fruit puree instead of jelly.

Crisp Coated Crepes

Ingredients as Blue Print opposite PLUS jam, jelly or fruit puree, oil or fat for deep frying and sugar.
Put a little of the crepe batter on one side, make and cook the crepes with the remainder of the batter as Blue Print. Keep warm. Spread with a little jam, jelly or fruit puree, then fold in the sides of the crepes and roll firmly. Dip each rolled crepe in the reserved batter and fry in hot deep oil or fat until very crisp and golden brown. Put onto a hot dish, top with sugar and hot jam, jelly or fruit. *Serves 4–6.*
To vary Dip in batter, then in fine soft bread crumbs or chopped nuts before frying.

Shrove Tuesday crepes

The crepe batter, covered by the Blue Print opposite, enables you to make a variety of savory and sweet dishes.

Savory Crepe Boat

Ingredients as Blue Print opposite MINUS fat for cooking and PLUS 2 tablespoons fat; 3–4 hard boiled eggs; 6 tablespoons butter or margarine; $\frac{1}{4}$ cup flour; $1\frac{1}{3}$ cups chicken stock; $\frac{2}{3}$ cup milk; seasoning; about 1 cup diced cooked chicken; 3–4 tablespoons light cream; 2–4 oz. ($\frac{1}{2}$–1 cup) button mushrooms; chopped parsley. To garnish: sprigs of watercress.
Make the batter as the Blue Print opposite. Heat the fat in a shallow pan, pour in the batter and bake for approximately 25–30 minutes towards the top of a hot to very hot oven, 450–475°F. Reduce the heat after about 15 minutes to moderate. Meanwhile slice the eggs, make a sauce with 4 tablespoons of the butter or margarine, the flour, chicken stock and milk. When thickened and smooth, add the seasoning, chicken and cream; do not allow to boil. Heat the remainder of the butter or margarine; sauté the whole or sliced mushrooms. Add most of the sliced eggs and mushrooms to the chicken mixture. Lift the crepe from the pan onto a hot serving dish; spoon the sauce mixture over this. Top with the remainder of the eggs, mushrooms and chopped parsley. Garnish with watercress. *Serves about 6.*

Orange Crepe Gâteau

Ingredients as Blue Print opposite PLUS 2 cans mandarin oranges, fresh orange juice (optional—see method), 2 tablespoons honey, 2 tablespoons sieved apricot jam, 1 table-

spoon arrowroot or cornstarch and 1 glacé, fresh or canned cherry.
Cook the crepes as the Blue Print opposite and keep hot. Strain the syrup from the cans of oranges to measure 2 cups. If insufficient, add a little fresh orange juice. Put most of the fruit syrup into a saucepan with the honey and jam; heat gently until the jam has melted. Blend the arrowroot or cornstarch with the remainder of the syrup, add to the mixture in the pan; stir until thickened and clear. Put the first crepe onto a hot dish, top with some mandarin oranges and sauce. Continue like this, ending with a crepe. Arrange a few orange segments and the cherry on top and coat with a little sauce. Serve cut into slices, like a cake. *Serves 6–8.*

Shrove Tuesday Crepes

Make the crepes as the Blue Print opposite. Serve in the traditional way with sugar and lemon slices. *Serves 4–6.*

New Look to Crepes

1 Flavor the batter with $\frac{1}{2}$ teaspoon ginger, cinnamon, allspice or grated lemon rind.
2 Fill the cooked crepes, fold the ends in and roll. This prevents the filling coming out. Dip in a stiffly beaten egg white blended with 1 teaspoon cornstarch and fry in deep fat or oil. If the filling is savory, roll in grated cheese after frying. If the filling is sweet, roll in chopped nuts or dried coconut.
3 Use crepes instead of omelettes in the recipe for Pastel de Tortillas (page 73).

A savory soufflé is ideal for the main course of a luncheon, the first course of a formal dinner or the pièce de résistance of a late supper party.

The Blue Print gives a fairly firm textured soufflé. If you are having this with vegetables, as a main course, I would increase the amount of liquid by up to an extra $\frac{1}{3}$ cup. This means that you have a very soft texture in the center which serves as a sauce with any vegetables.

Blue Print Recipe

Cheese Soufflé

2 tablespoons butter or margarine · 4 tablespoons flour · $\frac{2}{3}$ cup milk (see introduction above) · seasoning · 4 eggs · approximately 3 oz. ($\frac{3}{4}$ cup) grated cheese*.

*You can vary the cheese—Dutch Gouda gives a pleasant mild, creamy texture, a Cheddar or Gruyère a fairly definite taste and Parmesan a very strong taste and a drier texture. You can also combine cheeses, i.e. half Gruyère and half Parmesan.

To make Heat the butter or margarine in a large saucepan, stir in the flour then gradually blend in the milk. Cook until a thick sauce (if using the higher percentage of

Savory Soufflés

liquid it will be a coating consistency). Season well. Remove from the heat and add the egg yolks, then the cheese and finally fold in the stiffly beaten egg whites. Put into a greased soufflé dish which has been coated with grated cheese.

To cook Bake in the center of a moderate to moderately hot oven, 375–400°F, for approximately 30 minutes. If using the larger quantity of liquid use the lower temperature so the mixture does not overbrown before it is cooked.

To serve As quickly as possible. *All recipes based on this serve 4 for a main dish.*

● **AVOID** *Handling the mixture too much when putting in the egg whites, for this destroys the fluffy texture.*

● **TO RECTIFY** *You can tell if you are overhandling the mixture because you lose the very light appearance. If by chance you have been too rough, the best remedy is to incorporate an extra beaten egg white.*

● **SHORT CUT** *Instead of making the sauce, use $\frac{1}{2}$ to 1 whole $10\frac{1}{2}$ oz. can condensed soup,*

either mushroom, chicken or asparagus, to blend with the other flavoring.

● **TO REDUCERS** *This is a relatively low calorie, high protein dish.*

Storing and freezing *You cannot freeze or store a hot soufflé.*

Spinach Soufflé

Ingredients as Blue Print but substitute spinach puree for the milk. Cheese may be added if wished. Make and bake as the Blue Print.

Fish Soufflé

Ingredients as Blue Print but use flaked cooked fish (white fish, salmon or shellfish) in place of cheese and flavor the sauce to taste with a little anchovy paste. Make and bake as the Blue Print.

Smoked Haddock and Cheese Soufflé

This is a very pleasant combination.
Follow the Blue Print recipe but use only 2 oz. ($\frac{1}{2}$ cup) grated Parmesan cheese and 2–3 oz. cooked flaked smoked haddock. Substitute fish stock (or liquid from cooking the fish) for milk if possible.

Cream Soufflé

Follow the Blue Print recipe using the smaller quantity of milk and add 4–5 tablespoons heavy cream to the sauce with the egg yolks.

A soufflé omelette is made by separating the egg yolks and the whites, then beating the whites until very stiff and folding them into the egg yolks. In this way you produce a thick, ultra-light type of omelette.

A soufflé omelette makes an excellent basis for a hot dessert. Although you can add sweet fillings to the plain omelette on page 72, they blend better with the lighter texture of the soufflé omelette.

The savory fillings given on page 72 and 73 may be incorporated into this type of omelette, although I prefer more moist fillings as suggested on this page.

The points under AVOID and TO RECTIFY on page 72 also apply to this type of omelette.

Blue Print Recipe

To Make a Soufflé Omelette

2 or 3 eggs · seasoning or 1 teaspoon sugar for a sweet omelette · 1 tablespoon water · 2 tablespoons butter · filling or flavoring (see individual recipes).

To make Separate the yolks from the whites. Beat the yolks with seasoning or sugar and water. Beat the egg whites until

Making a Soufflé Omelette

very stiff; fold into the yolks.

To cook Heat the butter in the pan (see page 72). Switch on or light the broiler. Pour the fluffy egg mixture into the hot butter. Allow to set and work as the Blue Print on page 72. You will find this more difficult as the mixture is less liquid. When the omelette is about half cooked, put the pan under the broiler (with the heat to medium) and complete the cooking.

To serve Add any filling required. This thicker omelette is more difficult to fold (you cannot roll it) so make a shallow cut across the center, then fold, see Sketches 2 and 3 (page 72). Slide or tip on to the hot serving dish or plate. *All recipes based on this serve 1 as a main dish or 2 as a light hors d'oeuvre or dessert.*

SWEET FILLINGS
Nut Omelette

Follow the Blue Print and blend 1–2 tablespoons chopped blanched almonds, hazelnuts, pecans or walnuts with the egg yolks. Fill with hot sweetened apricot puree or jam.

Fruit Omelette

Use light cream instead of the water in the Blue Print. Fill with hot fruit puree or sliced uncooked sweetened fresh fruit. The fruit can be flavored with brandy or liqueur.

Jam Omelette

Make the omelette as the Blue Print and fill with hot jam (or jelly). A delicious omelette is made by adding finely grated orange or lemon rind to the egg yolks, then filling with hot marmalade.

SAVORY FILLINGS WITH SAUCES

Thick cheese, curry, mushroom or tomato sauce all make excellent fillings.

Vegetable Filling

Blend diced cooked vegetables with any of the sauces above or with a thick fresh tomato puree (made more piquant with the addition of a little canned tomato paste).

Fish and Meat Filling

Blend cooked ham, tongue, chicken, white-fleshed fish or shellish with the selected sauce and flavor with chopped fresh herbs.

Storing and freezing *You cannot store or freeze a soufflé omelette, but it is a good idea to freeze different fillings in small containers.*
To use leftovers *I quite like a cold soufflé omelette cut in strips and served in place of hard boiled egg.*

Making Short Crust Pastry

Short crust is undoubtedly one of the most useful of all types of pastry. It is quick to make, relatively simple, keeps well and is equally good with sweet as with savory ingredients.

Blue Print Recipe
Short Crust Pastry

2 cups flour · pinch salt · ½ cup fat* · cold water to mix.

*This can be lard, margarine, butter, shortening or a mixture.

To make Sift the flour and salt. Cut the fat into convenient-sized pieces, drop into the bowl. Rub in with the tips of your fingers until the mixture looks like fine bread crumbs. *Do not overhandle.* Lift the flour and fat as you rub them together so you incorporate as much air as possible and keep the mixture cool. *Gradually* add water to give enough moisture to bind the ingredients together. Use a spatula to blend. Flour varies a great deal in the amount of liquid it absorbs, but you should require about 2 tablespoons water. When blended, form into a neat ball of dough with your fingers. Put on to a lightly floured pastry board and roll out to a neat oblong or round about ¼-inch in thickness unless the recipe states to the contrary. Always roll in one direction and do not turn the rolling pin; instead lift and turn the pastry. This makes sure it is not stretched badly.

To cook As the individual recipes; generally short crust pastry needs a hot oven to set the pastry, but you may need to reduce the heat after a time.

● **AVOID** *Making the pastry too wet; this produces a tough instead of a crisp, short result. Overhandling the dough. Baking too slowly.*

● **TO RECTIFY** *If you have made the pastry overmoist either chill thoroughly (this does allow it to dry out slightly) or use a generous amount of flour on the pastry board; unfortunately the latter remedy spoils the basic proportions of the pastry.*

● **SHORT CUT** *Use ready-made frozen short crust pastry for the various dishes in this section.*

Old English Chicken Pie

Short crust pastry made as Blue Print. *For the filling:* small quantity of sage and onion stuffing or 1 cup packaged stuffing prepared according to directions. ¾ lb. (scant 2 cups) diced raw chicken meat; ½ cup flour; seasoning; 3 sausages (skinless if possible); 4 tablespoons butter or fat; 2 cups chicken stock or water and 1 chicken bouillon cube; 2 hard boiled eggs. *To glaze:* 1 egg.

Make the pastry as the Blue Print and put to one side while preparing the filling. Form the stuffing into 6 small balls. Toss the chicken meat in half the flour, blended with a little seasoning. Halve the sausages. Toss the stuffing balls, coated chicken and sausages in the hot butter or fat until golden brown. Remove from the fat and put into a 5–6 cup baking dish. Stir the remaining flour into any fat remaining in the pan, then gradually add the stock or water and bouillon cube. Bring to the boil, cook until thickened. Add the coarsely chopped eggs. Pour the sauce over the chicken, stuffing balls and sausages. Cool slightly, then cover with the pastry as the sketches below. Make a slit in the center of the pie to allow the steam to escape. (This encourages the pastry to crisp.) Decorate with pastry leaves made from the trimmings. Brush with the beaten egg and bake in the center of a hot oven, 425–450°F, for about 20–25 minutes until the pastry is golden brown. Reduce the heat to moderate and cook for a further 20–25 minutes. Serve hot. *Serves 6.*

To make tartlets
1. Cut the pastry into rounds (about 2-inches in diameter, but depending upon the size of the patty tins). Use a plain cutter for savory tarts and a fluted cutter for sweet tarts.
2. Put the rounds into the patty tins, press down and continue as the individual recipes.

Old English chicken pie

To make a pie
3. Put the filling into the pie dish. Cut a band of pastry to fit round the moistened edge of the pie dish. Brush the rim of pastry with a very little water.
4. Support the rest of the pastry over the rolling pin. Arrange on top of the pie (slip the rolling pin away).

5. Press the edges together, then cut away the surplus pastry.
6. Decorate the edges by fluting.

Savory Tarts and Pies

Corned Beef Plate Tart

Short crust pastry made as Blue Print opposite. *For the filling:* 24 oz. canned corned beef; 2 medium-sized onions; 1 tablespoon oil; seasoning; 1 teaspoon Tabasco sauce; 1 egg; 2–3 diced cooked or canned carrots; $\frac{1}{2}$ cup cooked or canned peas. *To glaze:* 1 egg. *To garnish:* parsley.

Make the pastry as the Blue Print opposite and put to one side. Flake the corned beef and put into a bowl. Peel and chop the onions, toss in the hot oil until tender; blend with the corned beef, seasoning, Tabasco sauce, egg and vegetables. Roll out the pastry, use half to line a 7–8-inch deep pie plate or dish. Cover with the filling and the rest of the pastry as sketches below and opposite. Decorate with leaves of pastry made from the trimmings and glaze with the beaten egg. Bake for 25–30 minutes in the center of a moderately hot to hot oven, 400–425°F, then lower the heat to moderate for a further 20–25 minutes. Serve hot or cold, garnished with parsley. *Serves 6.*

Note As you see by comparing the cooking temperatures of this tart with the Old English Chicken Pie opposite, it is advisable to use a slightly lower oven temperature and longer cooking time when you have pastry above and below a substantial filling. This ensures that the bottom pastry sets and browns as well as the top pastry. If the filling is fairly dry in texture, it is not essential to make a slit in the top of the pastry.

Chasseur Chicken Pie

Ingredients as Old English Pie opposite, but substitute a generous $\frac{1}{4}$ lb. mushrooms for the sage and onion balls and about 4 firm, halved peeled tomatoes for the hard boiled eggs.

Make as the Corned Beef Plate Tart in a pastry lined and covered pie plate. *Serves 6.*

Steak and Vegetable Pie

The pie shown on page 69 is made with steak and vegetables. Cook the steak as in the Steak and Kidney pie on page 85 for about 1 hour, then add about $\frac{3}{4}$ lb. diced uncooked vegetables and continue cooking until the steak is almost tender, i.e. approximately 2–$2\frac{1}{4}$ hours. Put into a deep pie dish and cover with flaky or short crust pastry. Cook as the instructions for that pastry. *Serves 6.*

Golden Crust Pie

Short crust pastry made with $1\frac{1}{2}$ cups flour etc. as Blue Print opposite. *For the filling:* 4 tablespoons butter; 1 large onion; 2 large tomatoes; 1 cup ground cooked meat or

chicken; seasoning; 1 tablespoon chopped parsley; $\frac{1}{2}$–1 teaspoon chopped thyme or pinch dried thyme; 2 eggs; 2 oz. ($\frac{1}{2}$ cup) grated Cheddar cheese.

Make the pastry as the Blue Print opposite. Roll out and line an 8-inch flan ring or pan. Bake blind in the center of a hot oven, 425–450°F, until crisp and just golden in color; this takes approximately 15–18 minutes. While the pastry is cooking, prepare the filling. Heat the butter in a skillet and cook the peeled chopped onion and tomatoes until soft. Add the meat or chicken, seasoning and herbs and heat thoroughly. Add the beaten egg yolks then spoon the hot filling into the hot pastry shell. Beat the egg whites until very stiff, fold in the cheese and seasoning, pile this over the meat mixture. Lower the temperature to 325°F and cook for 10 minutes. Serve at once. *Serves 4–5.*

To vary Omit the meat or chicken and add the same quantity of cooked or canned pea beans or white kidney beans.

Tuna Pie Florentine

Short crust pastry made with $1\frac{1}{2}$ cups flour etc. as Blue Print opposite. *For the filling:* 1 lb. fresh spinach or 10-oz. carton frozen spinach; 4 tablespoons butter; 2 tablespoons heavy cream; seasoning; medium-sized can water packed tuna fish; $\frac{2}{3}$ cup milk; 2

tablespoons flour. *To garnish:* 1 lemon.

Make the pastry as the Blue Print opposite. Roll out and line an 8-inch flan ring or dish. Bake blind as the recipe above but allow a little longer until golden brown. Meanwhile cook the spinach, drain well, puree or chop and blend with half the butter, the cream and seasoning. Open the can of tuna; drain this and blend the juice from the can with the milk. Make a thick sauce with the rest of the butter, flour and milk (plus tuna liquid). Add the flaked fish and seasoning. Put the creamy spinach at the bottom of the pastry, top with the tuna mixture. Garnish with lemon slices. Serve at once. *Serves 4–5.*

To make a plate tart

7. Cover the baking tin or pie plate with pastry, neaten edges, add filling. Cover with pastry as described under the pie, Sketches 4–6.

To make a flan

8. Lower the pastry into the flan ring on an upturned baking sheet, or put into a layer cake pan. Neaten edges by cutting or rolling.

Savory Cheese Flans

The best known of all the savory flans is a Quiche Lorraine, i.e. an egg custard filling flavored with cheese and crisp bacon. This is only one of the many interesting flans of the same type. A Quiche is an excellent hors d'oeuvre and ideal for buffet parties.

Blue Print Recipe

Making a Quiche

To make Prepare the pastry, roll out and line the flan ring (put this on a cookie sheet for easy removal) or use a cake pan or oven-proof serving dish. Prepare ingredients for the filling.

To cook Bake the pastry blind (see page 112) in a moderately hot to hot oven, according to the type of pastry used, until just set and pale golden; do *not* overcook. Remove the pastry from the oven and pour the *warm* filling into the *warm* pastry. Lower the heat to very moderate to moderate, as directed in the recipe, and continue cooking until the filling is set. The *greater* the depth of filling, the *longer* the cooking time and the *lower* the oven setting.

To serve Hot or cold.

● **AVOID** *Having pastry that is not crisp. Allowing the custard filling to curdle.*

● **TO RECTIFY** *Although not all recipes bake the pastry case blind, I find this the perfect solution. You have crisp pastry by baking in a hot oven, and a custard filling that is perfectly set but does not curdle by cooking the filled flan at a lower temperature, see the Blue Print.*

● **SHORT CUTS** *Use frozen pastry or pie crust mix. Use the quick method of filling as in the Onion and Cheese Flan.*

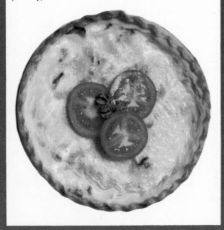

For Family Occasions

Shrimp and Cheese Quiche

For the pastry: 1½ cups flour; pinch salt; 6 tablespoons margarine, butter or shortening; water to mix. *For the filling:* 2 eggs; seasoning; ⅔ cup milk; ¼ lb. (1 cup) grated Gruyère cheese; ¼ lb. (½ cup) shelled chopped shrimp. *To garnish:* few whole shrimp; parsley.

Sift the flour and salt, cut in the fat then add sufficient water to make a firm rolling consistency. Roll out and line a *shallow* 8-inch flan ring, cake pan or oven-proof baking dish. Bake blind for about 15 minutes in the center of a hot oven, 425–450°F, until just set. Meanwhile beat the eggs with seasoning, add the *warmed* milk, cheese and chopped shrimp. Pour into the partially baked pastry shell, return to the oven and continue baking in a moderate oven, 350–375°F, for about 25–30 minutes until the filling is firm. Serve hot or cold garnished with whole shrimp and parsley. *Serves 4–5.*

Note This filling is rather shallow, as shown in the picture. This means it will set fairly quickly and is a firm filling, so ideal to cut and serve for a buffet. For a less firm filling you can use a *scant* 1¼ cups milk to the 2 eggs for an 8-inch, reasonably shallow, dish. Allow about 40–45 minutes to set the filling in a very moderate oven.

Quiche Lorraine

A simple Quiche Lorraine can be made in a very similar way to the Shrimp and Cheese Quiche above. Use crisply fried bacon in place of the shrimp. If preferred you can use grated Cheddar or crumbled Lancashire cheese in place of the grated Gruyère cheese.

For Special Occasions

Rich Quiche Lorraine

For the pastry: 2 cups flour; good pinch salt; ½ cup butter; 1–2 egg yolks and water to bind. *For the filling:* 4 large eggs; good pinch salt; shake pepper; pinch dry mustard; ⅔ cup milk and 1⅓ cups light cream or use all milk or all light cream or partly milk and partly heavy cream, but make the total amount 2 cups; ½ lb. (2 cups) grated Gruyère cheese; about 6 slices lean bacon (chopped, fried until crisp and well drained). *To garnish:* parsley.

Make the pastry as the Shrimp and Cheese Quiche, but binding with the egg yolks and water; then line a deep dish. I use a 5–6 cup deep pie dish or similar sized dish. Make sure you make the pastry sides fairly high. If you wish a more shallow Quiche then line a 9–10-inch pie plate instead. Bake blind in a hot oven for about 15 minutes. Prepare the filling as the Shrimp and Cheese Quiche, heating both the milk and the cream. Pour into the pastry shell. Lower the heat and

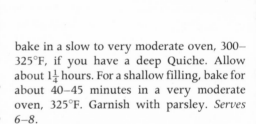

bake in a slow to very moderate oven, 300–325°F, if you have a deep Quiche. Allow about 1¼ hours. For a shallow filling, bake for about 40–45 minutes in a very moderate oven, 325°F. Garnish with parsley. *Serves 6–8.*

To vary Use shellfish in this filling in place of bacon.

Use cooked chopped ham or cooked chicken in place of the bacon.

Use a mixture of cooked vegetables,—sliced onions, mushrooms, potatoes, peas. Do not use tomatoes for they might cause the filling to curdle.

Onion and Cheese Flan

For the pastry: 1½ cups flour; good pinch salt; shake pepper; pinch dry mustard; pinch cayenne pepper; 6 tablespoons margarine or butter; 1 oz. (¼ cup) grated Parmesan cheese; 1 egg yolk and water to bind. *For the filling:* 2 large onions; little water; seasoning; 1 level tablespoon cornstarch; ⅔ cup milk; 2 eggs; 2 tablespoons cream; ¼ lb. (1 cup) grated Cheddar or Gruyère cheese.

Sift the flour and seasonings together. Cut in the fat, add the cheese then bind with the egg yolk and water. Roll out and line an 8-inch pan or flan ring or dish. Bake blind in a

Making a Pizza Pie

The famous Italian Pizza Pie has a yeast base but can be made with a baking powder dough. It is also possible to fill a short crust pastry flan with the savory mixture.

Blue Print Recipe

Pizza Pie

For the base: 3 cups flour · pinch salt · 1 tablespoon olive oil · scant $\frac{1}{2}$ oz. fresh or $\frac{1}{4}$ oz. (1 teaspoon) dried yeast · scant $\frac{2}{3}$ cup water. For the topping: 2 large onions · 1–2 cloves garlic · 1 tablespoon olive oil · $1\frac{1}{2}$ lb. (about 5 small) tomatoes · 1–2 tablespoons tomato paste · seasoning · $\frac{1}{4}$ teaspoon dried or 1 teaspoon fresh chopped oregano or marjoram · 4–6 oz. Mozzarella cheese · few anchovy fillets · few black olives · sprinkling grated Parmesan cheese.

To make Sift the flour and salt into a mixing bowl. Make a well in the center and add the oil. Cream the fresh yeast and add the tepid water, or sprinkle the dried yeast over the water. Pour the yeast liquid over the oil. Sprinkle flour over the yeast liquid. Cover the bowl with a cloth and leave in a warm place for about 15–20 minutes until the yeast liquid bubbles. Blend all the ingredients together and knead until smooth. Return to the bowl and cover. Leave in a warm place for about $1\frac{1}{2}$ hours until the dough has doubled its bulk. Knead again. Roll out to a 9–10-inch round then put onto a warmed greased baking sheet. While yeast dough is rising for the first time, prepare the topping.

Peel and chop the onions and garlic. Toss in the hot oil, then add the peeled, chopped tomatoes, the paste and seasoning. Simmer until the mixture is thick in an uncovered pan. Stir in the oregano or marjoram. Spread the tomato mixture over the yeast round. Top with the sliced Mozzarella cheese, the anchovy fillets, olives and a sprinkling of Parmesan. Allow to rise for about 20 minutes (although this stage is not essential).
To cook Bake in the center of a hot oven, 425–450°F, for about 15–20 minutes. If the yeast mixture is not quite cooked, then put a piece of foil over the topping to protect it, lower the heat to very moderate and leave a little longer.
To serve Hot or cold. *All recipes based on this serve 5–6 or up to 8 as an hors d'oeuvre.*

Speedy Pizza

Ingredients as Blue Print, but OMIT the yeast. Use 1 tablespoon baking powder. Blend the oil and water (or you can use milk) with the sifted flour, baking powder and salt. Knead lightly, roll into a round, add the topping and proceed as the Blue Print recipe.

Seafood Pizza

Ingredients as Blue Print PLUS about $\frac{1}{4}$ lb. (1 cup) shelled shrimp and use a whole can of anchovy fillets. Prepare as the Blue Print but add the shrimp and most of the anchovy fillets to the *cooked* tomato mixture. Proceed as Blue Print.

Anchovy and Onions Pizza

Ingredients for base as Blue Print, but OMIT the tomatoes and tomato paste from the topping and use double the amount of onions and garlic and a whole can of anchovy fillets. Cook the onion and garlic as the Blue Print, add the seasoning and herbs and spread over the dough. Continue as Blue Print.

Pizza Flan

Another way of serving the delicious pizza topping is as follows.
Make a really deep 8–9-inch flan with short crust pastry using 2 cups flour etc. Bake blind until crisp and just golden; *do not overcook*. Prepare the filling as the Blue Print. Spoon the hot tomato filling into the hot flan, top with the cheese, anchovies and olives as Blue Print. Return to the oven for a few minutes to melt the cheese.

Crisp Topped Pizza Flan

Make and fill the flan as above. Bring out of the oven when the cheese has almost melted and top with a layer of soft bread crumbs and grated Gruyère or Cheddar cheese. Either return to the oven to crisp the crumbs, or protect the pastry with foil and crisp under a moderate broiler.

Storing and freezing *The dough and filling should be stored separately in the refrigerator before baking. The unrisen dough keeps for 12 hours and rises very slowly in the refrigerator. Allow to stand at room temperature for about an hour before topping and baking. You can freeze the uncooked or cooked pizza. Allow to thaw out before cooking, but reheat from the frozen state if wished.*
To use leftovers *Heat gently so you do not dry the topping.*

---

moderately hot oven, 400°F, until quite cooked. Meanwhile cook the neatly sliced onions in just enough water to cover. Season, cover the pan tightly so the liquid does not evaporate. When the onions are cooked, blend the cornstarch with the milk, add to the onions and liquid and cook steadily until thickened. Remove the pan from the heat. Blend the beaten eggs with the cream, stir into the onion mixture and cook *without boiling* for about 3 minutes. Add the cheese and heat until melted. *If serving the flan hot:* put the hot filling into the hot pastry and serve as soon as possible. *If serving the flan cold:* allow the filling and pastry to cool then put the filling into the flan shell. *Serves 4–5.*

Storing and freezing *The uncooked pastry may either be stored overnight or for 1–2 days in a refrigerator or for some weeks in a freezer. The cooked Quiche keeps 2–3 days in a refrigerator or for some time in a freezer. The higher the proportion of cream used in the filling, the better the flan will freeze. Allow to defrost at room temperature.*

Quiche Lorraine (left)
Seafood Pizza (above)
Pizza (right)

Making Flaky Pastry

Flaky pastry has a light texture, should rise well, and is easier and quicker to make than puff pastry.

Blue Print Recipe

Flaky Pastry

2 cups flour · pinch salt · $\frac{3}{4}$ cup butter or other fat* · water to mix (as cold as possible).
*A favorite combination is half margarine and half lard.

To make Sift the flour and salt into a mixing bowl. Cut in one third of the fat. Add enough water to make an elastic dough. Roll out to an oblong on a lightly floured board. Divide the remaining fat in half; if hard soften by pressing with a knife, Sketch 1. Dot the top two thirds of the pastry with small pieces of fat, Sketch 2. Bring up the bottom third of the pastry dough and fold like an envelope, Sketch 3. Bring down the top third, Sketch 4.

Turn the pastry at right angles, seal the ends of the pastry then dent this at regular intervals with a lightly floured rolling pin—this is called "ribbing" the pastry, Sketch 5. Roll the dough out into an oblong shape again. *If you find it feels sticky and is difficult to roll then refrigerate for about 30 minutes. Repeat the process covered above and by Sketches 1–5. Refrigerate for another 30 minutes, or longer if wished. Roll out to the required shape.*

To cook As the individual recipe, but flaky pastry needs a hot to very hot oven to encourage the pastry to rise and to prevent it from being greasy.
To serve Hot or cold.

● **AVOID** *Overhandling the pastry both when cutting the small amount of fat into the flour and when folding. Pressing too firmly when you roll out the dough. Allowing the pastry to become warm and sticky.*

● **TO RECTIFY** *Cut the fat into the flour carefully as for short crust pastry, (see page 80). Lift the dough as gently as you can when folding. Use short sharp movements when rolling out the pastry. Put the pastry away in the refrigerator from time to time.*

● **SHORT CUT** *Although given a different name, i.e. rough puff pastry, this has the same proportions of fat to flour as flaky pastry and so can be considered a good alternative. The number of rollings and foldings for rough puff pastry is greater than when making flaky pastry, but the method of incorporating the fat is much quicker.*

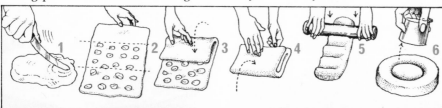

Chicken vol-au-vents

Rough Puff Pastry

Ingredients as the Blue Print.
Sift the flour and salt into a bowl. Drop in the fat; cut this into tiny pieces with 2 knives. Mix with water to an elastic dough. Roll out to an oblong as flaky pastry above, fold, as Sketches 3 and 4. Turn, seal the ends and rib as Sketch 5. Continue as flaky pastry but allow a total of 5 rollings and 5 foldings. Use as flaky pastry.

For Special Occasions

Vol-au-Vent Shells

Choose flaky pastry as the Blue Print, rough puff pastry, as above, or puff pastry (see page 86).
Roll out the pastry until about $\frac{1}{2}$-inch in thickness for fairly shallow shells or up to 1-inch for deep ones. Cut into required shape, or shapes, i.e. either 1 large round or square or a number of smaller shapes. Take a smaller cutter and press into the pastry as Sketch 6; let this cutter mark the pastry about half-way through. It will form the lid. Bake a large vol-au-vent shell in the center of a hot to very hot oven 450–475°F, for about 25–30 minutes, reduce the heat to very moderate, 325–350°F, after about 15 minutes. Small shell take from about 10 minutes (for cocktail size) to 15–20 minutes for the size shown on this page. There should be no necessity to lower the heat. Remove the pastry shell or shells from the oven. Lift out the pastry lid very carefully. If you find there is a little uncooked mixture in the center, return the shells to a very moderate oven until this is cooked.

If serving the vol-au-vent shells cold, then put the *cold* filling into the cold pastry. Place the lids in position, if wished. If serving hot, make quite sure both pastry and filling are very hot. Put together and serve at once.

Flaky or rough puff pastry made with 2 cups flour etc. as the Blue Print will give 1 large vol-au-vent to serve about 6 people, 6–8 medium-sized shells or about 12–14 tiny cocktail ones. Puff pastry made with 2 cups flour etc. produces rather more vol-au-vent shells.

Using Flaky Pastry

Although an excellent steak and kidney pie can be made with short crust pastry, I always feel the lighter texture of flaky pastry blends rather better with the meat filling.

For Family Occasions

Steak and Kidney Pie

For the filling: $1\frac{1}{4}$–$1\frac{1}{2}$ lb. round steak; about $\frac{1}{2}$ lb. beef kidney; scant $\frac{1}{4}$ cup flour; seasoning; 2–4 tablespoons fat; 2 cups stock or water and 1 beef bouillon cube. *For the flaky pastry:* $1\frac{1}{2}$ cups flour; pinch salt; $\frac{1}{2}$ cup plus 1 tablespoon butter or other fat (see Blue Print opposite); water to mix. *To glaze:* 1 egg plus 1 tablespoon water or a little milk.

Cut steak and kidney into neat pieces. Blend the flour and seasoning. Roll the meat in the seasoned flour then sauté gently in the hot fat. Use the higher amount of fat if the meat is exceptionally lean. Blend the stock into the mixture gradually. Bring to the boil and cook until thickened. Cover the pan *very* tightly and allow the meat to cook over a low heat until almost tender, 2–$2\frac{1}{4}$ hours. Make sure the liquid does not evaporate too much; add a little more stock if the gravy becomes too thick. Make the flaky pastry as the Blue Print opposite while the meat is cooking. Spoon the meat into a 5–6 cup baking dish, allow to cool, then cover with the pastry. Flake the edges with a knife to encourage the pastry to rise. Make a slit in the pastry so the steam escapes during baking and arrange pastry leaves, made from the trimmings, on top. Beat the egg (or use just the yolk) with the water. Brush over the pastry to give a shine when baked. Milk can be used in place of egg, but is not so effective. Place the pie dish on aluminum foil or baking sheet; this is a precaution in case any liquid bubbles over.* Bake in the center of a hot to very hot oven, 450–475°F, for 15–20 minutes. Reset the heat to moderate, 350–375°F, and continue cooking for a further 30–35 minutes until the pastry is brown and firm and the meat very hot. *Serves 6.*

*If you like a generous amount of gravy, then put a little into the pie with the meat and heat the rest to serve separately.

To vary   Add sliced onions or other vegetables to the steak and kidney.
Use a little red wine in the gravy in place of all stock.

Chicken Pie

Use raw chicken parts and diced vegetables in place of steak and kidney or a mixture of raw chicken and diced bacon.

Steak and kidney pie

Fillings for Vol-au-Vents

Savory   Blend diced cooked chicken, ham, cooked vegetables, flaked cooked fish or shellfish with a moderately thick sauce or with thick mayonnaise. The picture opposite shows chicken vol-au-vents.

Sweet   Fill with jam, lemon curd or well drained fruit.

Using Trimmings of Pastry

Often there are trimmings of pastry left which can be used for unusual savory or sweet tidbits which can be served either as cocktail snacks or with tea or coffee.
The baking temperature will be as the particular pastry, which is covered in the Blue Print on the various pages.

Sardine cigars   Mash sardines, season and flavor with lemon juice. Roll out narrow strips of pastry, put the fish mixture in the center, fold as sausage rolls (page 86) and bake for about 12 minutes in a hot to very hot oven, 450–475°F.

Jam fingers   Roll out the pastry to a square or rectangle; spread half with jam. Fold the unspread pastry over the top, brush with a very little water and sprinkle lightly with superfine sugar. Bake for about 15 minutes in the center of a hot to very hot oven, 450–475°F. Cut into fingers while warm. Mincemeat, honey and chopped nuts, chocolate spread and banana mashed with lemon juice and a little sugar, all make interesting sweet fillings. Use grated cheese and chopped dates or raisins for a savory filling.

Nut crisps   Roll out the pastry very thinly. Top with chopped nuts (fresh or salted peanuts, blanched almonds, walnuts, hazelnuts, brazilnuts or pecans) and bake until crisp.

Storing and freezing   *Uncooked flaky pastry keeps well for several days in a refrigerator. Wrap in foil or moisture-proof wrap to prevent the outside hardening. It freezes very well. Cooked flaky pastry keeps for several days but needs to be crisped for a short time in the oven. It freezes well, but naturally the success depends upon the filling. A steak and kidney pie is excellent.*
It is better to freeze the uncooked or cooked vol-au-vent cases without the filling and freeze the fillings separately. You cannot freeze fillings containing mayonnaise, and sauces are better if made with cornstarch rather than flour.

Puff is the richest of all pastries, yet, in spite of the high percentage of fat, it should not be greasy. The two important factors when making and cooking puff pastry are:

1 The way you roll the dough. Do not skimp on the number of rollings, for this blends the fat into the flour and incorporates air at the same time. You should see the bubbles of air forming in the dough as you roll. Read the comments about using the rolling pin in the same direction on page 80 and on handling flaky pastry on page 84. These are even more important when making puff pastry.

2 The baking temperature. Do not be afraid of using a very hot oven to encourage the pastry to rise and to seal in the fat. Reduce the heat as directed in the recipes to prevent overbrowning.

Blue Print Recipe

Puff Pastry

2 cups flour · pinch salt · water to mix (as cold as possible) · 1 cup butter.*
*Preferably unsalted. Other fats could be substituted. Soften slightly with a knife if very hard, see Sketch 1, page 84.

To make Sift the flour and salt into a mixing bowl. Gradually add enough water to make an elastic dough. Roll out to an oblong shape on a lightly floured board. Place the butter in the center of the pastry dough, Sketch 1. Fold the bottom part of the dough over the butter, Sketch 2; bring down the top part, Sketch 3. Turn, seal the ends and rib the pastry as described under flaky pastry (page 84). Continue rolling and folding as flaky pastry but allow a total of 7 rollings and 7 foldings. Puff pastry must be kept cool, so refrigerate between rollings.

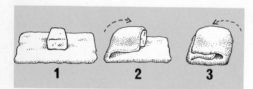

To cook As individual recipes, but puff pastry needs a very hot oven at the beginning of the cooking period. This enables it to rise well and prevents if from being greasy. It is suggested sometimes that puff pastry be cooked on damp baking sheets, but I have never found this necessary.

To serve Hot or cold. With sweet or savory ingredients.

- **AVOID** *Overhandling the pastry—see the comments on page 84.*
- **TO RECTIFY** *See page 84.*
- **SHORT CUT** *Frozen puff pastry is one of the most successful convenience foods. Remember though that when a recipe says puff pastry made with 8 oz. (2C) flour etc., or 8 oz. puff pastry you need to buy 1 lb. frozen pastry.*

Puff Pastry

The following recipes all use puff pastry. Several are equally successful with flaky or rough puff. An indication is given where the less rich pastries could be substituted.

Vanilla Slices (Mille Feuilles)

Puff pastry made with 2 cups flour etc. as Blue Print. *For the filling:* $1\frac{1}{3}$ cups heavy cream; sugar to taste; few drops vanilla extract; jam or jelly; little sifted confectioners' sugar (optional).
Roll the pastry out until water thin. Cut into about 15 or 18 fingers. Put on to cookie sheets; refrigerate for about 30 minutes; this makes sure they keep a good shape. Bake just above the center of a very hot oven, 475°F. Bake for approximately 10 minutes at this high temperature until well risen and golden, then lower the heat to very moderate, 325–350°F, or switch the oven off for about 5 minutes. Allow to cool, then trim the edges with a very sharp knife. Whip the cream, add a little sugar and vanilla extract. Spread one third of the slices with the cream, top with another slice, then the jam or jelly and a final pastry slice. Dust with sifted confectioners' sugar. (Illustrated opposite) *Makes 5 or 6.*
Note Flaky or rough puff are not as good in this recipe as puff pastry.

Napoleons

These are the same as Vanilla Slices above, except that both layers are filled with either whipped cream or Vanilla Cream (page 92) and the top slice covered with glacé icing (page 92). When the icing has dried, pipe thin lines of semi-sweet chocolate melted with a little water across the width of the slices. Run the point of a knife down the length of the slices twice, giving the chocolate a broken line.
To vary The three layers of pastry give a tall and very impressive portion, but two layers of pastry are often used, in which case spread the bottom layer of pastry with jam and then with cream and top with the second layer of pastry.

Maids of Honour

Puff, flaky or rough puff pastry made with $1\frac{1}{2}$ cups flour etc. (see above and page 84).

For the filling: little jam; $\frac{3}{4}$ cup cottage cheese; scant $\frac{1}{3}$ cup white raisins; $\frac{1}{2}$ teaspoon almond extract; 2 tablespoons ground or finely chopped almonds; 2 eggs. *For the topping:* scant cup confectioners' sugar; little water; few drops almond extract.
Roll out the pastry until wafer thin. Cut into 12–15 rounds, to fit into fairly deep patty pans about 3-inches in diameter. When gathering up the leftovers, lay these carefully one over the other and reroll to use for some of the rounds. Do not squeeze into a ball, as this spoils the pastry. Put a teaspoon of jam into each pastry shell. Sieve the cheese, add the other ingredients for the filling and beat well until a smooth mixture. Spoon into the pastry shells and bake for 10 minutes in the center of a hot to very hot oven, 450–475°F. Lower the heat to moderate, 350–375°F, and cook for a further 15 minutes, or until both pastry and filling are set. Allow to cool. Blend the confectioners' sugar with enough water to make a flowing consistency. Add a few drops of almond extract. Spoon a little into the center of each tartlet and leave to set. *Makes 12–15.*

Traditional Maids of Honour

Blend 1 cup ground or finely chopped blanched almonds with $\frac{1}{4}$ cup superfine sugar, the yolks of 2 small eggs and the white of 1 egg. Add 4 tablespoons flour or fine cake crumbs, then a teaspoon orange flower water or orange or lemon juice and a very little finely grated lemon rind. Use this filling in place of that given above. Do not ice.

Sausage Rolls

Puff, flaky or rough puff pastry made with 2 cups flour etc.* (see above and page 84); $\frac{1}{2}-\frac{3}{4}$ lb. sausage meat. To glaze: 1 egg plus 1 tablespoon water.
*this gives a very thin layer of pastry only.
Roll out the pastry and cut into strips; these should be sufficiently wide to cover the sausage meat. The pastry must be very thin if using the larger quantity of sausage meat. Form the sausage meat into long rolls. Lay on the pastry strips. Moisten the edges of the pastry and fold over the sausage meat. Press the edges together and flake these with the knife. Cut into the required lengths and make several slits on top if wished. Brush with the egg mixed with the water. Put on to baking sheets and bake in the center of a hot to very hot oven, 450–475°F, for 10–15 minutes, then lower the heat to moderate, 350–375°F, and cook for another 5–10 minutes, depending upon the size of the sausage rolls. Serve hot or cold. *Makes 8 large, 12 medium-sized or about 18 tiny rolls.*
Storing and freezing *See the comments on page 85 about uncooked pastry.*
Vanilla Slices freeze extremely well, but they should be served as soon as they have been defrosted at room temperature; otherwise the pastry becomes very soft.
Maids of Honour, Sausage Rolls etc., all freeze extremely well.

Maids of honour (left)   Vanilla slice (right)

An egg is an invaluable ingredient in many sauces. It adds flavor, food value and is either the sole thickening agent or helps the flour or cornstarch to thicken the mixture. Although Zabaglione is really a complete dessert rather than just a sauce, I have given it on this page, for the principles of making this frothy egg mixture are the same as the Blue Print recipe.

● **AVOID** *Having the water under the mixture too hot; this is essential, otherwise the eggs could set or curdle instead of being light and fluffy. Leaving the eggs without whisking; they could become hard around the sides of the cooking utensil.*

● **TO RECTIFY** *If the water begins to boil, remove from the heat and add a little cold water.*

● **SHORT CUT** *Soften the butter for the sauce; this means it is incorporated more readily.*

● **TO REDUCERS** *Although no sauce will help you reduce, the simple egg-thickened sauces are less fattening than those with a high percentage of flour.*

Hollandaise sauce
with asparagus

Blue Print Recipe

Hollandaise Sauce

3 egg yolks · salt · pepper · cayenne pepper · 2 tablespoons lemon juice* · 6 tablespoons butter.
*Or use white wine vinegar.

To make Put the egg yolks, seasoning and lemon juice into a bowl over a pan of hot water or into the top of a double boiler. Make sure the bowl or alternative utensil is sufficiently large to be able to beat well; a very narrow container hampers movement.
To cook Beat with a hand or electric beater or whisk until the mixture is light and fluffy. If using an electric beater, check that the egg mixture really is thickening well. To do this remove from the heat, if the eggs remain thick all is well. Sometimes one can beat so vigorously that the mixture *appears* to thicken, then flops as it has just been aerated, *not* cooked as it should be. When the eggs are thick, add a small piece of butter, beat hard until well blended. Continue like this until

all the butter is incorporated.
To serve Hot or cold over vegetables or with fish. This is an excellent sauce for cauliflower or broccoli. *All recipes based on this serve 6–7.*

Rich Hollandaise Sauce

Ingredients as Blue Print recipe PLUS extra 6 tablespoons butter. Method as the Blue Print but use the larger amount of butter.

Fluffy Hollandaise

Ingredients as Blue Print PLUS ½ teaspoon *prepared* English or Dijon mustard and ½–1 teaspoon sugar. Method as Blue Print. Add the mustard and sugar with the other seasoning. Allow the sauce to cool, then fold 3–4 tablespoons whipped cream into the egg mixture. Taste the sauce then add extra seasoning and lemon juice if required.

To give a more pronounced flavor, add the finely grated rind of 1 lemon to the egg yolks.

Tartar Sauce

Ingredients as Blue Print PLUS 1–2 teaspoons capers, 2–3 teaspoons chopped parsley and

2–3 teaspoons chopped gherkins (or use freshly chopped cucumber).
Make as the Blue Print recipe, then add the ingredients above. This is delicious with any fish.

Zabaglione

3 egg yolks; 4–6 tablespoons superfine sugar; 4–5 tablespoons Marsala.
Put the egg yolks and sugar into the container; beat as the Blue Print. When the mixture is thick, gradually beat in the Marsala. Serve warm by itself as a dessert or over fruit. *Serves 2.*
To vary
Orange Zabaglione Add the finely grated rind of 1–2 oranges to the egg yolks and flavor with 1 tablespoon curaçao and 2 tablespoons orange juice in place of the Marsala.

Storing and freezing *Although Hollandaise sauce can be stored for up to 24 hours, it does lose some of its light texture. It can however be frozen very successfully, but use as soon as possible after defrosting. Zabaglione is nicer served freshly made.*

There is a great sense of achievement in producing a perfect cake, homemade bread or a selection of cookies.

To ensure a perfectly baked product, the ingredients must be at room temperature and measured properly. Flour (all purpose unless otherwise stated) should be measured by scooping and leveling with a straight spatula. Use cream of tartar baking powder unless otherwise specified. Use large eggs and separate on removal from refrigerator; beat only after they have reached room temperature. The butter cakes which appear on pages 95 to 99 use butter (for which there is no flavor substitute) and the hand-mixing method, although they may also be mixed in an electric mixer following the same steps. The success of these cakes depends upon well-creamed butter and sugar. Unsalted butter is preferable to salted. Whole eggs may be added instead of separating the eggs, but the end product will not be as light. If using an electric mixer, add the flour at low speed or, better still, fold it in by hand.

If you wish to use the one-bowl method, choose quick creaming margarine or vegetable shortening. Put *all* the ingredients into a large mixing bowl. If creaming by hand, use a wooden spoon and beat gently for about $\frac{1}{2}$ minute so the

ingredients do not fly out of the bowl. When blended, increase the beating action and beat for 200 strokes. If using an electric mixer, set it to the lowest speed until the ingredients are just blended, then use medium speed for 2 minutes. To compensate for the very short creaming period, add 1 extra teaspoon of baking powder for each cup of flour.

The sponges and angel food cakes on page 100 depend for their leavening on the air beaten into them. The electric mixer is a boon for this prolonged operation.

It is important to bake the cake, loaf or cookies correctly and in the right size pan. When baking cookies, it is good to use at least two baking sheets as they must be

cool before the dough is put on them. It is essential to appreciate that individual ovens vary a great deal and that suggested temperatures in recipes can be based on the average oven only.

Baking too quickly will set the outside of a cake in too short a period, make it over-brown and prevent the heat penetrating to the center, so you may well have an overcooked cake or loaf on the outside and a nearly raw mixture in the center.

Baking too slowly can prevent a cake or loaf from rising properly and gives a heavy texture.

Take care when turning cakes out of the pans. Many a perfect cake is spoiled by a little part breaking away as it is turned out; this could probably be avoided. Allow all cakes to stand for 5–10 minutes, no longer, in the pan before turning out; this allows the mixture to contract slightly. Certain cakes and cookies should be cooled completely before being handled and this information is given in the recipes.

Perhaps you have never made your own bread; please try it once in a while as the Blue Print on page 107 gives very detailed instructions.

Baking is a very enjoyable form of cooking and I am sure your friends and family will enjoy the results.

On these two pages are some cookies for the youngsters – their favorites to eat and favorites to bake. They should become family favorites as well.

Ginger Drop Cookies

$\frac{1}{4}$ cup butter, margarine or shortening · $\frac{1}{2}$ cup sugar · $\frac{3}{8}$ cup molasses · 1 egg · $\frac{1}{2}$ cup buttermilk · $1\frac{1}{2}$ cups flour · 1 teaspoon baking soda · $\frac{1}{4}$ teaspoon salt · 1 teaspoon ginger · $\frac{1}{2}$ teaspoon cinnamon.

Cream the butter, margarine or shortening until fluffy; cream in the sugar a little at a time. Mix in the molasses, then the well beaten egg, and half the milk. Sift the flour, soda, salt and spices into the molasses mixture and mix well. Add the rest of the milk. Drop by teaspoonfuls on to a greased baking sheet, leaving about 2 inches between each. Cook in a moderate oven, 350°F for 13–15 minutes.
Makes about 42 cookies.

Fruit Cookies

$\frac{1}{2}$ cup butter, margarine or shortening; 1 cup brown sugar; 1 egg; $\frac{1}{2}$ teaspoon salt; $\frac{1}{2}$ teaspoon soda; $\frac{1}{4}$ cup buttermilk; $\frac{1}{2}-\frac{3}{4}$ cup pecans; $\frac{1}{2}-\frac{3}{4}$ cup glacé cherries; $\frac{1}{2}-\frac{3}{4}$ cup dates.
Cream the butter, margarine or shortening until fluffy. Cream in the sugar a little at a time. Add the well beaten egg. Sift the flour, salt and soda, alternating with the buttermilk, into the butter mixture, mixing well after each addition. Mix in the chopped nuts, cherries and dates. Drop by teaspoonfuls onto a well greased baking sheet (a nut may be placed on top of each cookie if liked). Bake in a moderately hot oven, 400°F for 10–13 minutes. *Makes about 30.*

Hermits

$\frac{1}{3}$ cup butter, margarine or shortening; $\frac{2}{3}$ cup sugar; 1 egg; $\frac{1}{4}$ cup milk; $1\frac{3}{4}$ cups flour; 2 teaspoons baking powder; $\frac{1}{4}$ teaspoon nutmeg; $\frac{1}{2}$ teaspoon cinnamon; $\frac{1}{4}$ teaspoon cloves; $\frac{1}{4}$ teaspoon mace; $\frac{1}{3}$ cup raisins.
Cream the butter until fluffy. Cream in the sugar a little at a time. When very smooth add the well beaten egg, then the milk. Sift the flour, baking powder and spices into the butter mixture and mix well. Drop by the teaspoonful onto a greased baking sheet and cook in a moderate oven 350°F for 13–15 minutes or until slightly brown. *Makes about 24 cookies.*

Oatmeal Cookies

$\frac{1}{4}$ cup butter, margarine or shortening; $\frac{1}{2}$ cup sugar; 1 egg; $\frac{1}{2}$ cup raisins; $\frac{1}{2}$ cup buttermilk; $\frac{1}{2}$ teaspoon baking soda; 1 cup rolled oats; 1 cup flour; $\frac{1}{2}$ tablespoon cinnamon; 1 tablespoon molasses.
Cream the butter, margarine or shortening until fluffy. Cream in the sugar a little at a time. Add the well beaten eggs, raisins and buttermilk. Sift the soda, oats, flour and cinnamon into the butter mixture; mix well, then add the molasses. Drop by teaspoonfuls onto a greased baking sheet. Bake in a moderate oven, 350–375°F, for 15–20 minutes. *Make 25–30.*

Brownies

2 oz. bitter chocolate; $1\frac{1}{2}$ cups brown sugar; 2 eggs; $\frac{1}{2}$ cup flour; $\frac{1}{2}$ teaspoon vanilla; $\frac{1}{4}$ cup chopped walnuts.

Melt the chocolate over hot water. Add the brown sugar to the slightly beaten eggs, then stir until no lumps remain. Sift in the flour; mix well. Add the melted chocolate, vanilla and walnuts. Spread evenly in a greased 8-inch square pan. Cook in a moderate oven, 350°F, for 15–20 minutes. Cut in squares immediately after taking from the oven and remove from the pan to a rack to cool. *Makes 16 squares.*

Christmas Bars

$\frac{3}{4}$ cup honey; 1 cup brown sugar; 3 eggs; $2\frac{1}{2}$ cups flour; 1 teaspoon cinnamon; $\frac{1}{4}$ teaspoon mace or nutmeg; $\frac{1}{4}$ teaspoon allspice; $\frac{1}{2}$ teaspoon cloves; $\frac{1}{4}$ teaspoon salt; 2 teaspoons baking powder; 1 tablespoon melted butter; 1 cup chopped walnuts.

Mix the honey and sugar until smooth, then add the well beaten eggs. Sift the dry ingredients into the honey mixture, mixing, then add the walnuts. Spread evenly in 3 well greased 8-inch square pans; cook in moderate oven, 350–375°F, for 25–30 minutes. Cut in squares immediately after taking from oven and remove from pan to a rack to cool. *Makes 4 dozen squares.*

To store Place in an airtight tin box with an apple and keep several weeks before using.

Date Nut Bars

3 egg yolks; 1 cup sugar; 1 lb. dates; $\frac{1}{4}$ lb. shelled walnuts; 1 cup flour; 1 teaspoon baking powder; $\frac{1}{8}$ teaspoon salt; 3 egg whites. Beat egg yolks until thick and lemon colored. Add sugar and mix until quite creamy. Sift the flour, baking powder and salt onto the cut dates and chopped nuts, mixing well

Refrigerator nut cookies in preparation and ginger drop cookies

until the dates are covered with flour. Add to the egg mixture. Fold in the stiffly beaten egg whites. Spread evenly in a well greased 9-inch square pan. Cook in a moderate oven, 350–375°F, for 25–30 minutes. Remove from pan, cut in bars then roll in confectioners' sugar.

Gingerbread Boys

1 cup molasses; $\frac{1}{2}$ cup butter, margarine or shortening; 3 cups flour; $\frac{1}{2}$ teaspoon soda; 1 tablespoon ginger; $1\frac{1}{2}$ teaspoons salt.
Heat molasses in a bowl over hot water; cool slightly. Add butter, margarine or shortening. Sift the flour, soda, ginger and salt together and add to the molasses; mix well. Shape into gingerbread boys or other figures on greased baking sheets. Bake in moderate oven, 350–375°F, for 25 minutes or until firm to the touch. *Makes 6 medium cookies.*

Blue Print Recipe

Vanilla Refrigerator Cookies

$\frac{1}{2}$ cup butter · $\frac{1}{2}$ cup confectioners' sugar · 1 teaspoon vanilla extract · $1\frac{1}{2}$ cups flour · 3 tablespoons cream.
To make   Cream the butter with the sugar. Add the vanilla and sift in the flour, add the cream and mix well. Shape the dough into 2 rolls 6 inches long and wrap in waxed paper. Chill at least 4 hours.
To cook   Cut roll into thin slices and place on an ungreased baking sheet, 1 inch apart. Bake in a 400°F oven for about 8–10 minutes or until lightly brown. Remove from baking sheet immediately. *Makes about 36.*

Nut Cookies

Ingredients as in Blue Print but roll the shaped dough in $\frac{1}{2}$ cup finely chopped walnuts, almonds, or pecans before chilling.

Pinwheel Cookies

Ingredients as Blue Print but when the dough is mixed divide it in two equal portions and add 1 oz. melted chocolate to one portion. Chill for 1 hour. On a floured surface roll white dough into a thin rectangle, approximately 7 × 11 inches. Roll the chocolate dough to the same size and place on top. Roll firmly together like a jelly roll. Wrap, chill and cook as Blue Print.

Marble Cookies

Ingredients as Blue Print but follow instructions for Pinwheel Cookies (above). When the two doughs have been rolled, fold in half and press together to marble. Proceed as Blue Print.

Lemon or Orange Cookies

Ingredients as Blue Print PLUS 1 teaspoon grated lemon or orange rind, working it into the dough. A few drops of food coloring may be added if liked. Cook as Blue Print.

The points listed below apply to all the rolled cookies on this and the next page.

● **AVOID** *Making the cookie dough too soft and sticky by adding excess liquid. You cannot overhandle most cookie doughs; the more you knead the better the texture and if the dough seems too dry, knead very well before adding extra liquid. You will probably find that handling produces the right texture. Baking too quickly; most cookie doughs need steady baking.*
● **TO RECTIFY** *If you have made a somewhat soft cookie dough, chill for several hours and then try to handle it. If the cookies seem to be baking too rapidly, lower the oven temperature immediately.*
● **SHORT CUTS** *Use quick creaming margarine or shortening which save time in blending.*

Blue Print Recipe

Orange Cookies

2 cups flour · $\frac{1}{2}$ cup plus 2 tablespoons margarine or butter · $\frac{1}{2}$–$\frac{3}{4}$ cup superfine sugar · very finely grated rind of 1 or 2 oranges.

To make   Put the flour into a mixing bowl. Lightly rub in the margarine or butter with the fingertips until like fine bread crumbs. Add half the sugar and orange rind. Knead

Hermits

firmly and work in the rest of the sugar. This dough should need *no* liquid but if necessary add a *few* drops orange juice.
Put the dough onto a very lightly floured pastry board. Roll out very firmly until about $\frac{1}{8}$-inch in thickness. Cut into rounds about 2–$2\frac{1}{2}$-inches in diameter. Put onto ungreased baking sheets. These cookies should not spread. Prick lightly with a fork.
To cook   Put as near the center of the oven as possible and bake for about 10–12 minutes in a very moderate oven 325–350°F Cool on the baking sheets.
To serve   With tea or coffee or as an accompaniment to ice cream. *Makes 14–18.*

Orange Laurel Rings

Ingredients as Blue Print PLUS angelica and a little sieved jam or marmalade (optional).
Prepare the dough as the Blue Print but cut into rings instead of rounds. Bake as the Blue Print. Decorate with pieces of angelica brushed first with a little jam or marmalade to make sure they stick onto the cookie. *Makes 18–20.*

Orange Cream Cookies

Ingredients as Blue Print PLUS 4 tablespoons butter, scant 1 cup sifted confectioners' sugar and finely grated rind of 1 orange.
Make the dough as the Blue Print. Roll out and cut an equal number of rounds and rings (the size to fit on top). Bake as the Blue Print, allow to cool. Do not decorate until the day you intend to serve these as the butter icing can soften the cookies. Cream the butter, nearly all the confectioners' sugar and grated orange rind together. Spread the rounds with a thin layer of the butter icing. Place the rings on top, dust with the remaining confectioners' sugar. Use the remaining butter cream to pipe rosettes into the center hole. *Makes 8–9.*

Currant crisps

Sugar Rings

Ingredients as Blue Print but MINUS grated orange rind and PLUS 1 egg white, $\frac{1}{4}$ cup superfine sugar and few drops vanilla extract.

Make up the dough as the Blue Print but cut into rings. Bake as the Blue Print for about 8–9 minutes until well set and nearly cooked. Remove from the oven. Beat the egg white until it begins to hold its shape. It must not be as stiff as a meringue. Fold in nearly all the sugar and the vanilla extract and spread over the nearly cooked cookies. Dredge with the remaining sugar. Return to the oven, but lower the heat to very cool,

250–275°F, and leave for about 40 minutes until the topping is very crisp but still white. *Makes 18–20.*

Currant Crisps

$\frac{1}{4}$ lb. butter, margarine or shortening; $\frac{1}{2}$ cup superfine sugar; 1 egg yolk; generous $\frac{1}{2}$ cup currants; 2 cups flour.

Cream the butter, margarine or shortening and sugar until soft and light. Add the egg yolk and beat again. Stir in the currants and flour. Knead well, then roll out until about $\frac{1}{8}-\frac{1}{4}$-inch thick. If using quick creaming margarine or shortening, put all the ingredients listed in the above recipe into a bowl. Beat for about 2 minutes then knead well, roll out and cut into shapes. Put onto lightly greased baking sheets. Bake for 10–12 minutes in, or near, the center of a very moderate oven, 325–350°F. Cool on the baking sheets. *Makes 20–24.*

To vary Add a little mixed spice to the flour. Use chopped glacé cherries.

Zebra Cookies

Ingredients as Currant Crisps above MINUS the currants and PLUS $\frac{3}{4}$–1 teaspoon instant coffee, little water and 2–3 oz. semisweet chocolate.

Cream the fat with the sugar. Blend the coffee with the egg yolk, mix well then beat into the creamed fat and sugar. Add the flour and

a few drops of water, if necessary. Roll out and bake as Currant Crisps; but there is no need to grease the baking sheets. Allow to cool. Do not ice until the day you serve.

Melt the chocolate in a bowl over hot, but not boiling, water. Put into a grease-proof bag with a small hole at the base or use a fine writing tube. Pipe lines of chocolate across the biscuits. *Makes 20–24.*

Chocolate Shortbreads

Ingredients as Currant Crisps above MINUS the currants and PLUS 3 tablespoons fat, 2–3 oz. semisweet chocolate and 1 teaspoon baking powder.

Cream the fat with the sugar, using the larger quantity of fat, but roll the mixture into about 15–16 balls. Put on the baking sheets allowing room to spread. Bake as the Currant Crisps but allow about 15 minutes. Leave to cool. Melt the chocolate in a bowl over hot, but not boiling, water. Spread the chocolate over the cookies placed on a wire rack and allow the chocolate to flow evenly and make thin lines on the biscuits.

To vary Make as above, but roll out and cut into small squares.

Storing and freezing *All these biscuits (unless coated with soft icing) store well in airtight tins away from cakes, pastry or bread. There is no point in freezing them.*

Left to right: Orange laurel rings, Cherry ginger cookies, Chocolate shortbreads, Sugar rings, Zebra cookies and Orange cream cookies

Viennese orange shortbreads

These piped Viennese shortbreads, delicately flavored with orange, are delicious for a special occasion. In order that they may hold their shape do not exceed the recommended amounts of butter and confectioners' sugar. If you do not wish to use a pastry bag, then roll in balls as the Cherry Ginger Cookies on this page.

Blue Print Recipe

Viennese Orange Shortbreads

Grated rind 1 large orange · 1 cup flour · 1 cup cornstarch · $\frac{3}{4}$ cup butter · nearly 1 cup sifted confectioners' sugar. *For the filling and coating of confectioners' sugar:* grated rind 1 large orange · 6 tablespoons butter · nearly $1\frac{1}{4}$ cups confectioners' sugar.

Piped Cookies

To make Put the grated orange rind into the mixing bowl. Make certain you have taken just the top orange zest, not the bitter white pith that lies under the skin. Sift the flour and cornstarch into a small bowl. Add the butter and confectioners' sugar to the orange rind and cream very well, by hand or mixer, until very soft and light. This is most important if you wish to pipe the mixture. Gradually beat in the flour and cornstarch. Put the mixture into a cloth pastry bag with a $\frac{1}{2}$-inch rose tube and press out about 14–16 large neat rose shapes on an ungreased baking sheet.
To cook Bake in the center of a very moderate to moderate oven, 325–350°F, for

about 15–20 minutes. Look at the shortbreads as they cook, for they must crisp without becoming too brown. Allow to cool on the baking tray. Cream the finely grated orange rind, butter and nearly all the confectioners' sugar together. Sandwich the biscuits together with the butter icing and dust with the remaining confectioners' sugar. *Makes 7–8 double shortbreads.*

Cherry Ginger Cookies

Use the recipe above for the cookie dough, but not the filling. Omit the orange rind and sift 1 teaspoon powdered ginger with the flour and cornstarch. Roll into about 14–16 balls, flatten into rounds and bake as the recipe above. When cold and ready to serve, top with icing made by blending about 2 cups confectioners' sugar with enough water to make a spreading consistency. Spoon the icing into the center of each cookie and top with a glacé cherry. *Makes 14–16.*

Macaroons and Meringues

These are delicious to serve not only with tea or coffee, but also as a dessert. They can be varied in many ways to give interest to meals and are suitable for both family and special occasions.

Macaroons may be topped with ice cream for a special occasion and meringues can be filled with whipped cream, whipped cream and fruit or ice cream.

Blue Print Recipe

Coconut Macaroons

2 egg whites · $\frac{5}{8}$–$\frac{3}{4}$ superfine sugar · nearly 2 cups dried coconut · rice flour or cornstarch (optional, see method). To decorate: glacé cherries.

To make Put the egg whites into a mixing bowl and beat lightly; do not overwhip; the whites should just be frothy, not stiff. Add the sugar (the amount given above is on the generous side and if wished you can use as little as $\frac{1}{2}$ cup. Stir in the coconut gradually; as egg whites vary in size, you may need a little less than the amount given. The mixture should just roll into balls. If you wish a firmer texture, then use a little less coconut and add 1–2 teaspoons rice flour or cornstarch. When blended, roll into about 10–12 balls. Grease baking

sheets lightly and put on the balls. Allow room for the mixture to flatten out during cooking. Press half a glacé cherry on top of each cookie.

To cook Bake in the center of a very moderate to moderate oven, 350–375°F, for about 18–20 minutes. If you like a slightly sticky macaroon, then put a pan of water in the bottom of the oven while cooking.

To serve Remove from the baking sheets when nearly cold. Serve with tea or coffee or top with a scoop of ice cream. I like to put the ice cream on about 5 minutes ahead of time so it softens the macaroon slightly. *All recipes based on this make 10–12.*

● **AVOID** *Cooking macaroons too slowly; otherwise they become too hard. Cooking meringues too quickly or they brown on the outside before becoming crisp.*
● **TO RECTIFY** *As you cannot rectify mistakes, check the baking carefully.*

Storing and freezing *Macaroons become dry after 1 or 2 days if stored in a tin. Meringues keep well for weeks. Macaroons can be wrapped and frozen and they store for some weeks without losing their soft texture inside. Meringues contain such a high percentage of sugar that they never become frozen.*
To use leftovers *Macaroons can be crumbled and added to trifles. Meringues can be put back into the tin, unless they are filled with cream, etc., when they will soften very quickly. You can therefore freeze leftover filled meringues.*

Put the egg whites into a bowl, free from any specks of dust or particles of egg yolk. Beat until very stiff. Gradually beat in half the sugar and fold in the remainder. Brush the baking sheets with a very little oil or butter and dust with flour. Either spoon or pipe the meringues onto the baking sheets as Sketches 1 and 2. Bake in the coolest part of a very slow oven, 225–250°F, for about 2 hours until crisp but still white. Lift from the baking sheet with a warm, but dry, spatula. Store in an airtight tin until ready to fill.

Coconut macaroons

The meringues may either be filled with whipped cream or with butter icing, see recipe on page 93 for orange butter icing. You can flavor with vanilla instead of orange or other extracts or a little sifted cocoa (as in the picture) or instant coffee. They are delicious if filled with fruit or ice cream. To incorporate more filling, press the base of each meringue gently so you break it slightly and make a hollow, then sandwich two together with the filling. A nest shape also enables you to use a generous amount of cream and other filling.

To tint meringues add a few drops of food coloring to the egg whites before they are quite stiff.
To flavor meringues add a few drops extract to the egg whites before they are quite stiff. If you wish to add cocoa or instant coffee, blend either of these with the sugar.

Meringues

Almond Macaroons

Flavor with almond extract, use ground almonds in place of coconut. Top with blanched almonds.

Oatmeal Macaroons

Use all rolled oats or half rolled oats and half coconut or ground almonds. Top with almonds or glacé cherries.

Crumb Macaroons

Use all dry, fine bread crumbs or half crumbs and half coconut or ground almonds. Flavor bread crumbs version well with extract i.e. almond, rum or vanilla.

Meringues

The Blue Print on page 113 gives details about making the meringue mixture but some of the most important points are repeated below.

2 egg whites; $\frac{1}{2}$ cup superfine sugar (or use half superfine and half sifted confectioners' sugar).

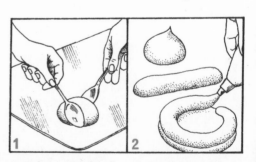

1. Take a spoonful of meringue mixture. Hold over the baking sheet and form into a neat shape with a second spoon.

2. Put the mixture into a pastry bag with a $\frac{1}{4}$-inch tube. Pipe into rounds, fingers or nest shapes.

White Cakes

White cakes are light and delicate butter cakes made with egg whites instead of whole eggs. When margarine is used in place of butter, it is an ideal cake for people on a low cholesterol diet. However, the baking powder should be increased by 1 teaspoon. This is the same batter used for the famous Lady Baltimore Cake.

Blue Print Recipe

White Lemon Cake

$\frac{3}{4}$ cup butter · $\frac{1}{2}$ cup superfine sugar · $2\frac{1}{2}$ cups flour · 3 teaspoons baking powder · $\frac{1}{2}$ teaspoon salt · $\frac{3}{4}$ cup milk · $1\frac{1}{2}$ teaspoons vanilla extract · 4 egg whites · pinch of salt.

To make Cream butter until fluffy. Add the sugar gradually, creaming after each addition. Alternately add the sifted flour, baking powder and $\frac{1}{2}$ teaspoon salt and the milk. Mix in the vanilla. Beat the egg whites with the pinch of salt until stiff and carefully fold into the batter.

To cook Pour into 3 well greased $7 \times 1\frac{1}{2}$-inch layer pans and bake in the center of a moderately hot oven, 375–400°F, for about 20 minutes. Cool in pans 5–10 minutes on cake racks. Remove from pans and cool completely.

To serve Fill with Lemon Curd and frost top and sides with White Icing (page 102). Sprinkle edge of top layer with grated lemon rind and place a twist of lemon in the center.

White Orange Cake

Recipe as Blue Print. Fill with Orange Filling (below) and frost with White Icing (page 102).

Lady Baltimore Cake

Method as Blue Print but double the ingredients. Cook in 3 well-greased $8 \times 1\frac{1}{2}$-inch layer pans in a moderately hot oven, 375–400°F, for about 25 minutes or until a toothpick inserted in the center comes out clean. *To fill and frost:* Triple the recipe for White Icing (page 102). Reserve a generous $\frac{1}{3}$ of the icing for the tops and sides. To the remainder add 1 cup finely chopped nuts, $\frac{1}{3}$ cup cut raisins, $\frac{1}{3}$ cup chopped glacé cherries, 4 chopped figs. Spread between the layers and frost with the reserved icing.

Lemon Filling

1 cup sugar; 4 tablespoons cornstarch; 1 cup water; $\frac{1}{2}$ cup lemon juice; $1\frac{1}{2}$ teaspoons grated lemon rind; $1\frac{1}{2}$ tablespoons butter; 1 egg yolk.
Mix the sugar and cornstarch thoroughly,

add boiling water and stir constantly over low heat until the mixture boils. Remove from heat and stir in the butter and beaten egg yolk. Blend well and cook, stirring, for 2 minutes. Do not boil. Remove from heat and add the lemon juice and rind. Let cool before filling the cake. If the filling seems runny, refrigerate before using. *Makes enough for a 3-layer 8- or 9-inch cake.*

Orange Filling

Make as Lemon Filling (above) but reduce the water to $\frac{3}{4}$ cup and the lemon juice to 2 tablespoons. Add $\frac{3}{4}$ cup orange juice and 2 teaspoons grated orange rind with the lemon juice.

For Special Occasions

Easter Cake

This cake delights children for any occasion. Use a 7-cup lamb or rabbit mold or any other 7-cup mold.
Ingredients and method as Blue Print. Pour batter into the front half of the *well* greased mold (use melted butter or cooking oil and a pastry brush to do this). Cover mold and cook in a moderate oven, 350°F, for about 1 hour. Remove from oven and let cool on a

White lemon cake

cake rack with the top removed. When cool, invert the cake onto a serving platter. Slip strips of waxed paper under the cake. Any pieces (such as the head or tail) which may have broken, can be glued back with the help of frosting and toothpicks. Spread with 7 Minute Frosting (below) using $1\frac{1}{2}$ times the recipe given. Press 1–2 cups fresh or canned grated coconut onto the icing. Encircle the neck with a collar of crystallized violets. If you prefer a "black lamb", use sprinkles instead of coconut to form his coat. Gum drops, cinnamon candies, chocolate bits, raisins or whatever your fancy may be used to make the eyes, nose and mouth.

Seven Minute Frosting

2 egg whites ($\frac{1}{4}$ cup); $1\frac{1}{2}$ cups sugar; $\frac{1}{4}$ teaspoon cream of tartar or $1\frac{1}{2}$ teaspoons light corn syrup; $\frac{1}{3}$ cup water; 1 teaspoon vanilla extract.
Combine all ingredients in the top of a double boiler and beat until well blended. Place top over, but not touching, boiling water and beat constantly for seven minutes. Remove from heat, add vanilla and continue beating for a minute or two until spreading consistency. *Makes enough filling and frosting for two 7- or 8-inch layers.*

To some people a cake is not a cake unless it's a chocolate cake smothered in chocolate frosting, the fudgier the better. I've tried to anticipate all tastes and hope you will enjoy this selection.

Chocolate Cakes

For Family Occasions

Light Chocolate Layer Cake

$\frac{1}{2}$ cup butter; 1 cup sugar; 2 egg yolks; 1 oz. bitter chocolate; $\frac{1}{2}$ cup milk; $1\frac{1}{2}$ cups flour; 1 teaspoon baking powder; pinch of salt; 1 teaspoon vanilla; 2 egg whites.

Cream the butter until fluffy. Add the sugar gradually, creaming after each addition. Beat in the well beaten egg yolks, then the melted chocolate. Sift the flour, baking powder and salt into the mixture alternately with the milk. Add the vanilla, then fold in the stiffly beaten egg whites. Pour into 2 well-greased 8-inch layer pans and cook in a moderately hot oven, 375–400°F, for about 25 minutes. Frost with any icing.

Banana Cocoa Layer Cake

Ingredients as Blue Print but OMIT chocolate and sift in $\frac{1}{3}$ cup cocoa with the flour. Cook as Blue Print. Fill with $\frac{1}{2}$ recipe Chocolate Cream (below) to which 1 sliced banana has been added, and frost with chocolate flavored Butter Icing (page 102).

Chocolate Cream

Follow the recipe for Pastry Cream (page 102) but add 1 oz. chocolate to the flour-milk mixture.

Chocolate Cup Cakes

Ingredients and method as Blue Print or batter for Banana Cocoa Layer Cake (above). Fill well-greased or paper-lined muffin cups $\frac{1}{2}$ full. Cook in a moderately hot oven, 375–400°F, for about 15 minutes. *Makes 18–24.*

Boston Cream Mocha Pie

1 cup sugar; 1 tablespoon butter; 1 teaspoon salt; $1\frac{3}{4}$ cups flour; 1 teaspoon baking powder; 5 teaspoons cocoa; $\frac{1}{2}$ cup boiling water.

Mix and stir all the ingredients into the boiling water. Pour in a well-greased 8-inch layer pan and cook in a moderate oven, 350°F, for 15 minutes. Cool. Split the cake and fill the cake with chocolate filling.

Chocolate filling: In a heavy saucepan place 2 oz. bitter chocolate, 1 cup sugar, 2 tablespoons cornstarch, 1 cup strong coffee and 1 tablespoon butter. Bring to a boil, stirring, and continue stirring until thick. Cool before using.

Icing: Work together 1 cup confectioners' sugar, 1 teaspoon cocoa, 1 tablespoon butter and 1 tablespoon strong hot coffee until spreading consistency. If the icing does not seem moist enough, add a little more coffee.

Marble Cake

This modest but pleasant loaf cake is good served with ice cream and a sauce.

$\frac{1}{2}$ cup butter; 1 cup sugar; 2 eggs; $1\frac{1}{2}$ cups flour; $1\frac{1}{2}$ teaspoons baking powder; $\frac{1}{2}$ cup milk; 1 oz. bitter chocolate.

Cream the butter until fluffy. Add the sugar gradually, creaming well between each addition. Sift in the flour, baking powder and salt alternately with the milk. Mix 1 cup of the batter with the melted chocolate. Cook in a 9 × 5-inch well-greased loaf pan in a moderately hot oven, 375–400°F, for about 25 minutes.

Rich Chocolate Cake

4 oz. bitter chocolate; $1\frac{3}{4}$ cups sugar; $1\frac{1}{2}$ cups buttermilk; $\frac{1}{2}$ cup butter; 3 eggs; $2\frac{1}{2}$ cups flour; $1\frac{1}{2}$ teaspoons baking powder; $\frac{3}{4}$ teaspoon soda; $\frac{1}{2}$ teaspoon salt; 1 teaspoon vanilla extract.

Melt chocolate over boiling water, add 1 cup sugar, $\frac{1}{2}$ cup buttermilk and stir until sugar is dissolved. Set aside to cool. Cream butter until fluffy. Add sugar gradually, creaming after each addition until mixture is light and fluffy. Add well beaten eggs and beat well. Sift the flour, baking powder, soda and salt twice. Mix about $\frac{1}{4}$ into the creamed mixture, then blend in the cooled chocolate mixture; add the remaining flour alternately with the 1 cup buttermilk, a small amount at a time. Add the vanilla. Pour the batter into two 9-inch layer pans and cook in a moderate oven, 350°F, for about 30 minutes. Frost and fill with Fudge Icing (below) or Seven Minute Frosting (page 95).

Black Chocolate Cake

1 cup sugar; $\frac{1}{2}$ cup butter; 2 eggs; 2 cups flour; 1 teaspoon soda; pinch salt; $\frac{1}{2}$ cup buttermilk; 1 teaspoon vanilla extract.

Cream the butter until fluffy; cream in the sugar gradually. Beat in the eggs. Sift in the flour, soda and salt alternately with the buttermilk. Mix in the vanilla. To $\frac{1}{2}$ oz. bitter chocolate melted in $\frac{2}{3}$ cup milk, add $\frac{1}{4}$ cup sugar beaten in 1 egg. Cook, stirring, until thick. Stir in 1 teaspoon vanilla. Add to the cake batter. The mixture will be very runny, but do not add additional flour. Pour into 2 well-greased 8-inch layer pans and cook in a moderately hot oven, 375–400°F, for about 20 minutes. Fill and frost with Cooked White Frosting (page 102).

Fudge Icing

Combine $1\frac{1}{2}$ cups sugar, 1 tablespoon light corn syrup, and dash of salt in a small saucepan; bring quickly to the boil, stirring only until the sugar is dissolved. Boil without stirring until the mixture reaches 238–240°F on a candy thermometer. Choose the lower temperature for a smooth coating icing, the higher when you wish the icing to stand in peaks or if the weather is damp. To test without the thermometer, drop a little of the hot mixture into cold water; when ready, it should form a soft ball. Melt 4 oz. chocolate in a medium saucepan over hot water, add 4 tablespoons butter, 1 teaspoon vanilla then stir until butter is melted and blended. Remove from heat and add syrup gradually, stirring constantly until smooth and thickened. Place again over boiling water and stir until frosting is softened and of spreading consistency. Keep over hot water to keep soft while spreading. The quantity above is enough to fill and frost two 9-inch layers.

Rich chocolate cake

Coconut fudge cake

Coconut Fudge Cake

This is a moist deep chocolate cake using oil instead of butter.

2 cups sugar; 1 cup cooking oil; 2 eggs; 3 cups flour; $\frac{3}{4}$ cup unsweetened cocoa; 2 teaspoons soda; 2 teaspoons baking powder; $1\frac{1}{2}$ teaspoons salt; 1 cup hot coffee or water; 1 cup buttermilk or sour milk; 1 teaspoon vanilla; $\frac{1}{2}$ cup chopped nuts. *For the Filling:* $\frac{1}{4}$ cup sugar; 1 teaspoon vanilla; $\frac{1}{2}$ lb. cream cheese; 1 egg; $\frac{1}{2}$ cup flaked coconut; 1 cup (6-oz. package)

semi-sweet chocolate pieces.

Prepare the filling; set aside. In a large mixer bowl, combine sugar, oil and eggs; beat 1 minute at high speed. Add remaining ingredients except filling; beat 3 minutes at medium speed, scraping bowl occasionally. Stir in nuts by hand. Pour half the batter into a generously greased and lightly floured 10-inch tube or Bundt pan. Carefully spoon the prepared filling over the batter; top with the remaining batter. Bake in a moderate

oven, 350°F, for 70 to 75 minutes until the top springs back when touched lightly in the center. Cool upright in pan for 15 minutes; remove from pan. Cool completely; drizzle with glaze made by combining 1 cup powdered sugar, 3 tablespoons cocoa, 2 tablespoons butter, 2 teaspoons vanilla and 1–3 tablespoons hot water. *To make Filling:* Beat sugar, vanilla, softened cream cheese and egg until smooth. Stir in coconut and chocolate pieces.

Yellow cakes use the whole egg. If you want to use the one-bowl method, see page 89.

Blue Print Recipe

Two-Egg Cake

$\frac{1}{2}$ cup butter · 1 cup sugar · 2 egg yolks · 2 cups flour · 2 teaspoons baking powder · $\frac{1}{4}$ teaspoon salt · $\frac{2}{3}$ cup milk · 1 teaspoon vanilla extract · 2 egg whites.

To make Cream the butter until fluffy. Add the sugar gradually, creaming after each addition. Gradually beat in egg yolks. Sift in the flour, baking powder and salt alternately with the milk. Beat in the vanilla. Carefully fold in the stiffly beaten egg whites. Divide the mixture between two 8–9-inch greased and floured layer pans.

To cook Bake above the center of a moderate oven, 350–375°F, for 20–25 minutes until just firm to the touch.

To serve Use any of the fillings and icings on pages 95–103.

● **AVOID** *Adding the sugar too quickly, or the cake will be grainy. Adding the eggs too quickly, for this could curdle the mixture. Overbeating the flour, as this spoils the texture.*

● **TO RECTIFY** *If the butter was hard, cream the mixture a little longer than you think necessary. If the egg yolks have been added too quickly and the mixture shows signs of curdling, blend in a little sifted flour.*

Yellow Cakes

● **SHORT CUTS** *Use the quick creaming margarines and shortenings and put all the ingredients into the bowl and beat for about 2 minutes. As less air has been beaten into the mixture it is advisable to sift an extra level teaspoon baking powder with each cup flour. This means, however, that the cakes tend to dry out more easily.*

One-Egg Cake

To vary

Ingredients as Blue Print but use 1 egg only and decrease shortening to $\frac{1}{3}$ cup. Use 8-inch layer pans. Cook as Blue Print.

Three-Egg Cake

Ingredients as Blue Print but INCREASE the butter to $\frac{2}{3}$ cup and the sugar to $1\frac{1}{4}$ cups. Use 3 eggs, 1 tablespoon baking powder and $\frac{1}{2}$ cup milk. Cook as Blue Print. Use two 9- or three 8-inch layer pans.

Spanish Cake

Ingredients as Blue Print but OMIT vanilla and substitute 1 teaspoon cinnamon.

Orange Layer Cake

Ingredients as Blue Print but OMIT the milk and vanilla and substitute $\frac{2}{3}$ cup orange juice and 1 tablespoon grated orange rind. Increase the baking powder to 1 tablespoon.

Cook as Blue Print. Fill and frost with Orange Frosting (below).

Make the sponge as the Blue Print, but mix the orange juice with the beaten eggs and bake in 7-inch pans.

Orange Frosting

$\frac{1}{2}$ lb. butter; $2\frac{1}{2}$ cups sifted confectioners' sugar; grated rind 2 oranges; little orange juice.

Cream the ingredients together, adding orange juice to make a spreading consistency.

Pineapple Butterscotch Cake (Upside Down Cake)

Ingredients as Blue Print. *For the topping:* 4 tablespoons brown sugar; 4 tablespoons butter; pineapple slices; Maraschino cherries.

Make cake batter as Blue Print. Cream the brown sugar and butter together, spread on bottom of greased but not floured 9-inch square pan. Cover with pineapple slices. Place a cherry in the center of each slice if desired. To serve, turn onto a serving dish, pineapple side up and garnish with whipped cream.

Pound Cake

The traditional proportions of this cake are 1 pound each of butter, sugar, eggs and flour. $\frac{1}{2}$ lb. butter; 1 cup superfine sugar; 4 egg yolks; 2 cups flour; 1 teaspoon baking powder; $\frac{1}{4}$ teaspoon nutmeg; 1 teaspoon lemon extract; 4 egg whites.

Cream the butter until fluffy. Add the sugar gradually, creaming well after each addition. Add the well-beaten egg yolks and lemon extract, beating thoroughly. Fold in the egg whites carefully. Grease a 9 × 5-inch loaf pan thoroughly, line the bottom with greased waxed paper. Pour in the batter and cook in a slow oven, 300–325°F, for $1\frac{1}{4}$–$1\frac{1}{2}$ hours.

Orange layer cake

Applesauce cake

Fruit Cake

Use half the recipe for Pound Cake above PLUS $\frac{1}{8}$ teaspoon cinnamon, 1 teaspoon allspice, 1 teaspoon cloves and $\frac{1}{4}$ cup apple jelly. Use $1\frac{1}{2}$ cups ($\frac{1}{2}$ lb.) raisins, $1\frac{1}{2}$ cups ($\frac{1}{2}$ lb.) currants and $\frac{1}{8}$ cup ($\frac{1}{8}$ lb.) citron. After the egg yolks have been beaten into the butter-sugar mixture, beat in the melted jelly. Mix the flour, baking powder and spices together. Toss the flour with the fruit to coat the fruit thoroughly. Stir into the batter. Fold the stiffly beaten egg whites in carefully. Grease a 9-inch tube pan well and line the bottom with well-greased waxed paper. Cook as Pound Cake.

Gold Cake

This moist cake keeps well and is a good way of using up extra egg yolks.

$\frac{1}{2}$ cup butter; $1\frac{1}{2}$ cups sugar; 4 egg yolks plus 1 whole egg; $2\frac{1}{2}$ cups flour; $2\frac{1}{2}$ teaspoons baking powder; about $\frac{3}{4}$ cup milk.

Cream the butter until fluffy. Add the sugar gradually, creaming after each addition until light and fluffy. Beat in the well beaten egg yolks and whole egg. Alternately sift the flour and baking powder into the mixture with the milk. Add only enough milk to make a dropping consistency. Bake in a well-greased 9 × 5-inch loaf pan in a moderate oven, 350°F, for $1\frac{1}{4}$ hours.

You will often find that large cakes made by rubbing in the shortening have a tendency to crack slightly on top as the cake on this page. This is not a fault in short, crumbly cakes that have a pleasantly crisp textured crust.

Spice Cakes

You will often find that large cakes made by rubbing in the shortening have a tendency to crack slightly on top as the cake on this page. This is not a fault in short, crumbly cakes that have a pleasantly crisp textured crust.

Blue Print Recipe

Granny's Spice Cake

3 cups flour · 3 teaspoons baking powder · 1–2 teaspoons allspice · $\frac{3}{4}$ cup butter · $\frac{3}{4}$–1 cup superfine or light brown sugar · 1–$1\frac{1}{2}$ cups mixed dried fruit · 2 eggs · milk to mix.

To make Sift the flour, baking powder and spice together. Add the butter then rub this into the flour with the tips of your fingers until like fine bread crumbs. Lift the mixture to incorporate air. Add the sugar, fruit, the beaten eggs and enough milk to make a sticky, dropping consistency. Put into a greased and floured 7–8 × 3-inch round cake pan, smooth flat on top.

To cook Bake in the center of a moderate oven, 350–375°F, for approximately 1 hour for an 8-inch pan, $1\frac{1}{4}$ hours for a 7-inch pan. Reduce the heat to very moderate, 325–350°F, after 45 minutes. Test by pressing quite hard on top; the cake is cooked when quite firm to the touch.

Orange Raisin Cake

Ingredients as Blue Print using all raisins, MINUS the spice and PLUS the grated rind of 2 oranges, which should be added with the sugar.

Bake as the Blue Print or bake in a 9 × 5-inch loaf pan as illustrated for barely 1 hour.

To vary Top the cake with warmed marmalade and cover with a thick layer of coconut.

Gingerbread

$\frac{1}{2}$ cup butter; $\frac{1}{2}$ cup sugar; $\frac{1}{2}$ cup molasses; 1 egg; $1\frac{3}{4}$ cups flour; 1 teaspoon baking soda; 1 teaspoon cinnamon; 1 generous teaspoon ginger; scant $\frac{1}{4}$ teaspoon cloves; $\frac{1}{4}$ teaspoon salt; $\frac{1}{2}$ cup boiling water.

Cream the butter until fluffy; add the sugar gradually, creaming after each addition then beat in the well beaten egg and molasses. Mix the flour, soda, spice and salt together and add. Add boiling water. Bake in a well-greased 8-inch square pan in a slow oven, 300°F, for 30–35 minutes. Serve warm, garnished with whipped cream. Hot or cold, this is an equally good as a breakfast cake.

Applesauce Cake

$\frac{1}{2}$ cup butter; $\frac{1}{2}$ cup sugar; $1\frac{1}{2}$ cups sweet applesauce; $2\frac{1}{2}$ cups flour; 1 teaspoon baking soda; $\frac{1}{2}$ teaspoon each cloves, cinnamon and nutmeg; 1 teaspoon vanilla.

Cream the butter until fluffy. Add the sugar gradually, creaming after each addition then add the applesauce. Add the flour, soda, spices and vanilla and beat well. Pour into a greased 9-inch square pan and bake in a moderate oven, 350°F, for 30–35 minutes. This moist cake keeps well for several days in an airtight tin.

...page depend for leavening ...ten into them and they contain ...ening. After mixing, turn gently ...the pan and cook immediately. If ...lowed to stand the mixture will fall. All of these cakes may be cut and filled or served plain with fruit and cream or ice cream.

Blue Print Recipes

1. Sponge Cake

6 egg yolks · 1 tablespoon lemon juice · 1 teaspoon grated lemon rind · 1 teaspoon vanilla extract · 6 egg whites · 1 cup sugar · $\frac{1}{4}$ teaspoon salt · 1 cup flour.

To make Beat the egg yolks until stiff and the beater leaves a ribbon on the surface of the eggs. Beat in the lemon juice and rind and the vanilla.
Beat the egg whites separately at low speed until frothy. Add the salt, increase the speed and beat until the whites form soft peaks. Continue beating, adding the sugar 1 tablespoon at a time, for about 5 minutes or until the meringue stands in stiff peaks.
Stir $\frac{1}{4}$ of the meringue into the yolk mixture. Pour the yolk mixture over the meringue, sift the flour over the top and gently fold in only until all the flour is incorporated.
To cook Bake in 3 ungreased 7-inch round layer pans, 2 round 9-inch layer pans or a 9 × 4-inch tube pan in a moderate oven, 350°F, for 35–40 minutes. Cool in pan.
To serve Fill the layers with cream and fruit or Lemon Curd. The ungarnished tube cake may be served with fruit as dessert or as an accompaniment to tea or coffee.

● **AVOID** *Overfolding the flour when blending into the meringue: it must be barely folded in, carefully and quickly.*
● **TO RECTIFY** *There is no remedy for a sponge where the flour has been overfolded. You are sure to have a rather heavy tight texture, instead of a light one.*

Orange Sponge Cake

Ingredients as Blue Print but substitute 2 tablespoons orange juice for the lemon juice and 1 teaspoon grated orange rind for the lemon rind. Make and bake as the Blue Print. Fill the layers with orange curd and a little whipped cream. Flavor the remainder of the cream with 1 tablespoon curaçao if liked. Pipe around the edge of the cake. The tube cake may be served as the Blue Print for dessert or with coffee.

Chocolate Sponge Cake

Ingredients as Blue Print MINUS $\frac{1}{4}$ cup flour and PLUS $\frac{1}{4}$ cup cocoa sifted with the flour. Fill with chocolate Butter Icing (page 102) or whipped cream.

Sponge and Angel Food Cakes

Jelly Roll

This is not a "true" sponge because it contains baking powder, but do not belittle this cake. It is very versatile.
4 eggs yolks; 1 teaspoon vanilla extract; 4 egg whites; pinch of salt; $\frac{3}{4}$ cup sugar; $\frac{3}{4}$ cup flour; 1 teaspoon baking powder.
Make as Blue Print. Bake in an 11 × 16-inch jelly roll pan lined with waxed paper in a moderately hot oven, 375°F, for about 13 minutes. Invert on a dish cloth sprinkled with confectioners' sugar, remove paper, trim edges and roll from the narrow end in the cloth. Cool on cake rack. Unroll and spread with the beaten jelly or filling of choice. Reroll and sprinkle with confections' sugar. *Makes 8–10 slices.*

Chocolate Roll

Ingredients as Jelly Roll (above) but use 6 tablespoons cocoa sifted with 6 tablespoons flour in place of the $\frac{3}{4}$ cup flour. Make as Blue Print. Bake in a moderately hot oven, 375°F, for about 13 minutes. Invert on a damp dish towel, trim the edges and let stand for a few minutes. Roll when cool. Fill and frost with Whipped Cream Cocoa Topping (below).
3 tablespoons cocoa; $\frac{1}{4}$ cup confectioners' sugar; 1 cup heavy cream; pinch of salt.
Sift dry ingredients, add cream and chill for 2 hours. Beat until stiff, being careful not to overbeat. *Enough to fill and frost two 8-inch layers or one rolled cake.*

2. Angel Food Cake

This all-American cake is tailor made for people on reducing or low cholesterol diets. It's also the perfect cake for any very special occasion.

$1\frac{1}{2}$ cups (10–11) egg whites · pinch salt · 1 teaspoon cream of tartar · $1\frac{1}{4}$ cups superfine sugar · 1 cup cake flour · $\frac{1}{2}$ teaspoon vanilla extract · $\frac{1}{2}$ teaspoon almond extract.

To make Beat egg whites at low speed until frothy then add salt and cream of tartar and beat at high speed until the whites have soft peaks. Add the sugar 1 tablespoon at a time and continue beating until the meringue holds stiff peaks. Sift the flour on top, about $\frac{1}{4}$ cup at a time, and gently fold in. Fold in vanilla and almond extracts. Push into an ungreased 10-inch tube pan and run a spatula through the batter to remove air holes.

To cook Bake in a moderately slow oven, 300°F, for 1 hour or until the top springs back when touched. Invert on cake rack and cool for $1–1\frac{1}{2}$ hours. Remove from pan.
To serve Plain with or without fruit or ice cream; cut in two layers, filled and frosted, or hollowed out and filled and frosted.

Chocolate Angel Food Cake

Ingredients and method as Blue Print but use $\frac{3}{4}$ cup flour only and sift with $\frac{1}{4}$ cup cocoa. OMIT almond extract and increase vanilla extract to 1 teaspoon. Bake as the Blue Print.

Daffodil Cake

Ingredients as Blue Print PLUS 6 egg yolks. Make as Blue Print. Fold half the batter into the egg yolks which have been beaten for about 5 minutes or until thick and the beater leaves a ribbon on the yolks. Bake as the Blue Print.

Raspberry Heaven

1 Angel Food Cake as the Blue Print; 1 package frozen raspberries; 3 cups heavy cream; 2 tablespoons confectioners' sugar. Cut a 1-inch slice from the bottom of the cake and hollow the cake out, leaving a 1-inch-thick wall on sides and bottom. Drain the partially defrosted raspberries, reserving the syrup. Whip $1\frac{1}{2}$ cups of the heavy cream and fold into the raspberries. Fill the cake with whipped cream and raspberries; replace the top. Whip the remaining cream with the sugar. Fold in enough of the reserved syrup to color the cream lightly. Frost the cake with this and serve before the raspberries become completely defrosted.

Berries on a Cloud

10-oz. package frozen strawberries or raspberries; 4 slices angel food or sponge cake; 1 tablespoon brandy; 1 tablespoon orange-flavored liqueur; 1 pint vanilla or strawberry ice cream or raspberry sherbet; 1 cup whipped cream or whipped topping mix.
Thaw fruit as directed on the package. Meanwhile, toast cake in the broiler just until golden brown—about 5 minutes. Combine the fruit with the brandy and liqueur, mixing gently to blend. Place the cake on serving plates, top each with a scoop of ice cream, about $\frac{1}{4}$ cup of the fruit mixture and a generous spoonful of whipped cream. *Serves 4.*

Storing and freezing *Sponges and Angel Foods should be baked as soon as possible after mixing. The cooked cakes tend to dry if kept more than 1 or 2 days, but freeze well.*
To use leftovers *These stale cakes are excellent for making trifles.*

Berries on a cloud

The recipes on this page can turn a simple layer cake (page 98) or light sponge (page 100) into a special gâteau. The Royal icing opposite is ideal for rich fruit cakes or as a glaze on tortes.

● **AVOID** *Using too heavy or stiff an icing on these delicate cakes, for they would break the sponge and make it difficult to cut.*
● **TO RECTIFY** *While one cannot change a firm icing, such as Royal icing, it is possible to make other icings softer in texture so they do not break the cake.*
● **SHORT CUT** *Do not bother to sift the confectioners' sugar for a simple water glaze (unless in very hard lumps); if mixed with the liquid and allowed to stand the glaze will be smooth. The confectioners' sugar must be sifted for other icings.*

Choice for Fillings and Toppings

Use sweetened whipped cream, flavored with 1 teaspoon of vanilla for every cup of unwhipped cream, as a filling or frosting. Another excellent filling for light cakes (as well as pastries) is the Pastry Cream, below. Butter icing is not only ideal to pipe on light cakes, but is excellent for fillings too.
Cooked White frosting, below, is as good for filling and frosting sponges as for fruit cakes. Water Glaze is one of the best icings for light cakes, but is rarely used as a filling.

Blue Print Recipes

1. Water Glaze

To 2 cups confectioners' sugar add 4 tablespoons melted butter and $1\frac{1}{2}$ teaspoons vanilla. Add 2–4 tablespoons hot water gradually, stirring until the glaze is the desired consistency. The larger amount will give a very runny icing that will trickle down the sides of the cake.
Flavorings can be given by using strong coffee or orange or lemon juice in place of the water and vanilla (plus $\frac{1}{2}$ teaspoon grated rind worked in with the melted butter), 2 oz. melted and cooled bitter chocolate added to the sugar or 4 tablespoons cocoa (increase the water a bit) added to the sugar; 2 tablespoons rum, cognac or liqueur may be added in place of the vanilla. Pour over the cake, letting it run down the sides. *Enough for a 10-inch sponge or angel food cake.*

2. Butter Frosting

This is made by creaming butter with *sifted* confectioners' sugar and flavoring. To $\frac{3}{4}$ cup butter add 3 cups confectioners' sugar and $1\frac{1}{2}$ teaspoons vanilla extract. Up to 2 tablespoons milk may be added for a softer consistency. Variants are given by adding 3 oz. melted and cooled bitter chocolate or 6 tablespoons cocoa (reduce sugar by 6 tablespoons); omitting the vanilla and adding orange juice (plus 2 teaspoons grated rind), lemon juice (plus 1 teaspoon grated rind) or

Mocha hazel-nut gâteau

extra strong coffee for the milk; $\frac{1}{2}$ cup maple syrup may also be substituted for the vanilla and milk. *Enough to frost and fill two 8- or 9-inch layers.* Any extract may be used to replace vanilla.

Mocha Hazelnut Gâteau

$\frac{3}{4}$ cup butter; $\frac{3}{4}$ cup superfine sugar; 3 large eggs; $1\frac{1}{4}$ cups flour; $1\frac{1}{4}$ teaspoons baking powder; 1 tablespoon cocoa; $\frac{1}{4}$ cup finely chopped hazelnuts; 1 tablespoon strong coffee. *For the filling:* $1\frac{1}{4}$–$1\frac{1}{2}$ cups butter; $3\frac{1}{2}$–$4\frac{1}{2}$ cups sifted confectioners' sugar; $1\frac{1}{2}$–2 tablespoons very strong coffee; 4–5 tablespoons chopped hazelnuts; whole hazelnuts to decorate.
Cream the butter and sugar, gradually add the beaten eggs, then fold in the sifted flour, baking powder and cocoa. Add the chopped hazelnuts and coffee. Divide between two 8-inch greased and floured round layer pans and bake for 20–25 minutes above the center of a moderate oven, 350–375°F, until firm to the touch. Turn out carefully. Allow to cool. Make the butter frosting as Blue Print 2. Use about $\frac{1}{4}$ of the mixture to sandwich the layers

Coating the sides of the cake

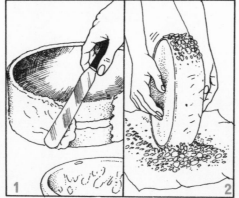

together and another $\frac{1}{4}$ to coat the sides, see Sketch 1. Roll the cake in the chopped nuts, see Sketch 2, then cover the cake with some of the remaining frosting and pipe rosettes on top with the last of the frosting. Decorate with whole hazelnuts.

Pastry Cream

$\frac{3}{4}$ cup flour; 2 tablespoons cornstarch; $1\frac{1}{2}$ cups milk; vanilla pod or $\frac{1}{2}$–1 teaspoon vanilla extract; $\frac{1}{4}$ cup superfine sugar; 2 tablespoons butter; 1 whole egg or 2 egg yolks; $1\frac{1}{2}$ tablespoons heavy cream or milk.
Blend the flour and cornstarch with the cold milk, put into a saucepan with the vanilla pod or extract and cook gently, stirring well, until thickened. Add the sugar and butter as the mixture begins to stiffen. Remove the pan from the heat, take out the vanilla pod (rinse in cold water and dry). Blend the egg or yolks with the cream or milk, add to the mixture in the pan and cook gently for several minutes without boiling. Stir from time to time as the mixture cools to prevent a skin forming. If wished, blend in $\frac{1}{3}$ cup lightly whipped heavy cream when the filling is cold. This is also known as Crème Patissière.
The quantity above fills about 12 good-sized puffs or would provide 2 thick or 3 thinner layers in a layer cake.

Cooked White Frosting

Stir 2 cups granulated sugar and 1 cup water over a low heat until the sugar has dissolved. Add a good pinch cream of tartar, then boil steadily until the mixture reaches 238–240°F. Choose the lower temperature for a smooth coating frosting and the higher temperature when you wish the frosting to stand in peaks, or if the weather is very damp. To test without the thermometer drop a little of the icing into cold water; when ready it should form a soft ball. Beat the syrup in the pan until slightly cloudy, then pour onto 2 stiffly beaten egg whites and beat well. Add 1 teaspoon vanilla. Spread the frosting over the top and and sides of the cake, either smooth flat or sweep up in peaks. *Enough for the top and sides of two 9-inch layers.*

Butter Cream

$\frac{2}{3}$ cup sugar; $\frac{1}{4}$ teaspoon cream of tartar; 5 tablespoons water; 5 egg yolks; 1 cup butter.
Combine the sugar, cream of tartar and water in a heavy saucepan and stir over low heat until the sugar is dissolved. Raise the heat and boil until a candy thermometer registers 238°F or until the syrup forms a soft ball in cold water. Beat the egg yolks in a large mixing bowl until light and fluffy. Add the sugar syrup in a steady stream, stirring continuously; beat until the mixture thickens. Cool and beat in the creamed butter. Flavor with 2–3 tablespoons rum, cognac or liqueur and/or 2–3 oz. melted bitter chocolate. *Enough to fill and ice two 9-inch layers.*

Blue Print Recipes

1. Marzipan

Although there are many variations of this recipe (you can increase the amount of sugar and decrease the quantity of ground almonds), the recipe I prefer is to blend 2 cups ground almonds with $\frac{1}{2}$ cup superfine sugar, 1 scant cup sifted confectioners' sugar, a few drops almond extract and 2 egg yolks or 1 large whole egg to bind. You can use a little less egg and some sherry. The marzipan is then rolled out on a sugared board and put onto the cake as shown in the sketches. The secret is *not* to overhandle the marzipan; if you do, the natural oils from the almonds seep through the icing and spoil the color. If you handle the marzipan lightly, you may ice the cake at once; if you feel it has been kneaded and rolled rather firmly, then allow it to dry out for 48 hours before putting on the icing.

The quantity above is sufficient to coat the top and sides of a 7–8-inch round cake (about $2\frac{1}{2}$-inches in depth).

The easiest way to calculate the amount of marzipan required is to take the *total* weight of the cake, then allow *half* this weight in marzipan.

Marzipan trimmings left from coating the cake may be colored and used to decorate the top of the cake.

Icings & Fillings

2. Royal Icing

This is the icing used on the wedding cake pictured on this page. It is essential to sift the confectioners' sugar. Do not overbeat, particularly in a mixer, for if you do you

Traditional two-tiered wedding cake

have large air bubbles which spoil the smoothness of the icing. Beat only until the mixture stands in soft peaks (for coating) and firm peaks (for piping).

Blend 1 lb. sifted confectioners' sugar with 2 lightly beaten egg whites and $\frac{1}{2}$–1 tablespoon lemon juice. To give a less hard icing add up to 1 teaspoon glycerine or use only 1 egg white and a little water to blend. If using water do not try and pipe the icing. The quantity above is sufficient to give one coating only on a 7–$7\frac{1}{2}$-inch round cake—with none left for piping.

The cake shown on this page would need Royal icing made with 5 lb. confectioners' sugar, etc. This would allow for two coats of icing and the piping as shown.

Storing and freezing *Icings harden with storage, and this makes them difficult to spread or pipe. Always cover bowls of icing with damp paper and keep surplus marzipan in a polyethylene bag or foil. Butter icings freeze well and many people find it an excellent idea to store small containers of different flavored butter icings. Cakes coated with water glaze and cooked white frosting can be frozen, but Royal icing keeps well without freezing.*

To use leftovers *Any icing left can be used at a later date if well covered, see above. Frosting tends to lose its fluffy texture if handled again so it is better to use all of this after making.*

1. Roll out the marzipan.
Cut a round the size of the top of the cake and a band the depth and circumference of the cake.

2. Brush the sides of the cake with sieved apricot jam or egg white.

3. Roll the cake along the strip of marzipan.

4. Brush the top of the cake and put on the round of marzipan.

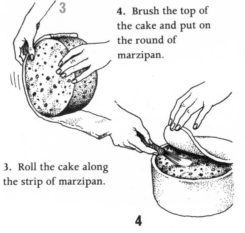

5. Roll the top of the cake lightly. Roll the sides of the cake with a jam jar.

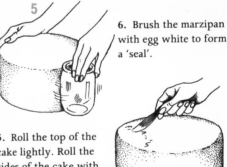

6. Brush the marzipan with egg white to form a 'seal'.

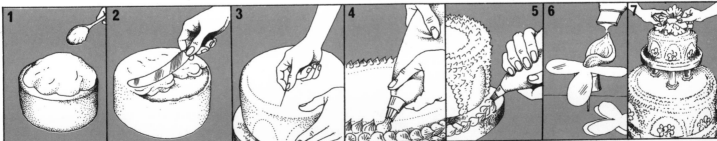

1. To coat the cake with icing, put the total amount for the first coating i.e. about $\frac{1}{3}$ on the cake.

2. Spread out until evenly coated with an icing spatula.
3. Let the first coat dry before putting on the second coat and when

this is dry 'prick out' the design with a fine needle.
4. Pipe the design with a fine rose or star tip.

5. When dry pipe the borders, you could use the same tip. Hold the bag at an angle as shown in the sketch.

6. To make flowers, put a piece of waxed paper on an icing nail Pipe out the petals.
7. Place the flowers in position and stand the

top tier on the pillars. Complete the cake with a spray of real flowers and ribbon on top.

There are few things more delicious than a feather-light, freshly baked biscuit, topped with plenty of butter or a hot muffin to start the day off right.

Blue Print Recipes

1. Baking Powder Biscuits

2 cups flour · 3–5 teaspoons baking powder* · 1 teaspoon salt · 2 tablespoons shortening · ¾ cup milk.

*Remember that the greater amount of baking powder gives a very well risen biscuit but I find it crisps less, so you can choose the amount you wish.

To make Sift the flour and baking powder with the salt. Cut in the shortening, then blend with milk to a soft rolling consistency. Use more milk only if needed to make the dough soft. The dough will make your fingers slightly sticky as you handle it. Turn out of the bowl on to a lightly floured board and knead very lightly for only ½ minute. Roll out to about ½-inch in thickness. Cut into triangles or rounds, or make one round. Lift the small biscuits or large round onto an ungreased baking sheet. Mark the round into 8 sections.

To cook Bake small biscuits towards the top of a hot to very hot oven, 450–475°F, for about 10–12 minutes until firm to the touch. The biscuit round should be baked in the center of the oven for about 20

Baking powder biscuits and bran and nut muffins

minutes. Reduce the heat to moderately hot, 400°F, after 10–12 minutes.

To serve When fresh, with butter, honey or jam. *All recipes based on this make 8–12 biscuits.*

To vary

Fruit Biscuits Add 2–4 tablespoons sugar plus 2½–4 tablespoons dried fruit.

Flavored Biscuits Add a little spice, grated lemon rind, etc. to the flour to flavor the mixture.

Cream Biscuits Mix with 1 egg and light cream instead of milk.

Cheese Biscuits Add a generous amount of seasoning to the flour and 4–5 tablespoons finely grated cheese.

Drop Biscuits Use 1 cup of milk.

Buttermilk Biscuits Use buttermilk in place of milk, omit baking powder and substitute ½ teaspoon soda.

● **AVOID** *Making the mixture, or any quick breads based on a biscuit dough, too dry; the mixture should be slightly sticky (see Blue Print). Baking too slowly.*

● **TO RECTIFY** *If the mixture is too dry be sure to add a little extra liquid. See baking instructions in Blue Print.*

● **SHORT CUT** *The large round biscuit is very speedy to prepare, although it takes longer to cook than small biscuits. Use a prepared biscuit mix.*

Strawberry Bonanza Shortcake

Ingredients as Blue Print, but increase the recipe by half, PLUS 3 tablespoons sugar added with the dry ingredients. Increase milk to 1½ cups in all. Prepare as Blue Print and roll out into three rounds. Cook as Blue Print. Halve 2 pints strawberries, reserving several for garnish. Whip 1½ cups heavy cream and sandwich the shortcake rounds with whipped cream and halved strawberries. Top with whipped cream and whole berries. Pictured on page 89.

Storing and freezing *The uncooked biscuits on this page may be stored in a refrigerator overnight before baking. All the biscuits freeze well when cooked. The popovers and muffins do not freeze quite as well.*

To use leftovers *Leftover biscuits, as on this page, can be freshened if you dip them in a little milk then heat in the oven for a few minutes. Otherwise split and toast.*

2. Muffins

2 cups flour · 2 teaspoons baking powder · ¼ teaspoon salt · 2 tablespoons sugar · 1 cup milk · 1 egg · 2 tablespoons melted butter.

To make Mix and sift together in a bowl all the dry ingredients. Add the milk to the well beaten egg in another bowl, then the melted butter. Mix in the dry ingredients and stir just enough to mix together. Fill greased medium muffin pans ⅔ full.

To cook Bake in a moderately hot oven, 400°F, for 20–25 minutes. *All recipes based on this make 10–12 muffins.*

Bran and Pineapple Muffins

Ingredients as Blue Print PLUS 1 cup bran substituted for 1 cup flour and ½ cup crushed pineapple. Increase baking powder to 2½ teaspoons. Make as Blue Print, adding the crushed pineapple with the dry ingredients. Bake in well-greased muffin pans in a moderately hot oven, 400°F, for 25–30 minutes.

Bran and Nut Muffins

Ingredients as Bran and Pineapple Muffins (above) MINUS the crushed pineapple PLUS ½ cup finely chopped pecans or walnuts. Make as the Blue Print, adding the nuts with the dry ingredients. Bake as Bran and Pineapple Muffins.

Corn Muffins

Ingredients and method as Blue Print PLUS 1 cup cornmeal and MINUS 1 cup flour. Increase baking powder to 3 teaspoons. Cook as Blue Print either in muffin pans or an 8- or 9-inch square pan.

● **AVOID** *Overmixing the dry ingredients; the muffins will be spoiled. The flour should be stirred in just enough to moisten it.*

Blue Print Recipe

Pancakes

1 cup flour · 1 teaspoon baking powder · $\frac{1}{4}$ teaspoon salt · 1 egg · 1 cup milk* · 2 tablespoons butter.

*Use more milk if a thinner pancake is desired.

To make Sift the flour and baking powder with the salt. Mix the well beaten egg with the milk and melted butter. Stir into the flour mixture only until flour is moistened. There will still be lumps.

To cook The old-fashioned griddle has become difficult to find, but modern versions are being made. The alternatives are to use the solid hotplate on your stove, if it has one, a cast iron skillet; or an electric frypan. Grease the griddle or substitute and warm. Test by dropping a teaspoon of the batter mixture on to the warm plate and the batter should set almost at once and begin to bubble within 1 minute. If this does not happen then heat a little longer before cooking the pancakes.

Drop from the tablespoon onto the griddle and cook for 1–2 minutes until the top surface is covered with bubbles (as shown in the picture). Put a pancake turner under the pancake and turn carefully and cook for the same time on the second side. To test if cooked, press gently with the edge of the knife; if no batter oozes out then the pancakes are cooked. Lift onto a clean teacloth on a wire cooling rack and wrap in the cloth until ready to serve.

Pancakes

Pancakes

To serve Warm topped with butter and jam, or cooked well drained fruit or maple syrup. They are also excellent if served with syrup and sausages or bacon. *All recipes based on this make 10–12.*

To vary

Buttermilk Pancakes

Ingredients as Blue Print MINUS the baking powder and PLUS $\frac{1}{2}$ teaspoon soda and using buttermilk or sour milk in place of milk. Make and cook as the Blue Print.

Oatmeal Griddlecakes

Method as Blue Print but use half flour and half quick-cooking rolled oats. Allow the batter to stand for several hours before cooking as the Blue Print. A tablespoon sugar can be added if wished.

Cornmeal Pancakes

Use half cornmeal and half flour.

Apple Pancakes

Add $\frac{1}{2}$ cup finely chopped apples to the batter.

Blueberry Pancakes

Add $\frac{1}{2}$ cup fresh blueberries to the batter.

Corn and Ham Pancakes

Add $\frac{1}{4}$ cup cooked or canned corn and $\frac{1}{4}$ cup chopped ham to the batter.

Ham and Cheese Pancakes

Add 1 cup grated Cheddar cheese and $\frac{1}{2}$ cup ham to the batter.

● **AVOID** *Making the batter too wet; otherwise the mixture spreads too much. Cooking too slowly.*
● **TO RECTIFY** *Add a little more flour if you have been generous with the liquid. Test heat of griddle, or pan, as described above.*

Cooking with yeast is most rewarding, for it produces delicious rolls and bread with the minimum of expenditure. Many people feel it takes a very long time to prepare, but for most of the time the yeast mixture is rising, or proving, and you have nothing to do but leave it until it is ready.

Blue Print Recipe

White Bread

13 cups all-purpose white flour · 3–7 teaspoons salt* · 1 oz. fresh yeast · 1 teaspoon sugar · approximately 4 cups lukewarm water.

*The first time you make bread use the smaller quantity of salt until you are sure how much you like. Remember refined table salt is less strong than coarse salt.

To make Sift the flour and salt into a warm bowl. Cream the yeast with the sugar, add *most of the liquid*. Make a well in the center of the bowl of flour, pour in the yeast liquid and sprinkle flour on top. Cover the bowl with a clean cloth and leave for about 20 minutes until the surface is covered with bubbles. Mix the liquid with the flour; if too dry then add sufficient lukewarm liquid to give an elastic dough. Turn out of the bowl on to a floured board and knead until smooth (see below for method of testing this). Either put back into the bowl and cover with a cloth or put into a large greased polyethylene bag. Leave to rise until almost double the original size. Turn onto the board again and knead. Form into the shape of loaves you like and place on a greased and floured baking sheet; for the loaf pan illustrated, grease, flour and warm the pans. Form the dough into an oblong shape, fold into three to fit the pan and lower into the pan. The dough should come just over halfway up the

pans. If you brush the loaves with a little melted butter or oil it produces an excellent crust. Cover the pans with a cloth or polyethylene; allow to rise for 20 minutes.

To cook Bake for about 20–25 minutes in the center of a hot oven, 425–450°F, after this lower the heat to very moderate, 300°F, and complete cooking. A 9 × 5-inch loaf pan takes a total of about 35–40 minutes.

To test Turn the loaves out of the pans; knock firmly on the base; the bread should sound hollow. If it does not, return to the oven for a little longer. *Makes 3 loaves.*

To vary

Richer bread Use half milk and half water and rub 2–4 tablespoons shortening into the flour.

Milk loaf Use all milk for mixing, plus an egg if wished and rub 4 tablespoons butter or margarine into the flour.

Brown bread Use half white and half wholewheat flour.

Wholewheat bread Use all wholewheat flour but this absorbs more liquid.

● **AVOID** *Putting the yeast mixture in too warm a place; room temperature is generally ideal. Overkneading the dough.*

● **TO RECTIFY** *If you have put the dough in too hot a place you have killed the yeast too early and the dough will not rise. Test to see if you have kneaded sufficiently, then* stop. *The way to test is to press with a lightly floured finger; if the impression comes out, the dough is ready for the next stage.*

● **SHORT CUT** *One can buy risen, partially cooked bread doughs.*

● **TO USE ACTIVE DRY YEAST** *Allow half the quantity of fresh yeast ($\frac{1}{2}$ oz. dried yeast = 1 oz. fresh yeast). Mix the sugar with the lukewarm liquid. Sprinkle the yeast on top, wait for about 10 minutes, stir well then proceed as fresh yeast.*

Lardy Bread

Ingredients as the Blue Print using $4\frac{1}{4}$ cups flour, etc. PLUS a little lard, sugar and dried fruit. Roll the risen dough out to an oblong shape. Spread with a very thin layer of

softened lard, about 2 tablespoons, the same amount of sugar and some dried fruit. Fold as puff pastry, then repeat this once or twice more adding the lard, sugar and fruit. Form into required shape loaf and score the top. Bake as the Blue Print, but allow a little longer cooking time.

Dough for Sweet Rolls

Most small sweet rolls are made as the Blue Print, but to each $4\frac{1}{4}$ cups flour rub in about 4 tablespoons shortening; add about $\frac{1}{4}$ cup sugar and mix with an egg and enough lukewarm liquid to bind.

Soft Topped Buns

Ingredients as the Blue Print PLUS a little milk and flour for topping.

Make the dough as the Blue Print; be quite sure it is a soft consistency. Allow it to prove in bulk as the Blue Print but form into small rounds instead of a loaf. Put onto warmed, lightly greased baking trays. Press the buns lightly with your hand to flatten, brush with milk and sprinkle with flour. Allow to prove for about 15 minutes. Bake for about 12 minutes near top of a hot oven, 425°F.

Fruit Loaf

Ingredients and method as Blue Print but add $\frac{1}{4}-\frac{1}{2}$ cup dried fruit to the flour.

Fruit Malt Loaf

Ingredients and method as Blue Print PLUS $1\frac{1}{4}-2\frac{1}{2}$ tablespoons powdered malt and $\frac{1}{4}-\frac{1}{2}$ cup dried fruit added to the flour.

Storing and freezing *This is a somewhat complex subject so consult your freezer book; but you can store the unproven dough overnight in the refrigerator where it will begin to rise slowly, or you can freeze both unbaked and baked yeast breads.*

To use leftovers *Stale bread can be freshened by heating in the oven or by dipping quickly in a little liquid if very stale and heating in the oven.*

The mixture for doughnuts may be either the bread dough or dough for sweet rolls opposite or the baking powder version below.

Blue Print

Perfect Doughnuts

To make   Choose the dough you prefer. For round doughnuts, roll into balls (remember those made with yeast dough rise to about twice the original size). Make a depression with the tip of your finger or the handle of a spoon and fill with jam, then reroll the ball to cover the jam. For ring doughnuts, roll out and cut into rings. Allow yeast doughnuts to prove as instructions opposite.
To cook   In deep fat or oil. Heat oil or fat until it reaches 370–375°F; a cube of bread should turn golden in 30 seconds. Slide the doughnuts into the hot oil or fat; put in as many as you can but allow space between to turn them over. Cook quickly until they

Making Doughnuts

rise to the surface and begin to color underneath, turn carefully and continue to cook until golden brown all over. Lift out carefully with a perforated spoon or slotted pancake turner. Drain over the pan for a few seconds, then on absorbent paper. Roll in sugar spread on a plate or drop into a bag of sugar and shake vigorously until coated.
To serve   When fresh with coffee, tea or instead of a dessert.
● **AVOID** *Making the dough too dry.*

● **TO RECTIFY** *Blend with enough liquid to give a soft pliable dough.*
Storing and freezing *See opposite.*
To use leftovers *If fried for 1 minute only, until very hot, you freshen a rather stale doughnut; of course the sugar coating spoils the oil or fat so it is wiser to warm through in the oven.*

Baking Powder Doughnuts

2 cups flour; 2 teaspoons baking powder; good pinch salt; 2 tablespoons melted butter or oil; 1 egg; 2–4 tablespoons sugar; approximately 8–9 tablespoons milk or better still use milk and water. *To fill:* jam (see Blue Print). *To cook:* oil or fat (see Blue Print). *To coat:* sugar (see Blue Print).

Sift the dry ingredients together. Add the butter or oil, the egg and sugar and mix; gradually add enough milk to make a soft rolling or handling dough. If slightly sticky, cover and stand for about 10 minutes. Prepare and cook as Blue Print. *Makes about 8.*

eight

PUDDINGS & DESSERTS

Few forms of cooking are more interesting and rewarding than producing a delicious pie or dessert, often with the minimum of effort, for some of the most interesting recipes are the simplest. The dessert rounds off the meal and helps to turn it into something exciting and memorable.

Pies are so much a part of American tradition that I have included a wide variety of them on pages 109–115. Families vary so much in size these days that I have given the proportions for 8-, 9-, and 10-inch pies. Excellent pie crust mixes and frozen crusts ready for baking make pies a simple task. The owner of a home freezer could on a rainy morning put up a number of fruit pies ready for use on a busy day or for unexpected guests.

Fruit flans are always a delight to look at, as well as to eat. And they add a touch of elegance to the dinner table. However, often a perfect fruit flan is spoiled because the cook is too impatient to put the ingredients together properly; the method on page 112 shows the right way to do this.

Meringue, custard, cream and chiffon pies are not neglected either. These are easy pies to make and a fitting end for any meal.

A baked or boiled custard may seem very homely fare but it is the basis of so many interesting and indeed quite exotic desserts. I have lost count of the number of people who ask me why custards curdle or why the pastry rises and the custard sinks in a pie. You will find the answers on page 117 in the Blue Print and the recipe for Custard Peach Pie.

On most pages I have given you a BLUE PRINT RECIPE, for if you know how to make the simple basic dish, upon which so many other recipes are based, you have unlimited scope for imaginative and varied desserts.

Have you ever made your own ice cream or fruit ices? They are ridiculously simple, but how delicious. If you own a home freezer then make these in larger quantities so they are always available.

With the development in freezing and excellent canning, practically every fruit can now be obtained in some form for most of the year, so fruit desserts should never be monotonous. A variety of these are on page 120. For those of you who are watching your weight and counting calories the fruit ice recipes are very helpful in adding interest to a reducing diet. So are the gelatin desserts on page 125.

I hope you will enjoy the varied selection of pies and desserts.

Making Plain Pastry

Although the short crust pastry on page 80 may be a little easier to handle because it contains less shortening, the recipe here is my favorite for everyday pies—dessert or savory. These proportions produce a tender flaky crust. Vegetable shortening, butter or lard may be used as the shortening according to your taste, but I prefer a mixture of half shortening and half butter or half lard and half butter or shortening.

The table gives proportions for two-crust 8-inch, 9-inch and 10-inch pies. Halve the ingredients for a one-crust pie.

Blue Print Recipe

Plain Pastry

	8″	9″	10″
Flour	2 cups	2½ cups	3 cups
Salt	½ tsp.	¾ tsp.	1 tsp.
Shortening	⅔ cup	¾ cup	1 cup
Water	4–5 tbsp.	5–6 tbsp.	7–8 tbsp.

To make Sift the flour and salt into a mixing bowl. Work in the shortening with your fingertips, two knives or a pastry blender until like fine bread crumbs. *Gradually* blend in the water until the pastry almost leaves the sides of the bowl. Gather into two equal-sized balls and flatten slightly. Roll out on a lightly floured pastry board using a lightly-floured rolling pin. The dough should be 2-inches larger than the inverted pie pan. Fold dough into quarters or roll around the rolling pin and ease into the pan. Do not stretch. Add the filling of your choice and trim the edge of the pastry so you have a ½-inch overhang. In the same fashion, roll out the remaining dough and place over the filling. Trim the edge of the pastry so you have a 1-inch overhang. Fold the top dough under the lower dough, roll and pinch to seal, leaving a raised edge. Flute or press with a fork. Cut slits in the top to allow the steam to escape.

To cook Bake in a 450°F oven 10 minutes, reduce heat to moderate, 350°F, and bake a further 25–30 minutes to make sure the fruit is cooked.

● **AVOID** *Overhandling the pastry. Using too much water; this produces a sticky dough which is difficult to handle and a tough crust.*

● **TO RECTIFY** *If the pastry is damp and sticky, flour the pastry board and rolling pin generously.*

Storing and freezing *Fruit pies and tarts are best eaten fresh. Baked and unbaked shells freeze well; unbaked shells need not be thawed before baking—just slip them into the oven. Unbaked fruit pies are apt to become soggy if frozen, but baked pies freeze well. Thaw before reheating in a 350°F oven.*

Simple fruit pie

th...
Spri...
tablesp...
with bu...
Prick or s...
sheet and co...
with whipped...
luxury touch, Ha...

a

Lattice-top Pies

Make plain pastry for ... two-crust pie (see Blue Print opposite). Roll out as Blue Print but allow 1-inch of pastry to overhang the bottom edge. Fill (see chart below). Cut the second rolled-out crust into thin strips with a knife or pastry cutter. Lay half the strips of pastry across the top of the pie. Turning back alternate strips and starting at the center of the pie, lay one of the remaining strips across it. Return the folded strips and turn back the alternate strips that were previously flat. Lay another strip across and continue weaving until the lattice is finished. Fold the overhang over the strips and build up a high rim; flute the rim. Place pie on a baking sheet and cook as Blue Print opposite.

	8″	9″
Apple Pie	5 cups sliced apples	6 cups sliced apples
	pinch salt	pinch salt
	½ cup sugar	¾ cup sugar
	1½ tbsps. cornstarch	2 tbsps. cornstarch
	½ tsp. cinnamon or nutmeg	1 tsp. cinnamon or nutmeg
	1 tbsp. lemon juice	1½ tbsps. lemon juice
	1 tbsp. butter	2 tbsps. butter
Beach Plum Pie	3 cups pitted plums	4 cups pitted plums
	1⅓ cups sugar	1½ cups sugar
	1½ tbsps. cornstarch	2 tbsps. cornstarch
	1 tbsp. lemon juice	1½ tbsps. lemon juice
	1 tbsp. butter	2 tbsps. butter
Blackberry Pie	3 cups blackberries	4 cups blackberries
	1 cup sugar	1¼ cups sugar
	2 tbsps. cornstarch	3 tbsps. cornstarch
	1 tbsp. lemon juice	1½ tbsps. lemon juice
	1 tbsp. butter	2 tbsps. butter
Blueberry Pie	3 cups blueberries	4 cups blueberries
	⅓ cup sugar	½ cup sugar
	2 tbsps. tapioca*	3 tbsps. tapioca*
	1 tbsp. lemon juice	1½ tbsps. lemon juice
	1 tbsp. butter	2 tbsps. butter
Cherry Pie	3 cups pitted red tart cherries	4 cups pitted red tart cherries
	1⅓ cups sugar	1½ cups sugar
	3 tbsps. tapioca*	¼ cup tapioca*
	¼ tsp. almond extract	½ tsp. almond extract
	1 tbsp. butter	2 tbsps. butter

*Use instant tapioca.

Fresh Apricot Pie

Pastry as Blue Print for a two-crust 8-inch pie; 8-10 apricots; $\frac{2}{3}$ cup sugar; 1 tablespoon lemon juice; 1 tablespoon butter.

Line an 8-inch pie pan as in Blue Print. Dip the fruit in boiling water 10–15 seconds, peel, halve and pit. Place apricot halves hole side down in the pan. Sprinkle with the sugar and lemon juice and dot with the butter. Weave a lattice top (above). Place the thumb on the pastry rim at an angle and pinch the dough with the knuckle of the index finger toward the thumb to make a roped edge. Place on Baking sheet and bake as Blue Print. (Illustrated on page 109.)

Hard Sauce

Cream 4 tablespoons butter with $\frac{3}{4}$ cup sifted confectioners' sugar. Gradually blend in 2 tablespoons brandy. Pile or pipe into a dish; chill thoroughly. *Serves 4–5.*

Mincemeat

2 lbs. beef; 1 lb. suet; 6 lb. apples; 3 lb. raisins; 2 lb. dried currants; $\frac{1}{2}$ lb. citron; 1 lb. brown sugar; 4 cups molasses; 2 quarts cider; 1 tablespoon salt; 1 tablespoon pepper; 1 tablespoon mace; 1 tablespoon ginger; 4 tablespoons cinnamon; 2 nutmegs grated; 2 cups brandy; 2 cups Madeira wine. Mix the chopped beef and suet, peeled, cored and sliced apples, raisins, currants, chopped citron, sugar, molasses, cider, seasonings and spices in a large kettle. Simmer for about 2 hours, stirring frequently. Cool and add the brandy and Madeira. Seal in jars. *About 8 quarts.* Allow to age at least 6 weeks before using.

Deep Dish Fruit Pies

Use $\frac{1}{2}$ recipe for a 9-inch two-crust pie. Roll out in a 9-inch square, large enough to cover an 8-inch square baking dish. Use 12 cups peeled sliced apples or peaches or 7–8 cups berries; 1–1$\frac{1}{2}$ cups sugar; 2 teaspoons cinnamon or nutmeg (optional); pinch of salt; $\frac{1}{4}$ cup cornstarch; 1$\frac{1}{2}$–2 tablespoons lemon juice; 2–3 tablespoons butter.

Prepare as fruit pie. Cover with dough and fold overhang under. Press against rim of pan with a fork to seal. Prick or slit top. Bake in a 450°F oven 10 minutes; reduce heat to

fruit tarts

350°F and continue baking 30–35 minutes until filling is bubbling and crust brown.

Fruit Tarts

Make $\frac{1}{2}$ recipe for Plain Pastry (see Blue Print) or 1 recipe Fleur Pastry (page 112). Roll out dough and cut into 5$\frac{1}{2}$-inch rounds. Place dough over inverted small muffin pans, fluting the sides to fit. If using individual tart pans, cut dough 1-inch larger than the inverted pan and place dough inside pans. Prick bottoms and bake in a 450°F oven for 10–12 minutes or until golden brown. Cool in pans, remove, then either fill with fruit and glaze as for a fruit flan (see page 112) or fill with fresh fruit, such as raspberries, strawberries or blackberries and top with whipped cream or ice cream.

Ingredients for Fruit Pies

10″	8″	9″	10″
8 cups sliced apple pinch salt 1 cup sugar 2$\frac{1}{2}$ tbsps. cornstarch 2 tsps. cinnamon or nutmeg	**Cranberry Pie** 2 cups halved cranberries 1 cup dried currants $\frac{3}{4}$ cup sugar 3 tbsps. tapioca* 1 tbsp. lemon juice 1 tbsp. butter	2$\frac{2}{3}$ cups halved cranberries 1$\frac{1}{3}$ cups dried currants 1 cup sugar $\frac{1}{4}$ cup tapioca* 1$\frac{1}{2}$ tbsps. lemon juice 2 tbsps. butter	3$\frac{1}{3}$ cups halved cranberries 1$\frac{2}{3}$ cups dried currants 1$\frac{1}{4}$ cups sugar $\frac{1}{3}$ cup tapioca* 2 tbsps. lemon juice 3 tbsps. butter
2 tbsps. lemon juice 3 tbsps. butter	**Mincemeat Pie** 1 9-oz. pkg. condensed mincemeat; or 3 cups canned or fresh	2 9-oz. pkgs. condensed mincemeat; or 4 cups canned or fresh	3 9-oz. pkgs. condensed mincemeat; or 5 cups canned or fresh
5 cups pitted plums 1$\frac{2}{3}$ cups sugar 2$\frac{1}{2}$ tbsps. cornstarch 2 tbsps. lemon juice 3 tbsps. butter	**Peach Pie** 5 cups sliced peaches $\frac{2}{3}$ cup sugar pinch of salt 3 tbsps. tapioca* 1 tbsp. lemon juice 1 tbsp. butter	6 cups sliced peaches $\frac{3}{4}$ cup sugar pinch of salt $\frac{1}{4}$ cup tapioca* 1$\frac{1}{2}$ tbsps. lemon juice 2 tbsps. butter	8 cups sliced peaches 1 cup sugar pinch of salt $\frac{1}{3}$ cup tapioca* 2 tbsps. lemon juice 3 tbsps. butter
5 cups blackberries 1$\frac{1}{2}$ cups sugar $\frac{1}{4}$ cup cornstarch 2 tbsps. lemon juice 3 tbsps. butter	**Raspberry Pie** 3 cups raspberries $\frac{1}{2}$ cup sugar 1 tbsp. cornstarch 1 tbsp. butter	4 cups raspberries $\frac{3}{4}$ cup sugar 2 tbsps. cornstarch 2 tbsps. butter	5 cups raspberries 1 cup sugar 3 tbsps. cornstarch 3 tbsps. butter
5 cups blueberries $\frac{2}{3}$ cup sugar $\frac{1}{4}$ cup tapioca* 2 tbsps. lemon juice 3 tbsps. butter	**Rhubarb Pie** 3 cups 1-inch sliced rhubarb 1$\frac{1}{4}$ cups sugar 2 tbsps. cornstarch 1 tsp. grated orange rind 1 tbsp. butter	4 cups 1-inch sliced rhubarb 1$\frac{2}{3}$ cups sugar 3 tbsps. cornstarch 1$\frac{1}{2}$ tsps. grated orange rind 2 tbsps. butter	5 cups 1-inch sliced rhubarb 2 cups sugar $\frac{1}{4}$ cup cornstarch 2 tsps. grated orange rind 3 tbsps. butter
5 cups pitted red tart cherries 1$\frac{2}{3}$ cups sugar $\frac{1}{3}$ cup tapioca* $\frac{3}{4}$ tsp. almond extract 3 tbsps. butter	**Strawberry Pie** 4 cups sliced strawberries $\frac{3}{4}$ cup sugar $\frac{1}{4}$ cup tapioca* 1 tbsp. lemon juice 1 tbsp. butter	5 cups sliced strawberries 1 cup sugar $\frac{1}{3}$ cup tapioca* 1$\frac{1}{2}$ tbsps. lemon juice 2 tbsps. butter	6 cups sliced strawberries 1$\frac{1}{4}$ cups sugar $\frac{1}{2}$ cup tapioca* 2 tbsps. lemon juice 3 tbsps. butter

These pies are filled with delicious, but unappetizing sounding, boiled custard. They are perfectly lovely when combined with fruit. I have also included a frozen pie. Go easy when serving this as it is very rich.

Blue Print Recipe

Cream Pie

½ recipe plain pastry for a 9-inch pie (page 170) · ½ cup sugar · ¼ cup cornstarch · ¼ teaspoon salt · 3 cups milk · 4 egg yolks · 2 tablespoons butter · 2 teaspoons vanilla.

To make Prepare the pie crust and bake blind (page 112). Stir the sugar, cornstarch and salt in an enamelled cast iron saucepan or the top of a double boiler. Combine the milk and lightly beaten egg yolks. Add gradually to the sugar combination.
To cook Place over low heat or boiling water, stirring constantly until the mixture thickens. It will thicken faster over direct heat but needs constant watching. Remove from heat and stir in butter and vanilla. Pour into baked pie shell and coat surface of custard filling with plastic wrap to avoid a skin forming on the top. Chill thoroughly.
To serve Garnish with whipped cream. This is particularly effective if the cream is piped onto the pie with a rose tube.
To vary Cover the hot filling with meringue (page 113) and bake the pie in a moderate oven, 350°F, for about 15 minutes.

● **AVOID** *Cooking the custard too rapidly: it will lump.*
● **TO RECTIFY** *If the custard shows any signs of lumping, remove from heat immediately and place in pan of cold water. You may whisk the lumps out, if possible, or strain the custard.*
● **SHORT CUT** *Use packaged pudding mixes.*

Storing and freezing *Cream pies are best eaten fresh. They do not freeze.*

Chocolate Cream Pie

Ingredients as Blue Print but use ⅓ cup sugar, 3 tablespoons cornstarch, pinch salt, 2 cups milk, 3 egg yolks, 1 tablespoon butter and 1 teaspoon vanilla. Make and serve as Blue Print.

8-inch Cream Pie

Ingredients as Blue Print but use ⅔ cup sugar, ⅓ cup cornstarch, ½ teaspoon salt, 4 cups milk, 5 egg yolks, 3 tablespoons butter and 1 tablespoon vanilla. Make as Blue Print.

10-inch Cream Pie

Ingredients as Blue Print PLUS 2 oz. melted bitter chocolate added with the butter and vanilla. Make and serve as Blue Print.

Banana Cream Pie

Ingredients as Blue Print PLUS 2 cups thinly sliced bananas. Make as Blue Print but cool the custard filling, covered with plastic wrap, in saucepan. Either fold the bananas into the cooled filling or line the bottom of the crust with bananas and pour cooled filling over.

Blueberry Cream Pie

Ingredients as Blue Print PLUS 1 cup blueberries. Cook the blueberries with the custard. Proceed as Blue Print.

Raspberry or Strawberry Cream Pie

Ingredients as Blue Print PLUS 1 cup sliced strawberries or whole raspberries. Make as Banana Cream Pie above.

Frozen Almond Pie

9-inch crumb crust made with macaroons (page 113); 2⅔ cups heavy cream; 3 egg whites; 3 egg yolks; ¼ cup sugar; ¾ cup finely ground macaroons; 1 teaspoon vanilla. Beat the cream and egg whites separately until stiff. Beat the egg yolks in a mixing bowl then add the sugar, macaroons and vanilla. Fold in the beaten egg whites and cream. Put in freezer 4–6 hours. Remove from freezer 10 minutes before serving.

Chocolate Rum Pie

Unbaked 9-inch crumb crust with graham crackers (page 113); 12 oz. cream cheese; ½ cup sugar; 2 eggs; 2 oz. bitter chocolate; 1 tablespoon rum. *For the topping:* 1 cup sour cream; 3 tablespoons sugar; 1 oz. bitter chocolate; 1 tablespoon rum.
Beat together the softened cream cheese, ½ cup sugar, beaten eggs and cooled 2 oz. chocolate melted with 1 tablespoon rum.
Bake in a 375°F oven for 20 minutes. Melt the chocolate with the rum, cool and mix with the sour cream. Spread over the cooked filling and bake 5 minutes more.

Sour Cream Lemon Pie

1 baked 9-inch pastry shell (page 109); 1 cup sugar; ½ cup corn starch; 1½ cups milk; 3 egg yolks; 1 teaspoon grated lemon rind; ⅓ cup lemon juice; ¼ cup margarine; 1 cup sour cream; whipped cream (optional). Mix sugar and corn starch in a 2-qt. saucepan. Gradually add milk, stirring until smooth. Stir in the slightly beaten egg yolks, lemon rind and lemon juice until blended. Add margarine. Cook over medium heat, stirring constantly, until mixture comes to a boil; boil 1 minute. Pour into bowl. Cover surface of pudding with waxed paper or plastic film. Chill. Fold in sour cream. Turn into baked pastry shell. Chill. Serve with whipped cream if wished.

Sour cream lemon pie

Cherry flan

Fruit Flans

There are various types of pastry you can use for the flan case but fleur pastry combines best with the fruit and glaze.

Blue Print Recipe

Fleur Pastry

Sufficient for one 8-inch flan ring: 6 tablespoons butter or best quality margarine · $\frac{1}{4}$ cup superfine sugar · 1 egg yolk · $1\frac{1}{2}$ cups flour · little cold water.

To make Cream the butter or margarine and sugar until soft and light. Beat in the egg yolk, add the sifted flour and blend with a pastry blender. Gradually stir in enough water to bind. Roll out to a circle about 10 inches in diameter.
If using a layer pan, grease lightly. If using a flan ring, stand on baking sheet.
Putting the rolling pin under the pastry to support it, lower into the pan or flan ring, see Sketch 1. Slip the rolling pin away as you do so, Sketch 2. Press the pastry into the ring with your fingers.
Either cut away any surplus pastry with a sharp knife, or else take the rolling pin backwards and forwards over the pastry, as Sketch 3.
To bake blind To keep the flan shell a perfect shape it should be weighted to prevent the pastry base rising and the sides losing their shape; this is called baking blind. The two best methods to use are either to prick the base of the flan shell, then put in a double thickness of foil and press firmly against the pastry. Or grease a round of waxed paper lightly and place greased side downwards into the flan shell. Fill with dried beans or rice, see Sketch 4.
Bake in the center of a moderate to moderately hot oven, 375–400°F, for 15–20 minutes, or until the pastry is just set. Remove the foil, or paper and beans or rice, then continue baking for a further 5–10 minutes until golden brown. Lift away the flan ring and if the pastry is a little pale return to the oven for a few minutes. Cool slightly on a wire cooling rack. When cold fill and glaze.
To Fill the Flan
You will need about 1 lb. of fruit. If using *cooked fruit*, poach carefully in syrup made with $\frac{1}{4}$ cup sugar to each $\frac{2}{3}$ cup water (use half the amount of water for soft fruits such as currants). Lift from the syrup and put in a strainer over a bowl. Retain the syrup. *Canned fruit* should be drained in the same way. *Frozen fruit* should be *almost* defrosted, then drained as above. It spoils the appearance and taste of *ripe cherries, raspberries and strawberries* if they are poached in syrup. Make a syrup from sugar and water (as above). Put the fruit into the syrup while it is still warm. Leave for 2–3 minutes, lift out and strain as above. Put the drained fruit into the flan shell carefully.
To Make the Glaze
If the flan shell is fairly shallow, use $\frac{2}{3}$ cup syrup, but if it is fairly deep, use $1\frac{1}{3}$ cups. Blend the syrup with 1 or 2 teaspoons arrowroot or cornstarch. Put into the saucepan, stir well and cook until thickened. Add a few drops of coloring if necessary, or about 2 tablespoons red currant jelly or strained raspberry jam for extra flavor. When thickened and clear, cool but do not allow to set. Brush or spread over the fruit, see Sketch 5. *Serves 6*.

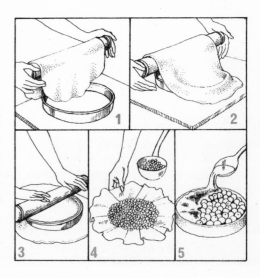

A meringue topping on a pie gives a look of luxury as well as a pleasant taste.

Meringue Pies

Blue Print Recipe

Lemon Meringue Pie

½ recipe plain pastry for 9-inch pie (page 109) · 1½ cups sugar · ¼ cup cornstarch · ¼ cup flour · 1½ cups boiling water · 4 egg yolks · grated rind 2 lemons · ½ cup lemon juice · 2 teaspoons butter.

To make Prepare pastry and bake blind (see page 112). Mix the sugar, cornstarch and flour together in the top of a double boiler and add boiling water, stirring constantly over heat until the mixture boils. Place the pan over boiling water and cook for 20 minutes. Add slightly beaten egg yolks and butter, blend well and cook for 2 minutes more. Remove pan from heat and add the grated rind and lemon juice. Fill baked pie shell and top with meringue (below). Push meringue to the edge of the pie shell so it will adhere and not shrink.

To cook Bake in a slow oven, 300°F, for 15 minutes or until lightly browned. Cool in a draught-free place.

Storing and freezing *Meringue pies are best eaten fresh although they may be stored for 1 day. They do not freeze.*

Meringue

3 egg whites; pinch salt; ¼ teaspoon cream of tartar; 6 tablespoons sugar; ½ teaspoon vanilla.

Beat egg whites at low speed in a completely dry and grease-free bowl. When frothy, add salt and cream of tartar and increase speed to medium. When the meringue holds soft peaks, add the sugar 1 tablespoon at a time and continue beating until stiff and glossy (about 5 minutes). Beat in vanilla. *Enough for a 9-inch pie.*

Meringue for 8-inch shell

Use 2 egg whites, pinch salt, ¼ teaspoon cream of tartar, ¼ cup sugar and ¼ teaspoon vanilla. Make as above.

Meringue for 10-inch shell

Use 4 egg whites, pinch salt, ¼ teaspoon cream of tartar, ½ cup sugar and ¾ teaspoon vanilla. Make as above.

Lime Meringue Pie

As Blue Print, but use ½ lime juice in place of lemon teaspoons grated lime rind.

Crumb Crust

Instead of the pastry shell make the crust of graham cracker or cookie crumbs. To 1½ cups crushed graham crackers add ½ cup melted butter and ¼ cup superfine sugar. Form into a 9-inch pie pan; do not bake. (If the contents of the pie are not to be further cooked, bake the crust in a moderate oven, 350°F, for 10 minutes.) Fill with the lemon or lime mixture, proceed as above. For an 8- or 10-inch crust, decrease or increase cracker crumbs by ¼ cup and sugar and butter by 1 tablespoon. If using cookie crumbs, omit sugar and halve butter.

Meringue Fruit Torte

3 egg whites; 1 cup sugar; ½ teaspoon vanilla; 2 teaspoons vinegar.

Beat the egg whites until they hold peaks. Beat in the sugar 1 tablespoon at a time until stiff and glossy (about 5 minutes). Beat in the vanilla and vinegar. Spread in a 9-inch pie pan rinsed out in cold water, pushing the meringue up the sides of the pan. Bake in a slow oven, 300°F, for 30 minutes. Fill with berries or sliced peaches and garnish with whipped cream.

Pumpkin-orange chiffon pie

Strawberry custard pie

While canned pumpkin makes pumpkin pie available throughout the year, I am one of those traditionalists who like to wait for the fall pumpkins before having my first pumpkin pie.

Blue Print Recipe

Pumpkin Pie

½ recipe plain pastry for 9-inch pie (page 109) · ¼ cup sugar · ½ teaspoon salt ½ teaspoon cinnamon · ½ teaspoon ginger · ½ teaspoon nutmeg · 1¼ cups steamed or canned pumpkin · 1 egg · ⅞ cup milk.

To make Line an 9-inch pie plate with plain pastry, making a high rim. In a large bowl, mix the sugar, salt and spices together. Gradually add the pumpkin, slightly beaten egg and milk; blend well. Pour into prepared pie pan.

To cook Bake in a hot oven, 450°F, for 10 minutes; reduce heat to moderate, 350°F, and cook for about 20 minutes longer or until a knife inserted in the center of the custard comes out clean. Cool.

Brandy Pumpkin Pie

Ingredients as Blue Print MINUS ½ cup milk PLUS ¼ cup brandy. Make and cook as Blue Print, adding brandy with the milk.

Rich Pumpkin Pie

Ingredients as Blue Print but use only 1 cup pumpkin, ½ cup milk, ½ cup heavy cream and 1 additional egg yolk. Make and cook as Blue Print.

Squash Pie

Ingredients as Blue Print MINUS pumpkin PLUS 1¼ cups steamed squash.

To Steam Squash or Pumpkin

Cut in half a large pumpkin or 4 acorn squash. Remove seeds and strings. Cut into smaller pieces and place face down in a rack over boiling water in a large kettle. Cover kettle tightly and steam until the pumpkin or squash is tender. Cool then scrape away the flesh and put through a food mill.

Pumpkin-Orange Chiffon Pie

½ recipe plain pastry for 9-inch pie (page 109); ½ cup sugar; 1 envelope unflavored gelatin; ½ teaspoon ginger; ½ teaspoon cinnamon; ½ teaspoon nutmeg; 3 egg yolks; ½ cup milk; 1¼ cups canned cooked pumpkin; 1 teaspoon orange rind; ¼ cup orange juice; 3 egg whites; ½ cup sugar; sweetened whipped cream; grated orange rind.

Prepare the pie crust, fluting the edge, and bake blind (page 112). In a 2-quart saucepan, stir together the sugar, gelatin, ginger, cinnamon and nutmeg. Beat together egg yolks and milk; add to saucepan. Cook over medium heat, stirring constantly, until mixture comes to a boil. Stir in pumpkin, orange rind and juice. Chill until partially set. Beat egg whites until frothy; gradually add sugar and beat until stiff peaks form. Fold egg whites into pumpkin mixture. Chill until firm (at least 6 hours). Serve with sweetened whipped cream, garnished with grated orange rind.

Pecan Pie I

½ recipe plain pastry for 9-inch pie (page 109); ¾ cup brown sugar; 1 tablespoon butter; 1 cup dark corn syrup; 3 eggs; pinch salt; 1 teaspoon vanilla; 1 cup coarsely chopped pecans.

Using a rotary beater, mix the sugar, melted butter, corn syrup, well beaten eggs and salt in a mixing bowl. When well blended, stir in the vanilla and nuts. Pour into a pastry-lined pie pan.

Bake in a moderate oven, 350°F, for about 50–60 minutes or until the filling is set. Cool.

Pecan Pie II

½ recipe plain pastry for 9-inch pie (page 109); ½ cup brown sugar; ¼ lb. butter; 3 eggs; ¼ teaspoon salt; 1 cup light corn syrup; ½ cup milk; ½ teaspoon vanilla; ½ cup finely chopped pecans. *For the topping:* ¾ cup heavy cream, ½ cup pecan halves.

Using a rotary beater, mix the sugar, melted butter, well beaten eggs, salt, corn syrup and milk in a mixing bowl. When well blended, add the vanilla dnd nuts. Pour the mixture into a pastry-lined pie pan.

Bake in a moderate oven, 350°F, for 40–50 minutes or until the filling is set. Chill. Cover the top with whipped cream and garnish with pecan halves.

Custard Pie

½ recipe plain pastry for 9-inch pie (page 109); 1 recipe Baked Custard (page 117).

Line a pie pan with the prepared pastry and bake blind (page 112). Pour the hot custard mixture into the hot shell and sprinkle with nutmeg.

Bake in a 325°F oven for 30–40 minutes or until the custard is set. Cool.

Strawberry Custard Pie

Prepare a pie shell of Fleur Pastry baked blind (see page 112). Fill it with Custard Sauce (page 117). Hull 2 pints of strawberries, selecting only the most perfect berries and mix gently with ¾ cup sugar. Place the berries point up in the custard sauce. *Serves 6.*

One of the airiest and lightest desserts you can serve is a chiffon pie. Leading in popularity is the Lemon Chiffon Pie, but do not neglect the others—they are delicious too. They are good with either a baked plain pastry shell (page 109) or a crumb shell (page 113).

Blue Print Recipe

Lemon Chiffon Pie

$\frac{1}{2}$ recipe plain pastry for 9-inch pie (109) or crumb crust (113) · 1 envelope unflavored gelatin · $\frac{1}{4}$ cup water · 4 egg yolks · $\frac{1}{2}$ cup sugar · $\frac{1}{2}$ cup lemon juice · 1 tablespoon grated lemon rind · 4 egg whites · $\frac{1}{2}$ cup sugar · $\frac{1}{2}$ cup heavy cream.

To make and cook Prepare the pie shell; if using plain pastry, bake blind (page 112). Soften the gelatin in the water. Mix the beaten egg yolks, sugar and lemon juice in the top of a double boiler. Place over boiling water and stir until the mixture is thickened. Remove from heat and stir in the lemon rind and gelatin; stir until gelatin is dissolved. Chill in the refrigerator until the gelatin begins to set. Beat the egg whites until they hold soft peaks. Beat in the sugar 1 table-spoon at a time making a thick meringue. Beat the cream in a separate bowl until thick. Fold the beaten egg whites and whipped cream into the thickening gelatin mixture. Pour into the pie shell and chill until set, about 3–4 hours.

● **AVOID** *Adding the beaten whites and cream before the gelatin mixture thickens; the eggs and cream will lose their airiness.*
● **TO RECTIFY** *If the whites begin to lose their airiness, stop adding immediately. Place the gelatin mixture over a bowl of ice cubes and stir until the mixture thickens more.*
● **SHORTCUT** *Chill gelatin mixture over a bowl of ice cubes, stirring occasionally, to hasten thickening.*

8-inch Lemon Chiffon Pie

Ingredients as Blue Print but use 2 teaspoons unflavored gelatin, 3 tablespoons water, 3 egg yolks, $\frac{1}{3}$ cup sugar, $\frac{1}{3}$ cup lemon juice, 2 teaspoons grated lemon rind, 3 egg whites, $\frac{1}{3}$ cup sugar and $\frac{1}{3}$ cup heavy cream. Make as Blue Print.

10-inch Lemon Chiffon Pie

Ingredients as Blue Print but use 4 teaspoons unflavored gelatin, $\frac{1}{3}$ cup water, 5 egg yolks, $\frac{2}{3}$ cup sugar, $\frac{2}{3}$ cup lemon juice, 4 teaspoons grated lemon rind, 5 egg whites, $\frac{2}{3}$ cup sugar and $\frac{3}{4}$ cup heavy cream. Make as Blue Print.

Orange Chiffon Pie

Ingredients as Blue Print MINUS water, lemon juice and rind PLUS $\frac{3}{4}$ cup orange juice and 1 tablespoon orange rind. Use $\frac{1}{4}$ cup orange juice to soften the gelatin. Make as Blue Print.

Lime Chiffon Pie

Ingredients as Blue Print MINUS lemon juice and rind PLUS an equal amount of lime juice and rind. Make as Blue Print.

Chocolate Chiffon Pie

Ingredients as Blue Print MINUS lemon juice and rind PLUS 2 oz. bitter chocolate, $\frac{1}{2}$ cup milk, $\frac{1}{2}$ teaspoon salt and 1 teaspoon vanilla extract. Soften the gelatin in water as Blue Print. Melt the chocolate with the sugar, salt and milk in the top of a double boiler. Add the beaten eggs. Proceed as Blue Print, adding vanilla when the mixture has thickened.

Coffee Chiffon Pie

Ingredients as Blue Print MINUS lemon juice and rind PLUS $\frac{3}{4}$ cup extra strong coffee. Soften the gelatin in $\frac{1}{4}$ cup of the cold coffee. Proceed as Blue Print.

Black Bottom Pie

$\frac{1}{2}$ recipe plain pastry for 9-inch pie; 1 envelope unflavored gelatin; $\frac{1}{4}$ cup water; $1\frac{3}{4}$ cups milk; 4 egg yolks; $\frac{1}{2}$ cup sugar; 4 teaspoons cornstarch; $1\frac{1}{2}$ oz. bitter chocolate; 2 tablespoons rum or brandy; 4 egg whites; $\frac{1}{4}$ teaspoon cream of tartar; $\frac{1}{2}$ cup sugar. *For garnish:* 1 cup heavy cream, chocolate shavings.
Prepare the pie crust and bake blind (page 112). Soften the gelatin in the water. Beat the milk and egg yolks together and stir gradually into the sugar and cornstarch. Cook over hot water, stirring constantly, until the mixture thickens. Remove 1 cup of the custard mixture; set aside. Dissolve the softened gelatin in the remaining hot custard. Chill. Add the melted chocolate to the 1 cup reserved custard and blend well; when cool, pour into the pie shell. When the gelatin mixture thickens and begins to set, beat in the rum or brandy. Beat the egg whites until frothy, add the cream of tartar and continue beating until whites hold soft peaks. Add the sugar 1 tablespoon at a time and beat until the meringue is thick and glossy (about 5 minutes). Fold into the thickened gelatin mixture and pour onto the chocolate custard. Chill 3–4 hours or until set. Garnish with whipped cream and chocolate shavings.

Lemon chiffon pie

115

Contrasting textures in food add interest to many dishes and both Brown Bettys and Crumbles are excellent examples of combining ultra crisp toppings and soft fruit. They are quick and easy to make and ideal for family or special occasions.

Blue Print Recipes

1. Brown Betty

1–1¼ lb. prepared fruit · little water · sugar to taste. For the betty mixture: 4–5 large slices bread · 6 tablespoons butter or margarine · ¼ cup sugar (preferably brown).

To make If using firm fruit, such as apples, plums, etc., cook in a covered saucepan with a *little* water and sugar to taste until softened. Berry fruit (such as raspberries, blackberries, etc.) may also be cooked first, but if you prefer these to remain firm then do not heat.

There are two ways of making a brown betty. The first is to remove the crusts and then cut the bread into neat fingers; the second method is to make fairly coarse crumbs from the bread. Heat the butter or margarine in a large skillet and sauté the bread in this until just golden colored. Put one third of the bread slices or crumbs into a pie or oven-proof dish, sprinkle with some of the sugar. Add half the fruit puree. If using uncooked soft fruit sprinkle with sugar. Put a second layer of bread and a sprinkling of sugar, then the rest of the fruit puree or fruit and sugar. Top with an even layer of bread and sugar.

To cook Bake for about 35–40 minutes in the center of a moderate oven, 350–375°F.

To serve In the dish or inverted on a hot serving plate and decorated with cooked or raw fruit.

To vary See below under Crumble.

2. Fruit Crumble

1¼ lb. prepared fruit · little water · sugar to taste. For the crumble: 1 cup flour · 4 tablespoons butter or margarine · ¼–⅓ cup sugar.

To make Put the fruit into a pie or oven-proof dish. If cooking soft berry fruit use no water or about 1 tablespoon if very firm; with harder fruit use 4–5 tablespoons. Add sugar to sweeten. Cook gently in the oven for 10–15 minutes. If you prefer berry fruit to be firm, do *not* cook this before adding the crumble topping. Sift the flour, rub in the butter or margarine, add the sugar. Sprinkle over the top of the fruit.

To cook Bake in the center of a moderate oven 350–375°F, for 25–30 minutes until crisp and golden brown.

To serve In the baking dish, with cream or custard sauce. It is nicer served hot rather than cold. *All recipes based on these Blue Prints serve 4–5.*

To vary Sift ½–1 teaspoon ground ginger, cinnamon or other spice with the flour, or add the grated rind of 1 or 2 oranges or lemons. Use the same flavorings in the brown betty and either mix with the crumbs and sugar or sprinkle over the fingers of bread after sautéing.

● **AVOID** *Too much butter or margarine in a crumble mixture; this prevents it becoming crisp. Too much liquid when cooking the fruit; this will spoil both the appearance and texture of the topping.*

● **TO RECTIFY** *If you find the fruit is too soft, strain away surplus moisture before adding the topping.*

● **SHORT CUT** *Use canned fruit or canned fruit pie filling.*

Apricot fruit crumble (above right) Cornflake Brown Betty (left)

Cornflake Brown Betty

Use Blue Print 1, but substitute 3–3¾ cups cornflakes for the bread crumbs. Toss the cornflakes lightly in the hot butter or margarine then mix with the sugar. Bake as Blue Print 1.

Coconut Crumble

Ingredients as Blue Print 2 PLUS 1 scant cup dried coconut.
Make the crumble, then add the coconut. Bake as Blue Print 2.

For Special Occasions

Choose the luxury fruits for either the Brown Betty or Crumble.

Apple Raisin Brown Betty

Use Blue Print 1 PLUS ½ cup seedless or pitted raisins, 1½ tablespoons brandy or lemon juice and 2½ tablespoons blanched chopped almonds.
Follow the Blue Print, but mix the raisins and brandy or lemon juice with the cooked fruit (in this case apples) and blend the chopped almonds with the bread crumbs before tossing in the hot butter or margarine. Bake as Blue Print 1 and serve with Hard Sauce (see page 110).

Chocolate Chip Crumble

Ingredients as Blue Print 2 PLUS 3 oz. semi-sweet chocolate bits.
Prepare the crumble as the Blus Print, add the chocolate bits with the sugar. Bake as Blue Print 2, but take care not to overcook to avoid scorching.

Storing and freezing *Both Bettys and Crumbles may be made the night before, stored in a cool place and cooked as the recipe. They may be frozen, wrapped and stored for 2–3 months. Thaw before cooking or reheating.*

Custards

Eggs or egg yolks have the ability to thicken liquids (generally milk), to make either a pouring sauce or quite a firm custard the higher the proportion of eggs used, the more solid the result; 2 eggs or egg yolks and $2\frac{2}{3}$ cups milk produce a lightly set custard or a custard sauce. However, 4 eggs or 2 whole eggs and 2 egg yolks, or 5 egg yolks and $2\frac{2}{3}$ cups liquid will give a custard sufficiently firm to turn out of the dish.

Blue Print Recipe

Baked Custard

$2\frac{2}{3}$ cups milk · 4 eggs · $\frac{1}{2}$ cup sugar · pinch salt · 1 teaspoon vanilla extract · nutmeg.

To make Scald the milk but do not let it boil; it should be about blood temperature. Beat the eggs and sugar together, then add the hot milk, stirring all the time.

To cook Strain into a greased 5–6 cup baking dish; grate a little nutmeg on top. Stand the dish in a pan containing cold water and bake on the lowest rack in a slow oven, 275–300°F, for approximately 45 minutes to 1 hour until the mixture is set.

To serve In the baking dish. This can be served plain or with cooked fruit.
All recipes based on this dish serve 4–5.

● **AVOID** *Overheating, which causes the mixture to curdle (separate). You can see when this has happened by the watery liquid in the dish. Pastry rising and custard sinking in a custard pie or tart. The recipe gives the best way of preventing this, i.e. to bake the pastry blind first and then to pour in the hot custard mixture.*

● **TO RECTIFY** *Whisk sharply, this is quite often effective in a sauce. If unsuccessful emulsify in a blender. This gives a thinner mixture. If time permits, beat in an extra egg or egg yolk, cook again to thicken. The only other alternative is to spoon the custard carefully from the dish, leaving the watery liquid behind.*

● **SHORT CUT** *Make a sauce with a packaged custard mix; when thickened add an egg or egg yolk. Simmer gently for 2–3 minutes only.*

Fruit queen of puddings

Custard Sauce

Ingredients as Blue Print but use only 2 eggs and 2 tablespoons sugar. Strain the custard into the top of a double boiler or bowl balanced on a pan, over *hot* but not boiling water. Cook gently, stirring well, until the custard coats the back of a wooden spoon. If serving cold, cover the surface with plastic wrap to prevent a skin forming.

Custard Peach Pie or Tarts

$\frac{1}{2}$ recipe plain pastry (page 109). Ingredients as Blue Print but use 2 cups milk, 3 eggs, $\frac{1}{3}$ cup sugar, pinch salt and $\frac{1}{2}$ teaspoon vanilla plus 1 package (10 oz.) frozen peaches. Line a 9-inch pie pan with the pastry. Bake blind (see page 112) in the center of a hot oven, 425–450°F, for 10 minutes to set the pastry and prevent it rising. Heat the thawed peaches in their juice, drain and cover the bottom of the hot pie shell. Prepare the custard as the Blue Print; pour the hot custard into the hot pastry shell over the peaches; top with grated nutmeg. Lower the heat to very moderate, 325–350°F, cook for a further 35–40 minutes until the custard is set. Serve hot or cold.
Small custard tarts are made in the same way. Set the pastry shells for 5 minutes, fill with fruit and custard, cook for 20–25 minutes.

Bread and Butter Pudding

Ingredients as Blue Print MINUS 2 eggs and use only 3 tablespoons sugar PLUS 4 large slices bread and butter and $\frac{1}{4}$–$\frac{1}{2}$ cup dried fruit.
Cut the bread and butter into triangles. Put into a pie pan with the fruit. Pour the custard over the fruit and top with the grated nutmeg, if wished. Bake as Blue Print.

For Special Occasions

Oeufs à la Neige or Floating Islands

Ingredients as Blue Print PLUS $\frac{1}{4}$ cup superfine sugar.
Pour the milk into a shallow pan or deep skillet. Separate the eggs. Beat the egg whites stiffly; cover the egg yolks to prevent them from drying. Gradually beat 2 tablespoons of the sugar into the egg whites. Heat the milk to about 190°F, i.e. until simmering. Drop spoonfuls of the meringue mixture on top of the hot milk, poach for 2 minutes. Turn with a perforated spoon and poach for the same time on the second side. Lift the meringues from the milk, drain on a towel. Meanwhile strain the milk on to the beaten egg yolks and remaining 2 tablespoons sugar. Add the vanilla extract. Cook as custard sauce on this page. Pour into a shallow dish, cool and top with meringue balls.

Fruit Queen of Puddings

$2\frac{1}{2}$ tablespoons jam; $\frac{1}{2}$ cup soft bread crumbs; 2 eggs; 2 cups milk; 6 tablespoons superfine sugar; 4 tablespoons fresh or canned fruit.
Spread half the jam in an oven-proof dish. Add the crumbs. Separate the egg yolks and make the custard as Blue Print using the 2 yolks, milk and 2 tablespoons sugar. Pour over the crumbs and bake as the Blue Print, until firm. Spread with the remaining jam and most of the fruit. Whip egg whites until very stiff, fold in remaining sugar. Pile onto the custard and top with the remaining fruit. Bake for 15 minutes in a moderate oven, 375°F. Serve hot.

Removing the crepe from the frying pan

For Family Occasions

Fruit Fritters

Ingredients as Blue Print PLUS 1 generous tablespoon flour; pan deep fat or oil for frying or $\frac{1}{2}$ cup fat for shallow frying; 4 good-sized cooking apples or bananas, 8 pineapple rings (drain canned pineapple well) or 12 plums; superfine sugar to coat.
Prepare the batter as the Blue Print in a large bowl (this makes it easier to coat the fruit). Put the flour on a large plate. Heat deep fat or oil. *Test if correct temperature*—a cube of bread should turn golden in 30 seconds. Lower the heat so the fat does not overheat. Peel and core apples, cut into $\frac{1}{2}$-inch rings. Halve large bananas. Coat the fruit first with flour (this makes sure the batter adheres well) and then in the batter. Lift out with a fork, hold over the bowl to allow surplus to drip into the bowl. Drop into the hot fat, cook steadily for 4–5 minutes until golden brown. Lift out, drain on absorbent paper, coat in sugar and serve hot. *If frying in shallow fat*, heat this *as* you coat the fruit. Turn the fritters after 2–3 minutes and brown other side. *Serves 4.*

Lemon Crepes

Ingredients as Blue Print (or economical variation) PLUS $\frac{2}{3}$ cup milk or milk and water, oil or fat for frying, 1–2$\frac{1}{2}$ tablespoons superfine sugar, 1 or 2 lemons.
Make the batter as the Blue Print, adding the extra liquid. Put 1–2 teaspoons oil or an equal amount of butter into a skillet, heat thoroughly. Pour or spoon enough batter into the pan to give a *paper-thin* layer. Cook

quickly for 1–2 minutes until brown on the under side, turn or toss, cook on the second side. Remove from the pan, see picture, put onto sugared paper, roll and keep hot on a plate over a pan of boiling water. Continue until all the batter is used. Serve with sugar and sliced lemon. *Serves 4.*

Syrup Waffles

Ingredients as Blue Print PLUS 1 teaspoon baking powder, scant 2 tablespoons melted butter or oil *and* butter, and butter or maple syrup for serving.
Make the batter as the Blue Print, sifting the baking powder and flour and adding the extra butter or oil and butter. Heat the waffle iron; oil if necessary. Spoon enough batter onto the iron to give a good coating. Close the lid, cook until the steaming ceases. Lift the lid, remove the waffle and serve hot topped with butter and syrup. *Serves 4.*

For Special Occasions

Almond Cream Fritters

Pit large plums, ripe apricots or small peaches. Fill with cream cheese and chopped blanched almonds. Omit 1 tablespoon milk from the Blue Print and add 1 tablespoon brandy instead. Coat, fry and serve as Fruit Fritters.

Chocolate Ice Cream Crepes

Make the crepes as directed. Keep hot until ready to serve. Fill with ice cream, top with hot chocolate sauce and serve at once.

The batter for crepes, pancakes, fritters and waffles is basically the same; it is just the consistency that varies. A batter for crepes has a higher percentage of liquid to give a wafer-thin result. When coating fruit with batter (for fritters), or making waffles, the batter needs to be thicker.

Blue Print Recipe

Fritter Batter

1 cup flour · pinch salt · 2 eggs · $\frac{2}{3}$ cup milk or milk and water · 1–2 teaspoons melted butter or cooking oil.
To make Sift the flour and salt. Gradually beat in the eggs and liquid giving a smooth thick batter. Add the butter or oil just before cooking.
To vary *For a lighter texture:* separate the eggs. Add the yolks to the flour, then the milk and oil. Fold the stiffly beaten egg whites into the mixture just before coating the fruit.
Economical batter: use 1 egg only.

- **AVOID** *Cooking too slowly; this makes a heavy mixture inclined to stick to the pan or waffle iron.*
- **TO RECTIFY** *If the first pancake or waffle cooks too slowly, heat the pan or iron to a higher temperature before adding more mixture. The method of testing the temperature is given in the recipe for Fruit Fritters.*
- **SHORT CUT** *Whirl ingredients in a blender. Put milk and eggs in first then add flour, etc.*
Storing and freezing *Batters may be stored for several days in a refrigerator. Wrap cooked crepes and waffles in aluminium foil, store for several days in a refrigerator or 10–12 weeks in a home freezer. Reheat as required.*

Apple fritters

A hot sweet soufflé is one of the most delicious desserts. It is so light in texture that it is a perfect choice after an elaborate main dish. The secrets of success are to make a smooth sauce and to incorporate the egg whites carefully, folding them gently but thoroughly into the mixture with a metal spoon or rubber scraper. If you choose a large-sized saucepan, in which to prepare the mixture, it gives room to do this well.

Soufflés are economical as well as interesting and can be varied in so many ways. If you like a firm-textured dessert, use the smaller quantity of liquid. For a more delicate and moist texture use the larger amount.

Blue Print Recipe
Vanilla Soufflé

1 tablespoon cornstarch · $\frac{2}{3}$–1 cup milk · vanilla pod or vanilla extract · $\frac{1}{4}$ cup sugar · 1 tablespoon butter · 4 eggs (see To vary) · little confectioners' sugar.

Hot Soufflés

To make   Butter a 6–7-inch soufflé dish or prepare as the Blue Print opposite (this is not essential for a hot soufflé, unless using a very small soufflé dish). Put the cornstarch into a bowl and blend with $\frac{1}{4}$ cup cold milk. Heat the remainder of the milk in a large saucepan with the vanilla pod or extract. Pour over the cornstarch, stirring well, then return to the pan. Remove the vanilla pod. Bring to the boil, add the sugar and butter, stir well and cook steadily until a thickened smooth mixture. Remove from the heat. Separate the eggs and gradually beat in the egg yolks. Beat the egg whites until stiff and fold into the mixture, see photograph. Spoon into the greased soufflé dish; smooth the top.

To cook   Bake in the center of a moderate oven, 350–375°F, for approximately 25 minutes until well risen. Have the confectioners' sugar ready.

To serve   Take the dish from the oven, shake the confectioners' sugar through a sieve as quickly as possible, remove the paper (if you have used this) and serve at once. To give a pleasant caramellized top to the soufflé, pull the oven shelf out gently and carefully about 6 minutes before the end of the cooking time. Dredge the soufflé with the confectioners' sugar and push the shelf back into the oven. *All recipes based on this dish serve 4–5.*

To vary   A lighter soufflé results if you use 3 egg yolks and 4 egg whites. If you care to omit the yolks completely and use just the egg whites, the soufflé has less flavor but sinks far less rapidly.

● **AVOID** *Too slow cooking. Keeping the cooked dish waiting—this means that you should time the cooking carefully so the soufflé can be served as soon as it is finished.*
● **TO RECTIFY** *A fallen soufflé (and it will fall if kept waiting) never rises again. The flavor is still very pleasant though, providing the mixture is still hot.*
● **SHORT CUT** *Cook in individual dishes for 10–12 minutes only.*

Chocolate Soufflé

Although one can make a chocolate soufflé as the Blue Print, adding 2 oz. melted bitter chocolate or 3 tablespoons sifted cocoa to the sauce *before* the egg yolks, the following variation gives a light and very moist soufflé. Melt 3 oz. bitter chocolate in $1\frac{1}{3}$ cups milk. Heat 6 tablespoons butter in a large pan. Stir in $\frac{1}{4}$ cup cornstarch or $\frac{1}{2}$ cup flour and cook for several minutes. Gradually blend in melted chocolate. Bring to boil and cook until thickened. Beat in $\frac{1}{4}$ cup sugar and 4 egg yolks. Fold in the 4 beaten egg whites. Proceed as Blue Print but bake for 40 minutes. Dust with sifted confectioners' sugar if wished, and serve with cream.

Coffee Soufflé

Recipe as Blue Print, but use either *all* strong coffee instead of milk, or half coffee and half milk. Make and cook the soufflé as the Blue Print.

Liqueur Soufflé

Follow the Blue Print recipe but reduce the amount of milk by $2\frac{1}{2}$–4 tablespoons and

use $2\frac{1}{2}$–4 tablespoons liqueur instead. Some of the most suitable are Apricot Brandy, Cherry Brandy, Curaçao, Crème de Menthe, Tia Maria (which can be used with milk, as in the Blue Print, or with coffee). Bake as Blue Print.

Fruit Soufflé

There are several ways of incorporating fruit flavors into hot soufflés.

If using citrus fruits, i.e. orange, tangerine, lemon or lime. Follow the Blue Print recipe but use fruit juice (or fruit juice PLUS fruit

liqueurs such as Curaçao or Apricot Brandy) instead of milk PLUS 2–3 teaspoons very finely grated fruit rind.

With most other fruits, particularly apricots, black currants and gooseberries, use the Blue Print recipe but substitute thin smooth fruit puree for milk.

Cooked or canned cherries and canned pineapple make excellent soufflés. Follow the Blue Print recipe but use $\frac{2}{3}$ cup of the syrup instead of the milk; reduce the amount of sugar if wished. When the sauce has been prepared, add 4–5 tablespoons well drained diced fruit *before* the egg yolks and whites. Bake as Blue Print.

Folding in the egg whites (left)
Chocolate soufflé (far left)

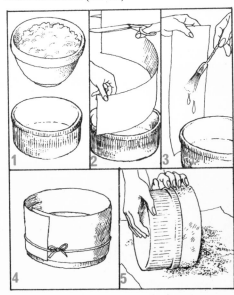

Put together beaten eggs, heavy cream, flavoring (this can be fruit, rich chocolate or coffee) and bind them with gelatin and you have the ingredients to produce one of the most elegant of desserts—a cold soufflé. Naturally any soufflé is a fairly expensive dish, which is why I have included a simple family adaptation: Orange Soufflé.

Blue Print Recipe

Five Stages to a Perfect Soufflé

Stage 1 Separate the egg yolks from the whites; put the yolks, sugar, flavoring and liquid (where used) into a bowl over a pan of very hot water. Beat until thick and creamy.

Stage 2 Soften the gelatin in some cold liquid. Add to the mixture above, stir over the heat until the gelatin has dissolved. Cool and allow to stiffen slightly.

Stage 3 Whip the cream lightly, fold into the thickened mixture.

Stage 4 Beat the egg whites until stiff but not too dry; fold into the mixture. Spoon into the prepared soufflé dish.

Stage 5 Allow to set and remove the paper slowly and carefully. Decorate the top and sides with whipped cream, finely chopped nuts or macaroons.

Preparing the Soufflé Dish

It is traditional that a cold soufflé should look as if it has risen in the dish, as the hot soufflé opposite. In order to achieve this result, choose a soufflé dish with a smaller capacity than the amount of mixture produced, see Sketch 1. A 6-inch dish is ideal for all the recipes on this page.

Cut a band of foil or waxed paper three times the depth of the dish, see Sketch 2.

Fold the paper to give a double thickness and brush the part that will stand above the dish with a very light coating of melted butter, see Sketch 3.

Tie or pin the band of paper *very securely* round the outside of the soufflé dish, see Sketch 4.

● **AVOID** *Overwhipping the cream, this makes it difficult to incorporate. Beating the egg whites until* too stiff. *Adding the cream and egg whites too early; wait until the gelatin mixture is lightly set.*

● **TO RECTIFY** *If the cream or egg whites have been beaten too stiffly, then soften with a few drops of water. Fold this in gently and carefully.*

● **SHORT CUT** *Use the mixer to beat the egg whites; do not overbeat. Make a smooth fruit puree in the blender.*

Storing and freezing *Keep in a cool place immediately before serving. The cold soufflé with the high percentage of cream may be frozen, but tends to lose some of its light texture. The hot soufflé cannot be stored or frozen.*

To use leftovers *Put spoonfuls of the soufflé into glasses and top with a whirl of whipped cream.*

Lemon Soufflé

Finely grated rind of 2 lemons; 5 tablespoons lemon juice; 3 eggs; $\frac{1}{2}-\frac{3}{4}$ cup superfine sugar; 1 envelope unflavored gelatin; 5 tablespoons water; $1\frac{1}{3}$ cups heavy cream. *To decorate:* small macaroons.

Put the lemon rind, juice, egg yolks and sugar into a bowl. Beat as Stage 1 in Blue Print. Soften the gelatin in the cold water, add to the egg yolk mixture and continue as Blue Print. Press some finely crushed macaroon crumbs on to the sides, see Sketch 5, and decorate the top with macaroons. *Serves 5–6.*

Fruit Soufflé

If using soft fruit, such as raspberries and strawberries, puree the raw fruit and measure. If using firm fruit, such as apricots, black currants and gooseberries, cook in the minimum of water until soft, puree and measure. If sugar has been used in cooking the fruit, omit a little in the recipe below.

$\frac{1}{2}$ cup thick fruit puree; 3 eggs; $\frac{1}{2}$ cup superfine sugar; 1 envelope unflavored gelatin; $\frac{1}{4}$ cup water; $1\frac{1}{4}$ cups heavy cream. *To decorate:* nuts and cream.

Put the fruit puree, egg yolks and sugar into a bowl. Beat as Stage 1 in Blue Print. Soften gelatin in the cold water, add to egg yolk mixture and continue as Blue Print. Chop a few nuts very finely, press against the sides of the soufflé, see Sketch 5. Decorate the top of the soufflé with cream.

Chocolate Soufflé

4 oz. semi-sweet chocolate; $2\frac{1}{2}$ tablespoons milk; 3 eggs; 6 tablespoons superfine sugar; 2 teaspoons unflavored gelatin; $2\frac{1}{2}$ table-spoons water; $1\frac{1}{4}$ cups heavy cream. *To decorate:* grated chocolate and cream.

Break the chocolate into pieces, put into a bowl with the milk, egg yolks and sugar. Beat as Stage 1 in Blue Print. Soften the gelatin in the cold water, add to the egg yolk mixture, continue as Blue Print. Decorate with coarsely grated chocolate and whipped cream. *Serves 5–6.*

Orange Soufflé

Dissolve a 3-oz. package orange flavored gelatin in $1\frac{3}{4}$ cups boiling water. Add grated rind of 1 orange and 2 tablespoons orange juice. Cool slightly. Beat 1 egg yolk and pour on the warm orange jelly. Allow to cool and stiffen slightly then fold in 2 tablespoons cream or evaporated milk (lightly whipped) and 1 beaten egg white. Put into a 5-inch soufflé dish. Decorate with cream. *Serves 4–5.*

Lemon soufflé

Although one can buy excellent ice cream, the homemade variety enables you to add any flavoring you wish. It also provides a nutritious dessert for the family. The Blue Print is for a fairly rich ice, creamy yellow in color. You will also find variations under the Blue Print.

If you have a home freezer, it is a good idea to make up a larger amount than that given in the Blue Print. Several different flavors, i.e. coffee, chocolate and fruit, can of course be made from the basic mixture.

Blue Print Recipe

Basic Ice Cream

2 large eggs · 4–6 tablespoons sugar (preferably confectioners' sugar) · $\frac{2}{3}$ cup heavy cream · $\frac{2}{3}$ cup light cream · flavoring.

To make Beat the eggs and sugar until thick and creamy. Whip the heavy cream until it *just begins* to hold its shape then gradually beat in the light cream. Add flavoring required. Fold into the egg mixture.

To freeze Spoon into the freezing tray or other utensil and freeze until firm. This mixture does not need beating during freezing. If using an electric mixer, beat the eggs and sugar, pour the heavy cream onto the beaten eggs and sugar, continue beating until thick again, then gradually beat in the light cream and flavoring.

Ice Cream

To serve Spoon or scoop into serving dishes. *All recipes based on this serve 4 or 6 with other ingredients, such as fruit.*

To vary *For a whiter ice cream* use the egg whites only. Whip these until very stiff and fold into the whipped cream.

For a more economical ice cream use the egg yolks to make a custard sauce (see page 117) with $1\frac{1}{3}$ cups milk and sugar. Cool, fold in the whipped cream, flavoring and finally the stiffly beaten egg whites.

Use $1\frac{1}{3}$ cups evaporated milk in place of the heavy and light cream. To whip evaporated milk boil the can of milk in water for 15 minutes, chill then beat until thick.

Flavorings for ice cream

Add $\frac{1}{2}$ – 1 teaspoon vanilla or other extract.
Add 1 tablespoon liqueur (remember this is very sweet and adjust sugar accordingly).
Add 2–4 teaspoons sweetened coffee extract.
Add $1\frac{1}{2}$ – 3 tablespoons sifted cocoa.
Add $\frac{2}{3}$ – $1\frac{1}{3}$ cups thick fruit puree. The most suitable fruits are raw pureed strawberries, raspberries and bananas, or cooked, pureed apricots (shown in the picture), black currants, gooseberries and damsons.

● **AVOID** *Too slow freezing. A recipe too low in fat content encourages the formation of ice crystals in the mixture as it freezes.*

Too solid a mixture.
● **TO RECTIFY** *Modern refrigerators and home freezers are sufficiently cold to freeze ice cream without adjustment. The older refrigerators freeze more slowly and should be turned to the coldest position at least half an hour before freezing the mixture and returned to normal setting when the ice cream is firm. Use a high percentage of cream or evaporated milk in the recipe to provide the fat content. Do not overbeat the cream. You have a lighter consistency by using half heavy and half light cream and by aerating the eggs or egg whites.,*
● **SHORT CUT** *Use commercial ice cream in some of the ice cream desserts.*

Apricot ice cream

For Special Occasions

Poires Hélène

Chocolate sauce: 4 oz. sweet German chocolate; 1 tablespoon butter; $2\frac{1}{2}$ – 4 tablespoons water. 4 small pears or large pear halves; ice cream as Blue Print or 4 portions bought ice cream.

Melt the chocolate in a bowl over *hot* water with the butter and water. Stir. Peel and core pears (do this at the last minute to prevent discoloration). Put scoops of ice cream into individual dishes with the pears and pour over the sauce. *Serves 4.*

Harlequin Flan

Fill a sponge or pastry flan with lightly whipped cream. Top with chopped glacé cherries, crystallized ginger, angelica and chocolate ice cream. *Serves 6–8.*

Storing and freezing *Freeze as instructed on this page. Store in the freezing compartment of a refrigerator for several days or in a home freezer. If a little hard, stand at room temperature for a short time before serving.*

Harlequin flan and a simple ice cream coûpe

Fruit Ices

Fruit ices are some of the most refreshing desserts, giving the flavor of fresh fruit in an interesting way.

Sorbets, or fruit ices, were originally served in the middle of the dinner to freshen the palate before proceeding to the next course. Although at some elaborate dinners this practice is still occasionally continued, it is more conventional now to serve them as a dessert.

Blue Print Recipes

1. Orange Ice

3 large oranges · 1 small lemon · 2 cups water · minimum $\frac{1}{2}$ cup sugar · 2 teaspoons unflavored gelatin · 1 egg white.

To make Pare the rind thinly from the oranges and lemon (do not use the white pith which would give a bitter flavor to the ice). Put into a saucepan with the water and sugar, simmer for 8 minutes. Squeeze the juice from the oranges and lemon. Soften the gelatin in 2 tablespoons cold orange juice, add to the liquid in the pan, stir until dissolved, strain and add to the remainder of the fruit juice. Taste; add a little extra sugar if required but do not make the mixture too sweet. Cool, then freeze.
To freeze Pour into freezing trays or a deeper utensil. Freeze on the normal setting in the refrigerator or home freezer. Leave until lightly frosted. Remove and blend with the stiffly beaten egg white. If wishing to serve as the picture on this page, pile the mixture into the orange shells (you will need 6 shells altogether) and support in individual dishes or cups. If preferred, spoon the mixture back into the freezing trays or original utensil. They also look most attractive served in a ring mold with fresh or canned fruit in the center or in a decorative mold.
To serve In orange shells or sundae glasses. *All recipes based on this serve 6.*

2. Apple Ice

1 lb. cooking apples · 1 lemon · $1\frac{1}{4}$ cups water · $\frac{1}{2}$ cup sugar · 2 teaspoons unflavored gelatin · coloring · 1 egg white.

To make Wash and chop the apples; do not remove peel or cores as these give flavor. Put into a saucepan with the thinly pared lemon rind, water and sugar. Simmer until the apples are very soft. Purée the mixture; return to the pan to keep warm. Soften the gelatin in the cold lemon juice, add to the warm apple mixture, stir until dissolved. Taste; add extra sugar if desired, or if the apples are rather sweet add a little more lemon juice. Tint a delicate shade of green or pink. Cool, then freeze.

To freeze As Blue Print 1. When lightly frosted, remove and blend with the stiffly beaten egg white. Return to the freezing compartment or freezer and continue freezing.
To serve In glasses, or pile into canned peach halves and decorate with mint leaves. The combination of the sharp apple mixture and the sweet peach is delicious. *All recipes based on this serve 6; when served with other ingredients, such as peaches, serve 8.*
To vary Use other fruit in place of apples. Plums, damsons, rhubarb, gooseberries, etc., should be cooked. Raspberries, strawberries and other soft fruits should be used raw then blended with the syrup, made by heating the water, sugar and lemon rind. Two fruits can also be blended together, e.g. apples and raspberries; rhubarb and orange juice.

● **AVOID** *The formation of ice splinters; the mixture should be smooth when frozen. Too hard a texture.*

● **TO RECTIFY** *Use a little gelatine in the mixture; this prevents splinters of ice forming: Add an egg white to the mixture to give additional aeration. Never serve the ice when too solid; allow time at room temperature for it to soften.*
● **SHORT CUT** *Use canned fruit juice or a smooth canned fruit puree. The canned fruits sold for baby foods are an excellent basis for fruit ices.*
● **TO REDUCERS** *Sweeten with sugar substitute and you have a low calorie desert.*

For Family Occasions

Lemon Ice

3 large or 4 smaller lemons; 2 cups water; $\frac{3}{4}$ cup sugar; 2 teaspoons unflavored gelatin; 1 egg white.
Method as Blue Print 1.
To vary Use pineapple, grapefruit and other juices as Blue Print 1.

For Special Occasions

Orange Curaçao Sorbet

Ingredients as Blue Print 1 PLUS $1-2\frac{1}{2}$ tablespoons Curaçao and 2 *additional* egg whites. Make the orange ice mixture as Blue Print 1, but use only $\frac{1}{4}$ cup of the sugar when simmering the orange and lemon rinds. Add the Curaçao just before freezing for the first time. Freeze until lightly frosted. Beat 3 egg whites until very stiff. Gradually beat in the remaining $\frac{1}{4}$ cup sugar. Fold the meringue mixture into the orange ice and freeze again. Serve in glasses or freeze and serve in orange shells as described in Blue Print 1.

Orange ice

Melon Ice

Ingredients as Blue Print 2, but substitute the flesh from a ripe honeydew or watermelon for apples and reduce the amount of water to $\frac{1}{3}$ cup.
Make the syrup with the water, sugar and lemon rind, add the gelatin, softened in the lemon juice, and stir until dissolved. Cool. Halve the melon, discard the seeds and puree the pulp. Blend with the lemon syrup, continue as Blue Print. Serve in glasses or the melon shell. Decorate with cherries or other fruit. The mixture can be tinted if wished and given additional flavor by adding a little dry sherry or white wine.

Cream and Cold Desserts

So many desserts are improved by topping or decorating with cream, or incorporating cream among the ingredients. However, the piping or dessert itself can be less than perfect because the cream has been overwhipped.

Blue Print Recipe

To Whip Fresh Cream

Put heavy cream into a bowl. Use an electric or hand beater or a fork to whip the cream. The latter is slow, but safer if the cream is very rich. Whip slowly and steadily until the cream *begins* to stand in peaks. This consistency is ideal when adding cream to desserts. If using the cream for piping, the cream should be stiffer and stand in peaks.

To make a lighter cream
1. Whip as Blue Print and then fold in an equal quantity of light cream. Whip again until it stiffens. This will be rarely firm enough to use for piping.
2. To each $\frac{2}{3}$ cup heavy cream add one egg white. Whip the cream and egg white in separate bowls and fold together *just before* serving. You can pipe this, although it tends to be much softer than heavy cream alone.

● **AVOID** *Overwhipping cream because if you do it will separate, giving you a solid butterlike substance and watery liquid.*
● **TO RECTIFY** *If the cream begins to separate, add a little milk or water and fold gently into the mixture.*
● **SHORT CUT** *Use an electric mixer for beating but choose a very low speed and watch the cream as it thickens to avoid overbeating.*

For Special Occasions

Banana Cream Syllabub

3 ripe firm bananas; $2\frac{1}{2}$ tablespoons lemon juice; $2\frac{1}{2}$ tablespoons white wine; $2\frac{1}{2}$ tablespoons superfine sugar; $1\frac{1}{3}$ cups heavy cream.
Peel the bananas and mash with the lemon juice, wine and sugar. Whip the cream as the Blue Print. Fold into the banana mixture. Spoon into serving dishes and chill before serving. *Serves 4–6.*

Creamy Apple Crunch

This recipe, somewhat similar in texture to Brown Betty (page 116) uses sour cream to give additional interest to the apple mixture. $\frac{1}{2}$ cup superfine sugar; $\frac{2}{3}$ cup water; 4 or 5 medium-sized cooking apples; $1\frac{1}{4}$ cups sour cream; 3 tablespoons brown sugar; 4–6 gingersnaps; $2\frac{1}{2}$ tablespoons chopped blanched almonds.
Make a syrup with the superfine sugar and water in a large pan. Peel, core and slice the apples and poach in the syrup until just tender, but unbroken. Lift the apple segments into a bowl, blend with the sour cream and $2\frac{1}{2}$ tablespoons brown sugar. Spoon into a heat proof dish. Crush the gingersnaps with a rolling pin; do this between 2 sheets of waxed paper or put the cookies into a large bag. Blend with the almonds and remaining brown sugar. Sprinkle over the fruit and brown for 2–3 minutes only under a hot broiler. Serve cold. *Serves 4–6.*

Apple Surprise Pie

One of the old fashioned farmhouse traditions, when making a fruit pie, was to cover the fruit with heavy cream before baking. Apples, plums or peaches are the most suitable fruits for this purpose.

Either put the prepared fruit into the pie plate with sugar, thickener and flavoring as page 110, or, to give a firmer fruit layer, poach the fruit for about 10 minutes with the sugar and a little water in a saucepan. Lift out the fruit with a slotted spoon (serve the liquid with the pie if wished) and put into the pie plate. Whichever method is used, top the fruit with $\frac{2}{3}$–$1\frac{1}{3}$ cups whipped cream, then with the pastry. Bake as the fruit pie on page 110.

Storing and freezing *Dairy cream, and any desserts using cream, must be used when fresh unless stored in a home freezer.*

Banana cream syllabub

Special Gâteaux

On this and the following page you will find a selection of gâteaux. They are all simple to make, and are based on Blue Prints in this book.

Fruit Cream Bande

This and the following recipe are based on puff pastry (see page 86).
$\frac{3}{4}$ lb. puff pastry made with $1\frac{1}{2}$ cups flour etc.; $2\frac{1}{2}$ tablespoons cornstarch; $1\frac{1}{3}$ cups milk; $2\frac{1}{2}$ tablespoons sugar; $\frac{2}{3}$ cup heavy cream; 6–8 sweet plums; 1 red-skinned eating apple; 1 sweet pear; 4–5 tablespoons apricot jam.
Roll out about $\frac{2}{3}$ of the pastry into a rectangle about 11 inches × 8 inches. Put on a baking sheet or tray. Roll out the rest of the pastry into a long strip, cut 2 pieces 11 inches × $\frac{1}{2}$–$\frac{3}{4}$ inch wide and 2 pieces $6\frac{1}{2}$–7 inches × $\frac{1}{2}$–$\frac{3}{4}$ inch wide. Damp the edges of the pastry rectangle and press the bands into position. The pastry shell should look like a picture frame. Bake just above the center of a very hot oven, 450–475°F, for about 5 minutes, then lower the heat to moderately hot, 400°F, for a further 15 minutes or until the pastry is golden brown. Allow to cool. Blend the cornstarch with the milk. Put into a saucepan with the sugar and cook gently, stirring all the time until thickened. Allow to cool, stirring from time to time to prevent a skin forming. Blend with the whipped cream; spread over the pastry. Halve the plums, remove the pits, slice the apple and peeled pear. Arrange on the cream layer and top with the warmed and pureed jam at once to keep the fruit a good color. *Serves 5–6.*

Raspberry Milles Feuilles

$\frac{3}{4}$ lb. puff pastry made with $1\frac{1}{2}$ cups flour, etc.; 4 cups raspberries; sugar to taste; $\frac{2}{3}$ cup heavy cream; $\frac{2}{3}$ cup light cream.
Roll out the pastry very thinly, cut into 3 equal-sized rounds and 1 ring to fit over the top, as shown in the picture. Put on a baking

sheet or tray and bake as the recipe above, allowing about 12–15 minutes only. Allow to cool. Mash about half the raspberries with sugar. Whip the heavy cream, add the light cream and whip again. Spread the first layer of pastry with mashed fruit and cream, put on the second layer of pastry, spread with cream, add third layer, spread with cream and top with the pastry circle. Fill the center with the whole fruit. *Serves 5–6.*

Peach Gâteau

Half the ingredients as Blue Print on page 100 (3 egg yolks, etc.); about 8 canned peach halves and some of the syrup; 4–5 tablespoons sherry; 5–6 tablespoons raspberry jam; $\frac{2}{3}$ cup heavy cream; little angelica.
Make the mixture as the Blue Print on page 100. Grease and flour a 9-inch round layer pan, put in the mixture, bake for about 35–

40 minutes in a moderate oven, 350°F. Allow to cool. Lift the peach halves from the syrup, blend about 4 tablespoons syrup and the sherry. Put the cake on or in a dish, spoon the syrup and sherry over this. Arrange the peach halves on top. Warm and sieve the jam and glaze the fruit with this. When glaze is quite cool, whip the cream and pipe, as in the picture. Decorate with angelica. *Serves 6.*

To vary Instead of using angelica decorate with macaroons. To make about 24, beat 1 egg white lightly, add $\frac{3}{4}$ cup ground almonds, $\frac{1}{4}$ cup superfine sugar and a few drops almond extract. Roll mixture into tiny balls, put on a greased baking sheet and bake for 6–8 minutes in the center of a very moderate oven, 325–350°F.

Fruit Gâteau

Ingredients as Blue Print 1 on page 100, and bake in two round 9-inch layer pans as for Peach Gâteau above. When cold, sandwich the cakes together with approximately $1\frac{1}{2}$

cups whipped cream and chopped canned and fresh fruit. Top with a selection of fruit as in the picture. Heat 4–5 tablespoons apricot jam and spoon over the fruit, to give a generous layer of glaze. *Serves 8–10.*

Peach gâteau (right); Blackberry milles feuilles (below)

Gelatin, obtainable both flavored and un-flavored, can be used to set clear liquids such as fruit juices, fruit purees, milk and/or cream mixtures. However, it is not always used as successfully as it might be, so Blue Print 1 covers the correct way to dissolve and incorporate it into other foods. Flavored gelatins are favorites with all the family and make interesting dishes with the minimum expenditure of time and trouble.

Blue Print Recipe

1. To use Gelatin

The instructions on the packet will give exact quantities. Generally one uses 1 enve-lope, which is $\frac{1}{2}$ oz. or 1 tablespoon to 2 cups clear liquid or half this quantity for thick-ened liquids (see page 123).

To dissolve Put the gelatin into a bowl, add $\frac{1}{4}$ cup *cold* liquid from the 2 cups. Stand the bowl in, or over, a pan of hot water, leave until the gelatin has dissolved. There is no need to stir *as* the gelatin softens; do this just before blending with the other in-gredients. Heat the remainder of the liquid, pour over the gelatin, stir until well blended.

To set Rinse a mold or bowl in cold water, leave damp. Pour in the gelatin; when set invert on to a *damp* serving dish. This means you can slide the gelatin easily into the cen-ter of the dish. *All recipes based on this serve 4.*

Fruit snow

Blue Print Recipe

2. Molded Fruit Gelatin

1 package flavored gelatin · water and fruit juice or syrup from a can · canned, cooked or fresh fruit.

Read the instructions on the package for the exact amount of water or liquid required; this can vary slightly according to different makes. If using canned or cooked fruit strain off the syrup, dilute with water to make up to the quantity given on the package *less* about 1 tablespoon. This is because the fruit is moist and will dilute the strength of the gelatin. If using fresh fruit such as bananas or berries you can use the full quantity of water because these are firm. If you wish to use a little fresh orange or lemon juice then this counts as part of the total amount.

Dissolve the gelatin according to the in-structions. Pour a little into the rinsed mold (see Blue Print 1). Allow this to become near-ly set and arrange the first layer of fruit on top. It is easier to do this if you dip the fruit in liquid gelatin. When set pour over a little more gelatin and continue filling the mold like this to give an interesting design. Allow to set and turn out as Blue Print 1.

- **AVOID** *Adding gelatin to hot liquids; soften first (see Blue Print 1).*
- **TO RECTIFY** *If gelatin does not dissolve well, due to putting it into hot liquid without softening, allow to stand until cool, stir well and reheat gently.*
- **SHORT CUT** *To speed the setting of gelatin, use some crushed ice instead of the same quantity of water.*
- **TO REDUCERS** *Many gelatin recipes are suitable for low calorie desserts. Use sugar substitute instead of sugar.*

Fresh Orange Gelatin

2–3 large oranges; 1 small lemon; water; 4–6 tablespoons sugar; 1 envelope un-flavored gelatin.
Pare the rind from the oranges and lemon, put into a saucepan with about $\frac{3}{4}$ cup water. Simmer for 10 minutes, strain, add sugar while hot. Squeeze the juice from the fruit and measure. The juice *plus* fruit liquid should give 2 cups. Soften the gelatin in a little cold liquid as Blue Print 1. Heat the

rest of the liquid, pour over the gelatin mix-ture. Stir until dissolved, then follow Blue Print 1 for setting and turning out the gela-tin.

Fresh Lemon Gelatin

Recipe as above but use 2 large or 3 medium-sized lemons.
You will note I added a lemon to the orange gelatin above. You may like to omit this but it does *not* conflict with the orange flavor, and it seems to give a more refreshing gelatin.

Fruit Snow

$1\frac{1}{4}$ cups thick sweetened fruit puree*; 1 tea-spoon unflavored gelatin; 2 tablespoons water or fresh fruit juice; $\frac{2}{3}$ cup heavy cream; 3 egg whites.
*In the picture apple puree was used and tinted with a little green coloring.
Warm the puree gently, soften the gelatin

in the water or fruit juice as Blue Print 1. Mix with the puree, stir until dissolved. Allow to cool, fold in half the lightly whipped cream and 2 stiffly beaten egg whites. Spoon into 4–6 serving glasses and allow to set lightly (this will never be sufficiently stiff to turn out). Whip the remainder of the cream and the third egg white in separate bowls; fold together and pile on top of the dessert. De-corate with lemon slices if wished. *Serves 4–6.*

Gooseberry Sparkle

Method as Blue Print 2. Choose canned gooseberries and a lime gelatin. Decorate with whipped cream, chopped glacé cherries and chopped crystallized ginger.

Gooseberry sparkle

Complete Index